PAUL GAUGUIN
THE SEARCH FOR PARADISE

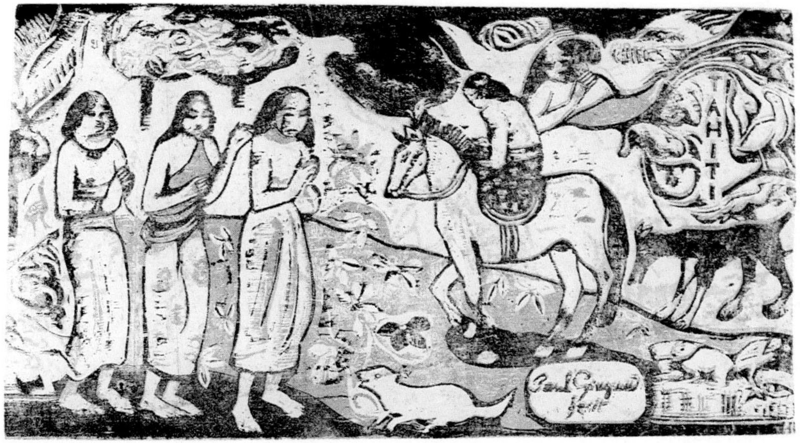

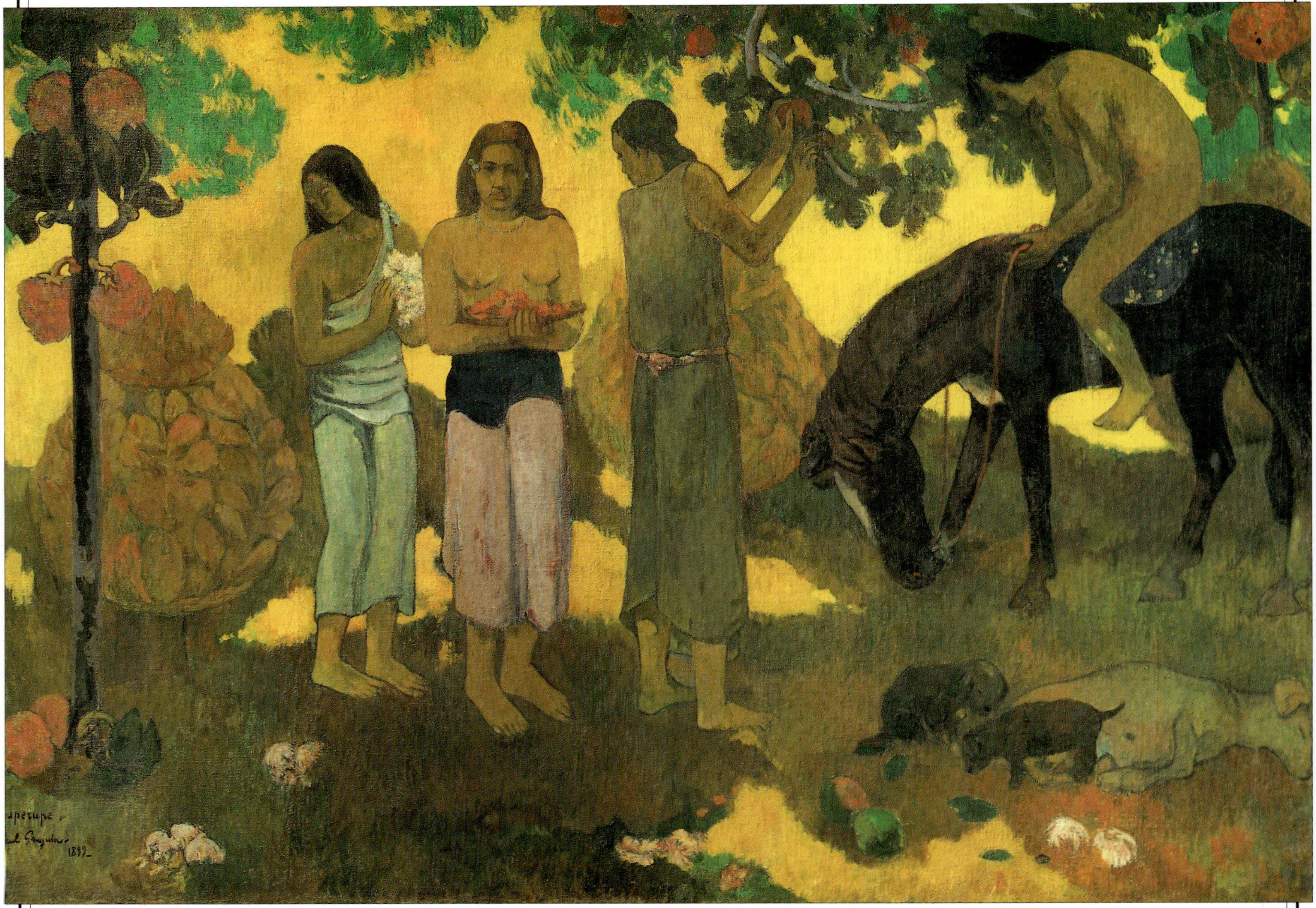

PAUL GAUGUIN
THE SEARCH FOR PARADISE
Letters from Brittany and the South Seas

Selected and introduced by Bernard Denvir

PB
PARKGATE
BOOKS

FRONT COVER: THE QUEEN OF THE NOBLE WOMAN (TE ARII VAHINE), 1896.

BACK COVER: *A page from Gauguin's Tahitian journal,* Noa Noa, *with a sketch for 'The Spirit of the Dead Watching' (Manau tupapau) painted in 1892.*

First published in 1990

This edition published in 1998 by
Parkgate Books Ltd
Kiln House
210 New Kings Road
London SW6 4NZ
Great Britain

9 8 7 6 5 4 3 2 1

First published by Collins & Brown in 1990 at £14.99

British Library Cataloguing in Publication Date:
A catalogue record for this book is available from the British Library.

ISBN 1 85585 392 2

Printed and bound in China by Sun Fung Offset Binding Company Limited.
Produced in association with the Hanway Press, London.

FRONTISPIECE: GATHERING FRUIT (RUPE RUPE), 1899 *This painting from Gauguin's last stay in Tahiti presents one of his favourite motifs: statuesque women with their domesticated animals.*

HALF TITLE: CHANGE OF RESIDENCE, 1898–9 *One of a suite of woodcuts printed by Gauguin and sent to the dealer Vollard in January 1900 which were probably intended to be used in juxtaposition to form friezes or patterns.*

Contents

FOREWORD
THE SEARCH FOR PARADISE
6

INTRODUCTION
A QUEST FOR INNOCENCE
7

CHAPTER 1
EARLY LIFE, 1848–1885
10

CHAPTER 2
BRITTANY AND MARTINIQUE, 1886–1890
22

CHAPTER 3
THE FRAGRANT LAND, 1891–1892
56

CHAPTER 4
INTERLUDE, 1893–1895
90

CHAPTER 5
'WHERE HAVE WE COME FROM? WHAT ARE WE? WHERE ARE WE GOING?', 1896–1900
100

CHAPTER 6
THE LAST CHANCE, 1901–1903
138

GAUGUIN: A BIOGRAPHICAL CHRONOLOGY
154

FRIENDS AND ACQUAINTANCES: A BIOGRAPHICAL INDEX
156

ACKNOWLEDGEMENTS
159

FOREWORD

The Search for Paradise

THIS BOOK IS MEANT TO BE neither a biography of Gauguin nor an evaluation of his work, but rather an attempt to describe, in his own words, the notions he held about himself as a 'savage' seeking a paradise which would fuel his creativity, vindicate the superiority of feeling over thought, the primitive over the sophisticate, and establish himself as the Messiah of a new artistic dispensation. In the places he chose for this quest he succeeded in finding something closer to purgatory—if not to hell—than to heaven, but he also produced paintings and writings which were to have a potent influence on the art of the twentieth century, and without which Fauvism and Expressionism, for instance, might have taken on a very different form. More interestingly too, he provided the twentieth century with one of its great archetypes, a cultural hero, almost as powerful in his hold on the imagination of subsequent generations as was his erstwhile friend Van Gogh.

A prolific writer, producing a very large number of letters, autobiographical excursions, journals, reflections on art, art history and on Catholicism in modern times, as well as a considerable body of journalism, Gauguin wrote vividly, vigorously and sometimes a trifle incoherently, in a free-flowing and usually legible script.

I have, on the whole, given more prominence to his letters, which reveal more of his personality, with all its ambiguities and pathos, than to his more studied writings, concerned as they usually are with the presentation of some argument, or the denunciation of some real or imaginary enemy.

Even with the former, a degree of ruthlessness in selection has been necessary, not only to achieve the avowed purpose of the book, but to avoid boring the reader with all the pleas for money and general details of his financial affairs that play so dominant a part in, for instance, the copious correspondence with his agent, Daniel de Monfreid.

To avoid encumbering the pages with the frequently complex notes that would be needed to explain all the references in the text, I have kept these to a basic minimum. Further enlightenment, however, about the people to whom the letters were addressed and others mentioned by Gauguin can be achieved by reference to the biographical index.

I must acknowledge how much I owe to those who have been involved in the production of this book: to Gabrielle Townsend, whose initial idea it was; to Sarah Bloxham, whose patient, accurate and helpful editing have been beyond praise; and, above all, to Sara Waterson, whose assiduous and imaginative pursuit of illustrations and the captioning of them have given the publication the major part of any merit it may possess.

BERNARD DENVIR
LONDON, 1992

A Quest for Innocence

In the autumn of 1910 Virginia and Vanessa Stephens, who would later be known by the names of their respective husbands, Woolf and Bell, attended a fancy-dress ball to celebrate the closing of the Post-Impressionist exhibition at the Grafton Gallery as Tahitian maidens draped in curtains borrowed from their home in Hyde Park Gate. It seemed a curious choice: Tahiti was not even part of the British Empire, and the cinema was still too technically naive to be able to popularize exotic island paradises. Their gesture, however, was one of the first, if not the most significant, of tributes to what was to be a legend of irresistible potency: the rejection by an artist of the flesh pots of civilization for the unsullied innocence of the primitive. Moreover, it had been presented with a vigour and a freshness of an extraordinary kind in the thirty-seven paintings by Paul Gauguin of Breton and Tahitian scenes which formed the very core of the Grafton Gallery exhibition. Nine years later, when Somerset Maugham published his *The Moon and Sixpence*, a novel about a London stockbroker, who, deciding to become an artist, abandons his wife and family for painting on a South Sea island, he opened up to what would be millions of readers a more accessible version of the legend, converting it into one of the more seductive myths to have fascinated modern man.

Gauguin can be seen as one of a long line of seekers of freedom. The search for paradise was as old as Adam. From early Christian hermits to medieval monks, the quest for heaven on earth was perennially attractive. It took on more tangible forms when in the fifteenth and sixteenth centuries European man discovered new worlds other than his own, where men lived untrammelled by the artificial restraints of civilization, their needs provided for by an abundant nature, their freedoms unhampered by political limitations. This was the spirit which made America, and which ensured the popularity of books such as Daniel Defoe's *Robinson Crusoe*. Further impetus was given to the cultivation of the motion of an accessible Eden by that cluster of movements that in the middle of the eighteenth century produced Romanticism, with its emphasis on personal sensibility and freedom from intellectual as well as political restraints and its preference for the dominance of the heart over the mind.

By the beginning of the nineteenth century, the application of steam power to the printing press, which made book production cheaper and easier, combined with the growth of the illustrated popular press to make the glamour of distant places accessible to a rapidly expanding population. In addition, all the detritus of industrialism had created a new ugliness and opened up the gulf between rich and poor, so that the incentives to escape were more potent than ever before.

Gauguin was to build his career as an artist around this passion to escape, moving first to Brittany and then to Tahiti, but in doing so he was motivated by reasons other than a mere romantic desire to find peace and beauty in a remote island refuge. Firstly, his Peruvian up-bringing and time in the navy had made a traveller of him, and secondly he needed new stimulus to fire himself as an artist. His first important appearance on the Paris art scene had been at the Impressionist exhibition of 1880, and he was happy enough to paint for a while in that particular idiom. But the reign of Impressionism was over, and an artist of his age—he was thirty-two at the time—was no longer able to continue expressing himself in a style which was coming to be looked on as conventional. He needed a new and personal credo.

At the end of his first stay in Tahiti he wrote: 'I have escaped everything that is artificial and conventional. Here I enter into truth, become one with Nature. After the disease of civilization, life in this new world is a return to health.' And the theme echoes constantly throughout his letters. This was to be his dogma, this the source of his art and his iconography, the main plank in the almost constant publicity campaign he waged in his letters and elsewhere. But he saw it as involving much more than what his traditionalist predecessors, who had visited and painted in places such as the Pacific islands, had done. The image he had of himself was as the noble savage—Degas, to his great delight, had once described him as 'a collarless wolf in a forest'. This presentation of himself as the champion and exponent of the primitive and the instinctive could not have been better timed to fit in with the temper of the age.

In the past, primitive art had been despised because it failed to come up to the representational standards of the West. But by the latter half of the century, a new, craft-inspired emphasis on the importance to be attached to the influence of the material used in making an artefact on its form, the opening of various anthropological and oriental museums, and the books of writers such as Alois Riegl, who were propounding the notion that naturalistic imitation was an ideal entirely alien to primitive art, which had to be judged on its own terms, had made possible a new attitude to the art of savage innocence. Gauguin had every justification for drawing on the resources of this art for his style, and for seeking his subject matter in remote places. As he wrote to his daughter Aline, in the *Cahier* he composed for her in 1892, 'You will always find nourishing milk in primitive art. In the civilized arts I doubt you will.'

The only thing that really hindered him was lack of money. His continual battle against poverty, and later his ill-health, was a source of great suffering and resentment to him. He saw his role in the world as that of a Messiah, in an almost literal sense, painting himself when he was in Brittany both as the crucified Christ and as Christ in the garden of olives. It was the suffering Messiah that he emphasized in his letters, implying that this was the extent of the sacrifice he was making for the good of the world in general, and art in particular. He presented himself as a 'savage Messiah', a man the magnitude of whose achievements was matched only by the burden of his sufferings. This was also the justification for his abandonment of his family, and for the tone of many of his letters to his wife Mette, which varies from kindliness to querulous attacks about her lack of support. He saw his Messianic achievement quite clearly, uncontaminated by modesty, unhedged by qualifications: 'I created this new movement in painting, and many of the young people who have profited are not without talent, but once more it is I who shaped them. Nothing in them comes from themselves, but through me.' It is an extraordinary statement, with a clear God-like note reverberating through the last sentence. His supporters were disciples—recipients of his *dicta* and servants of his needs. Throughout the letters to his agent Daniel de Monfreid, to his friends and fellow artists, William Morice and Émile Schuffenecker, and, of course, to his wife Mette, there runs a constant stream of orders and commands. Not only are there never-ending instructions about getting money, sending artist's materials, and exhibiting and selling his paintings, but requests for things such as woollen vests, new shoes, mandolin strings and a homeopathic medicine set, all to be paid for out of highly hypothetical funds.

Gauguin's judgements on his contemporaries are often ungenerous and intolerant. Even his own followers are only 'not without talent', and an artist such as Puvis de Chavannes, seen as the father-figure of much Post-Impressionist painting, though occasionally praised, is put securely in his place (see page 136–7). Pissarro, without whose teaching and active promotion he might never have made a start as a painter, is dismissed as a time-serving stylistic opportunist; and even when he praises what the loyal De Monfreid is doing, he refers to his 'little paintings'. Whole movements are dismissed with scorn, though on one occasion he does make a mildly adulatory reference to Impressionism. Degas is the only one who escapes this barrage of condemnation, but that, it would seem, is largely because he had bought his paintings, spoken well of him, and was seen by Gauguin as an influential figure in the Paris art world. Nor was he in any way tolerant of its supporting figures; contumely is hurled at the heads of those small dealers such as Bauchy and Lévy who sold his pictures when they could. Not only is Vollard, who towards the end provided him with a regular income and supplies of artist's materials, described as an unscrupulous schemer, but for good measure his father is dragged into the condemnation. Even Théodore van Gogh, who did so much for him, is described as 'a calculating Dutchman'.

His low opinion of others was matched only by his high opinion of himself. 'I am indeed a great artist,' he wrote to Mette from Tahiti. 'You are right; you are not mad. I am a great artist, and I know it. It is because I am what I am that I have to endure so much suffering. One has to be a colossus to do what I am doing.' But there was doubt and ambivalence in his nature, too. As he recounts in his Tahitian journal, *Noa Noa*, describing his journey with a young man to collect wood for a statue, 'I was exhausted by the male role of having to be strong and protective, of having to have broad shoulders, just to support everything. Just for once to be the weak one, who loves and obeys.' (When Gauguin first arrived in Tahiti the natives thought he was a *mahu*, a man-woman, because of his long hair.) Yet it could be argued that his flight to Tahiti, his desire to be a 'savage', an 'uncollared wolf', were all attempts to reject, not support, the burdens and responsibilities of society, whether they consisted of paying taxes, supporting a family or conforming to accepted modes of behaviour. The problem, of course, was that, despite his Peruvian ancestry, despite his attempts to identify with the life and beliefs of a primitive society, he was a Parisian, an artist drawing the syntax of his art from a specifically European tradition. The conflict was always there. But, as he wrote in his autobiographical excursus of 1903, *Avant et Après*:

> 'You wish to know who I am; my works are not enough for you. Even at this moment as I write, I am only revealing what I want to reveal. What if you often do see me quite naked? There is no problem; it is the inner man you want to see. Besides I do not always see myself very clearly.'

CHAPTER I

Early Life

1848–1885

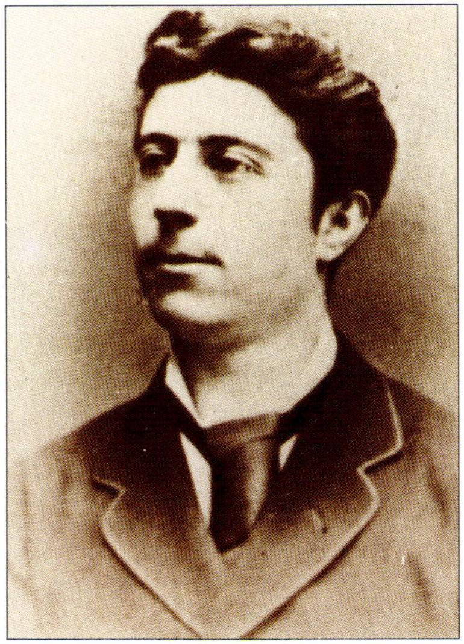

ABOVE: *A photograph of Gauguin taken in 1873, the year of his marriage to Mette Sophie Gad, possibly on the occasion of their engagement.*

MUCH OF GAUGUIN'S PERSONALITY and later preoccupations, his desire to travel and to discard respectability and responsibility, stemmed from his background. He came from a bohemian family and had a correspondingly unconventional childhood. His maternal grandmother, Flora Tristan, whose memory he cherished with special fervour and in whom he saw a prototype of himself, was descended from an ancient Peruvian family. Proud, fiery and independent, she was a socialist blue-stocking, a woman of great political fervour, who eventually migrated to France. Her husband, the engraver André François Chazal, was imprisoned for twenty years in 1838 on an unproven and dubious charge of attempting to murder her, an incident which Gauguin never once mentions in his writings. Gauguin's mother, Aline, whose portrait he always kept in his room, right to the end of his life, had been born in 1825 and married Clovis Gauguin, a republican journalist from Orléans. She bore him two children, Marie and, on 7 June 1848, Paul. In 1849 the family set sail for Peru, but Paul's father died on the journey, and, on arriving at Lima, they lived with Aline's great-uncle, Don Pio.

RIGHT: *Lima, the capital city of Peru, in the mid-nineteenth century. Gauguin spent his earliest years in the city; he was eighteen months old when he arrived with his mother and sister and six when they left. His memories of this exotic place and its colourful population remained with him throughout his life.*

A LIMA CHILDHOOD

My eyes have always been remarkable for their ability to remember things, and I remember from my childhood our house and a whole group of happenings: the presidential monument, the church whose dome had been placed on top, ready-made and all sculpted in wood.

I can still see our little negress, she who had to carry the prayer mat on which one prayed to church. I can also see our Chinese servant, who was so good at ironing. It was he who found me in the

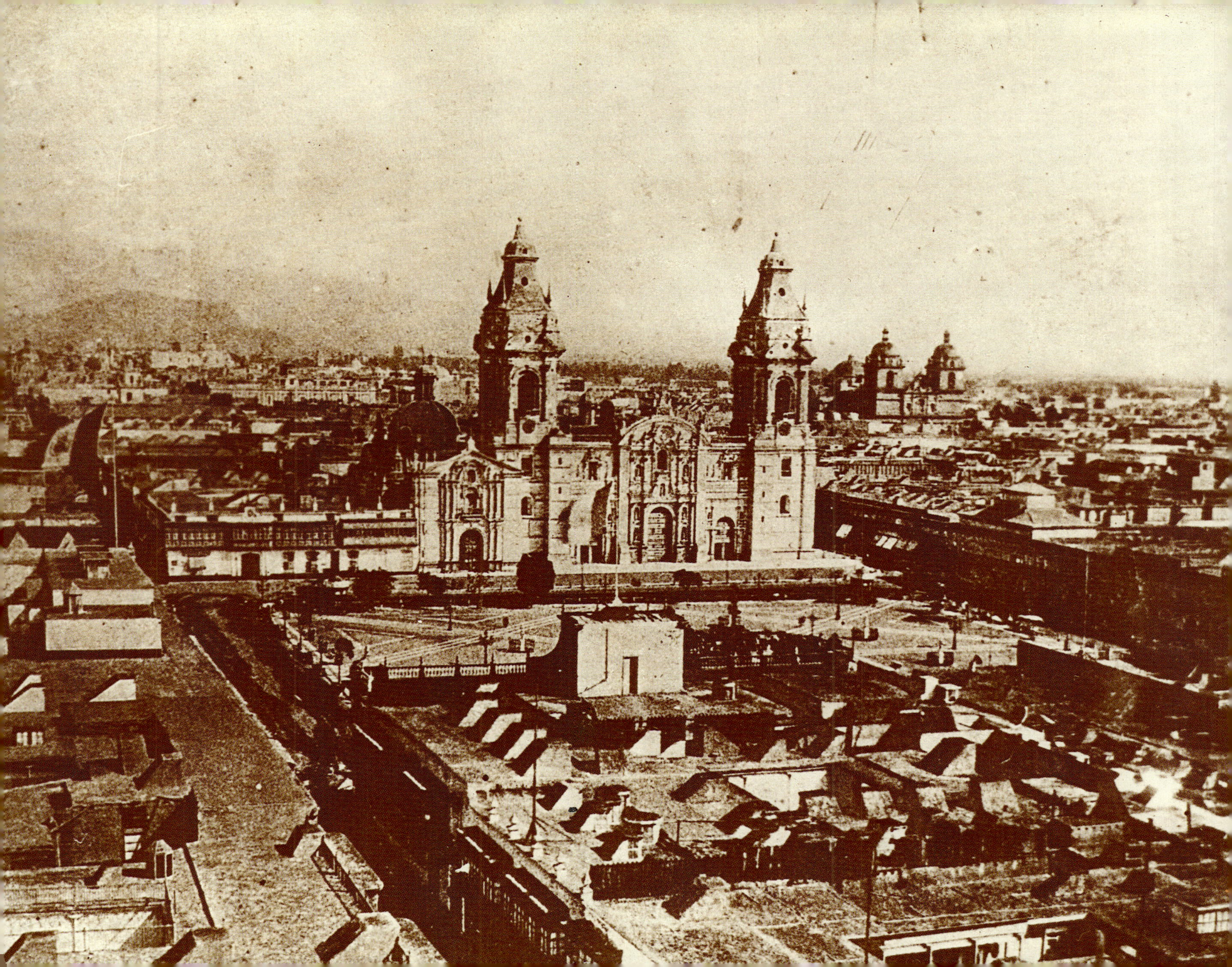

grocery shop where I was engaged in sucking sugar cane, seated between two barrels of molasses, whilst my mother was running round everywhere looking for me. I have always had a bit of a thing for escapades of this kind, for at Orléans, when I was nine, I had the idea of making off into the forest of Bondy, with a handkerchief packed with sand at the end of a stick, which I carried on my shoulder. It is an image that has always seduced me, that of a traveller, his stick and his bundle on his shoulder. Beware of images. Happily, the butcher took my hand and brought me back home, calling me a young rascal. As she was a Spanish lady of noble stock, my mother was very violent, and I was given a slapping with a tiny hand as supple as rubber. It is true that a few minutes later, in tears, she hugged and kissed me.

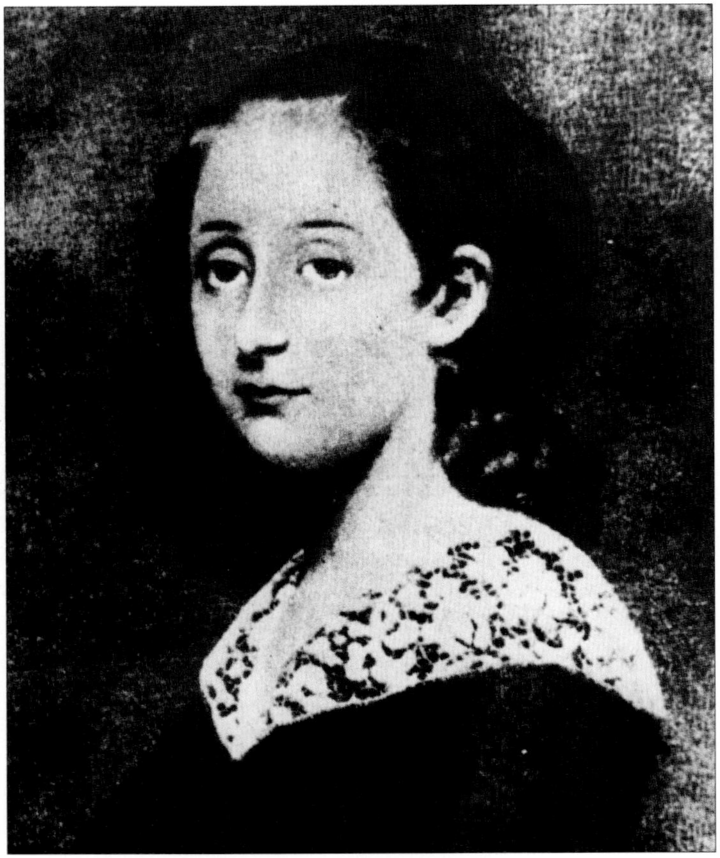

LEFT: *A photograph of Gauguin's mother, Aline, which he kept with him after her death and from which he painted a portrait in which her Spanish features are flattened to resemble his ideal Polynesian type.*

But let us not anticipate, and return to our city of Lima. In Lima at this time, in that delicious country where it never rains, the roof was a terrace, and the owners used to do something crazy; that is to say that upon the terrace they would keep a lunatic, attached by a chain to a ring, and the owner or tenant had a duty to provide him with a certain amount of basic food. I remember one day my sister, the little negress and I, sleeping in my room, the open door of which gave out on to the interior courtyard, were awakened and we could see just opposite us the face of the lunatic, who had climbed down the ladder. The courtyard was bathed in moonlight. None of us dared utter a word. I saw, and can still see, the lunatic enter our room, look at us and then climb back on to the terrace.

Avant et Après

RIGHT: *Gustave and Zoë Arosa with their daughters Marguerite, seated, and Irène with her husband Adolfo Calzado. Gauguin's mother nominated the genial banker and art collector her children's guardian after her death in 1867. In 1872 Arosa recommended Gauguin to the stockbroker Bertin, who gave him a job. Through him he also met his wife, Mette.*

IN 1855, ON THE DEATH of Paul's paternal grandfather, Guillaume, who had left them a trust fund, they returned to Orléans, where Paul was sent to a Jesuit seminary school which he abhorred. In the meantime, his mother had moved to Paris to work as a seamstress, and he joined her there in 1862. His first ambition was, significantly, to become a sailor. He passed the entrance exam for the merchant navy, making two trips to Rio de Janeiro and a thirteen-month journey around the world on *Le Chili*, visiting India and China and getting his first glimpse of Tahiti.

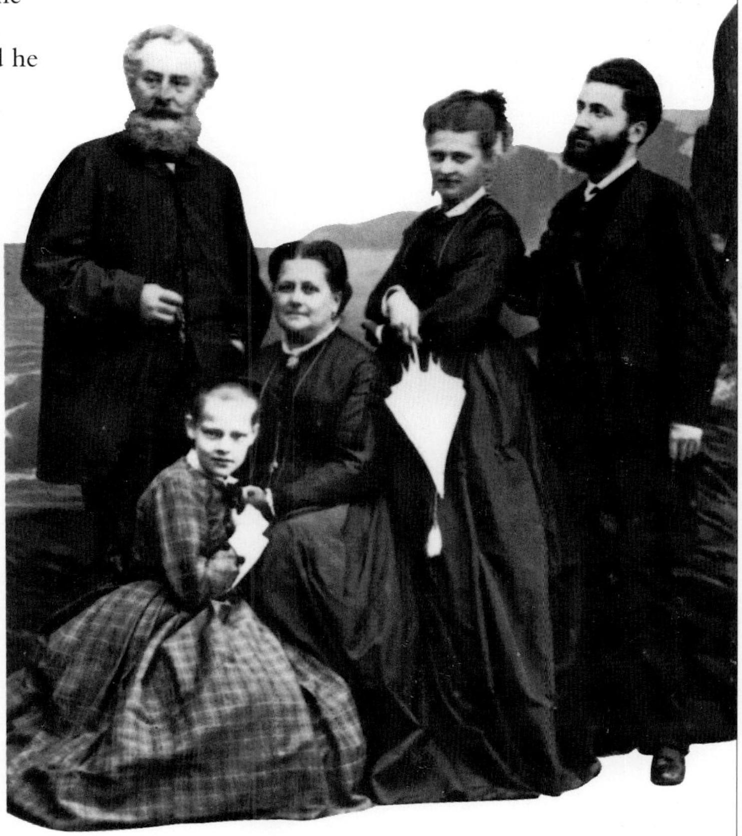

His mother died in 1867 and Gauguin transferred to the French navy, serving on board the *Jérôme-Napoléon* in the Mediterranean and the Black Sea, and, on the outbreak of the Franco-Prussian war in 1870, in the North Sea. In the meantime, he had inherited money and property in Orléans from his mother and paternal grandfather, and in 1871 settled in Paris under the tutelage of Gustave Arosa, a friend of his grandmother, who secured him a job in the stockbroking office of Bertin. Arosa was a friend and patron of a clutch of up-and-coming young artists calling

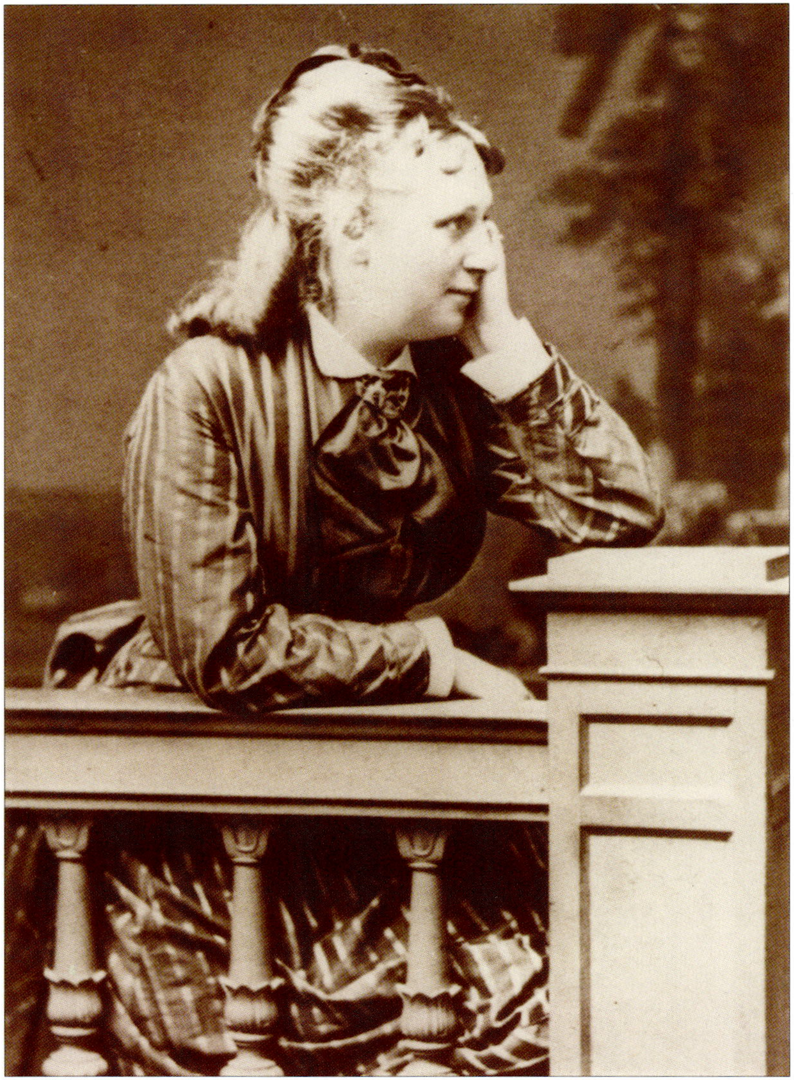

LEFT: *Mette Sophie Gad, captured just before her marriage to Gauguin in November 1873.*

themselves the Batignolles Group. Among them was Camille Pissarro, in whose style Arosa's daughter Marguerite taught the young Paul to paint. Another part-time artist in Bertin's office was Émile Shuffenecker, destined to become Gauguin's life-long friend and supporter.

In the spring of 1873, at a *pension* owned by a friend of the Arosa family, Gauguin met a twenty-two year old Danish girl, Mette Sophie Gad, whom he married in November. Over the next ten years they produced five children: Émile, Aline, Clovis, Jean and Pola. They lived in a comfortable flat in the Impasse Frémin, later moving to a more suburban house at Vaugirard. His views on the institution of marriage, however, were to remain sceptical throughout his life.

MARRIAGE

The institution of marriage is breaking up on all sides. There are two ways of defending this institution. The first is that all children would be abandoned without marriage, and in corroboration one points to the great number of children abandoned by their fathers outside wedlock. It would be easy to reply that this abandonment comes precisely in the greatest number of cases from the institution itself, from the shame of adultery, from the shame that comes from any illegal creation. One could also say that in modern society a woman, an inheritor of wealth like a man, having every facility to create a position for herself in all careers, can largely play her part in the education of the children. Death can quite quickly take away a father, and still the children are brought up. I myself, who am writing this, was deprived of my father when I was two. Finally, there is a financial problem to be resolved. If a rich young woman, say Mlle Rothschild, has an infant by her coachman, the child will be a bonny one, and will have no cause to complain about being abandoned by its father. And since in this matter the heart counts for nothing, but only financial considerations, let us see if such interests are harmed as a result of this noble institution. What is the lot

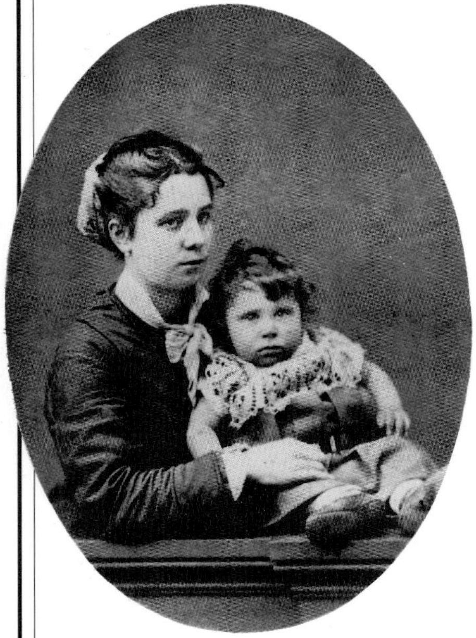

ABOVE: *The Gauguins' nursemaid, Justine, with their first child Émile, born in 1875, proving that the family lived in comfortable circumstances before the stockmarket crash of 1882.*

reserved for a young girl in 1900? If she has no dowry, three fates await her. A marriage can be arranged for her; her astute parents, by means of dirty tricks of varying degrees, can persuade some functionary, who does not have a great salary but an assured one and who is already middle-aged, to marry her. They will be marrying a treasure and the young girl, in the name of Morality, bowing her head before maternal authority, will do what her mother, her grandmother and her ancestors did: she will marry for permission to have a child, no more. She will be happy or unhappy, but she will always be a respectable woman.

Alternatively, she will be condemned to perpetual virginity, which from the point of view of her happiness, her health, from the point of view of the role that a human creature should play in society, is a morbid monstrosity.

Or again, she can flee her parents' house, take a lover, or two or three, and be dishonoured in the eyes of society and in her own. Finally, she will become a prostitute (hunger drives the wolf from the wood).

It follows from this observation that more than half of society, by reason of financial necessities, cannot marry and can only live by prostitution. In the other half of society, the wealthy, only half the young girls marry, because they are not beautiful and suitable husbands are becoming more rare. So only one in four women are truly eligible for marriage. You must admit, having observed how many divorces there are, or how many marriages that are unhappy, that there can't be many people left to proclaim the benefits of this noble institution.

Noa Noa

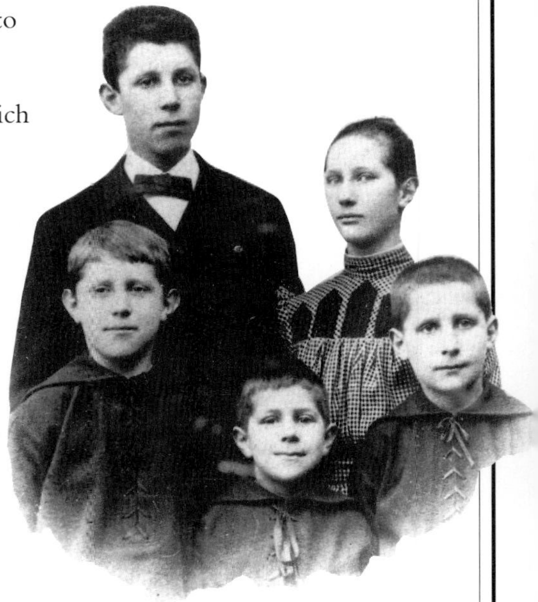

ABOVE: *After his separation from Mette, Gauguin constantly asked for photographs of the children, whom he greatly missed. This one, taken in Copenhagen c.1889, shows all five: Émile, Aline, Clovis, Jean-René, and Paul, known as Pola.*

GAUGUIN'S CAREER AS A BUSINESSMAN was not markedly successful, but his interest in painting was growing. This could not have happened at a more exciting time for, almost simultaneously, an enthusiastic coterie of young painters, who had been pupils of Marc Charles Gabriel Gleyre (1806–74)—Monet, Renoir, Sisley and

Bazille—was establishing connections with another group which included Pissarro, Cézanne, Berthe Morisot and Guillaumin. Under the tutelary leadership of Manet, these artists met in the cafés of the Batignolles quarter to form a movement which took shape, in the year that Gauguin's son Émile was born, in a group exhibition. The *bon mot* of a critic, after Monet changed the title of one of his Le Havre paintings to 'Impression: Sunrise', endowed them with the largely unwanted name of 'Impressionists'. Their beliefs were various, their personalities different, but they had in common a desire to record immediate experience, to capture the immediate visual impression, as it existed, not, as academic painters believed, as it was supposed to exist. They concentrated on painting subjects out of doors at one go before the light should change, and on eliminating the black lines and black shadows which traditional painters had used to define and organize their concept of visual experience. Gauguin, largely through the influence of Pissarro, was enraptured with these ideas—if for no other reason than that they were unconventional. Nor was his support simply theoretical; he amassed a considerable collection of works—by Manet, Renoir, Sisley, Monet, Pissarro, Guillaumin and Cézanne, for whose work he had an especial regard, even though his own style most clearly reflected that of Pissarro (as the critics were not slow to point out).

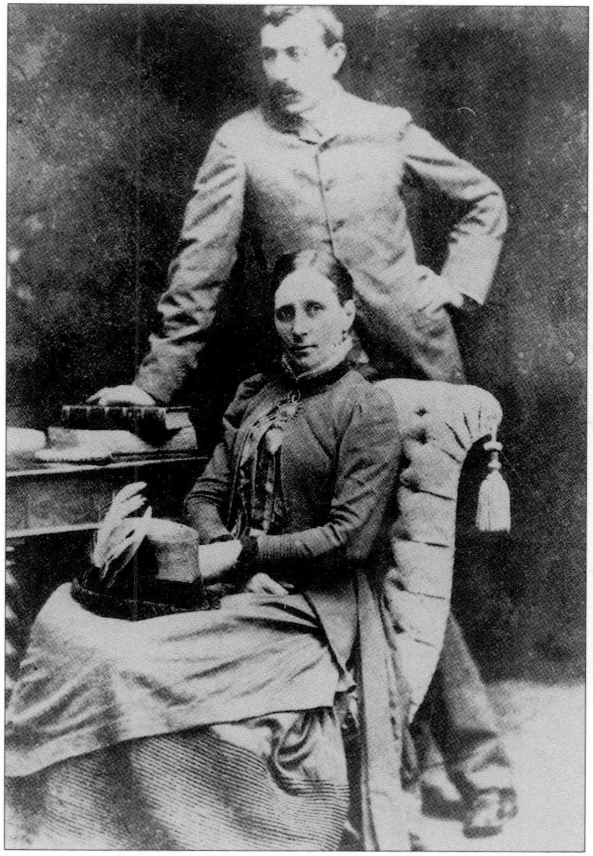

RIGHT: *A formal portrait photograph of Mette and Paul Gauguin in Copenhagen in 1885, looking every bit the bourgeois couple her family had expected.*

Copenhagen **To Émile Schuffenecker** ***14 January 1885***

Look at Cézanne, the misunderstood, an essentially mystic Eastern nature (he looks like an old man of the Levant). In his methods, he affects a mystery and the heavy tranquillity of a dreamer; his colours are grave like the character of orientals; a man of the south, he spends whole days on the mountain top reading Virgil and looking at the sky. So his horizons are lofty, his blues most intense, and with him red has an amazing vibration. Virgil has more than one meaning and can be interpreted as one likes; the literature of his pictures has a parabolic meaning with two conclusions; his backgrounds are equally imaginative and realistic. To sum up: when we look at one of his pictures, we exclaim, 'Strange.' But he is a mystic, even in drawing . . .

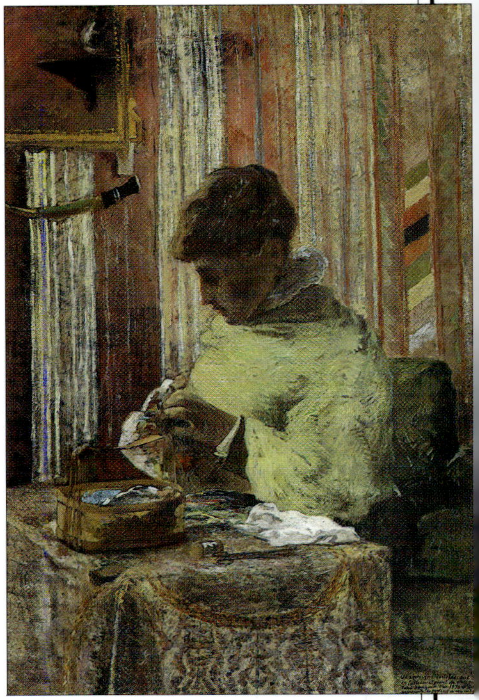

GAUGUIN'S FIRST EXHIBITED PAINTING was 'Sous-bois à Viroflay', accepted by the Salon of 1876. In the following year he began to take sculpture lessons from his neighbour, the academic Bouillot. He first made an appearance of sorts, by lending works from his own collection of Impressionist paintings, at the fourth Impressionist exhibition in 1879, the year in which he moved from the brokerage firm of Bertin to the bank run by André Bourdon. Henceforth, his appearances at the Impressionist exhibitions were regular and extensive: in 1880, seven paintings and one marble bust; in 1881, eight paintings and two sculptures; in 1882, twelve paintings; and at the last exhibition in 1886, no less than nineteen paintings. Nor was recognition slow in coming. In reviewing the 1881 exhibition, the influential J. K. Huysmans wrote, 'I do not hesitate to assert that amongst contemporary painters who have worked on the nude not one has been able to render it with such vivid realism as Gauguin who is the first artist in years who has attempted to represent the woman of our day in a bold and authentic painting.' Moreover, Durand-Ruel, the promoter of Impressionism, bought three of his works for 1,500 francs.

Emboldened by these successes, he forsook banking, and decided to devote himself entirely to painting and sculpture, accompanying Pissarro on expeditions to Pontoise and Osny. But he was already beginning to feel economic pressures, exaggerated by the recession

LEFT: METTE SEWING, *c.*1879–80 *This conventional genre portrait of Mette was made during the period of Gauguin's closest collaboration with the Impressionist group. The cosy domestic interior, among their favourite subjects, was soon abandoned by Gauguin as his own family life disintegrated.*

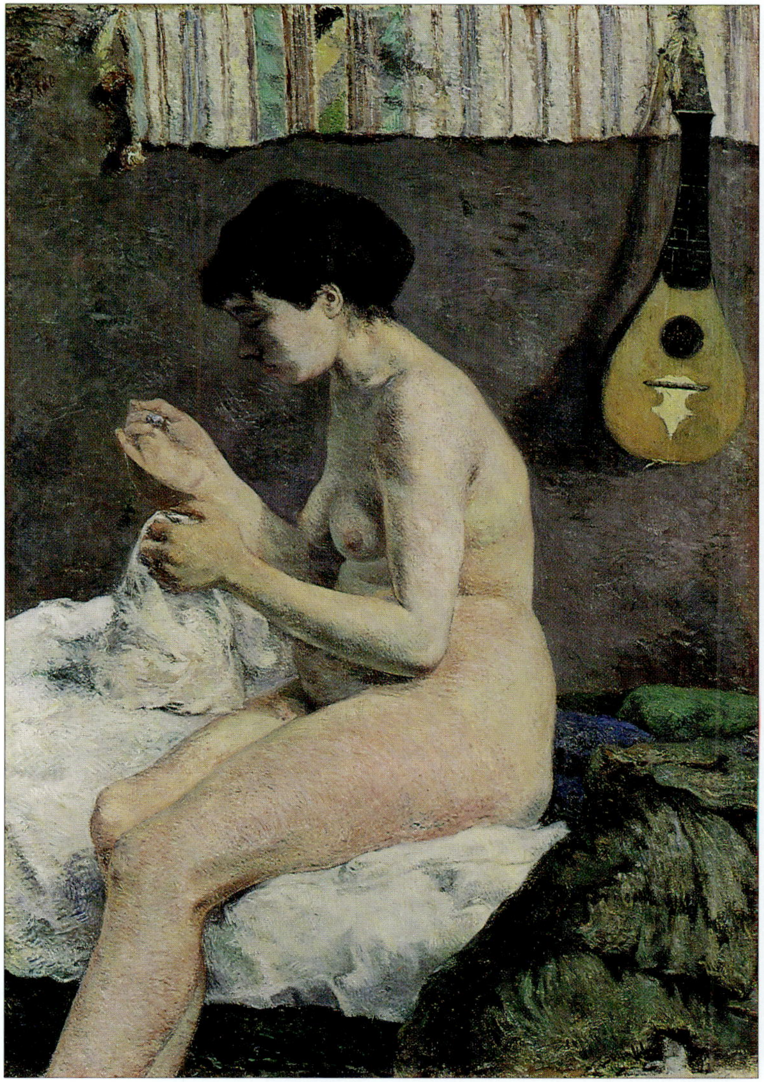

LEFT: SUZANNE SEWING (NUDE STUDY), 1880 *Gauguin probably used a professional model for this nude, painted before he became a full-time artist. The critic Huysmans called it a '. . . woman of our day . . . a bold and authentic canvas'. Described later by Pola as the 'first symptom of the return to Primitivism' in his father's work, it was at first so disliked by Mette she would not have it hung in the house.*

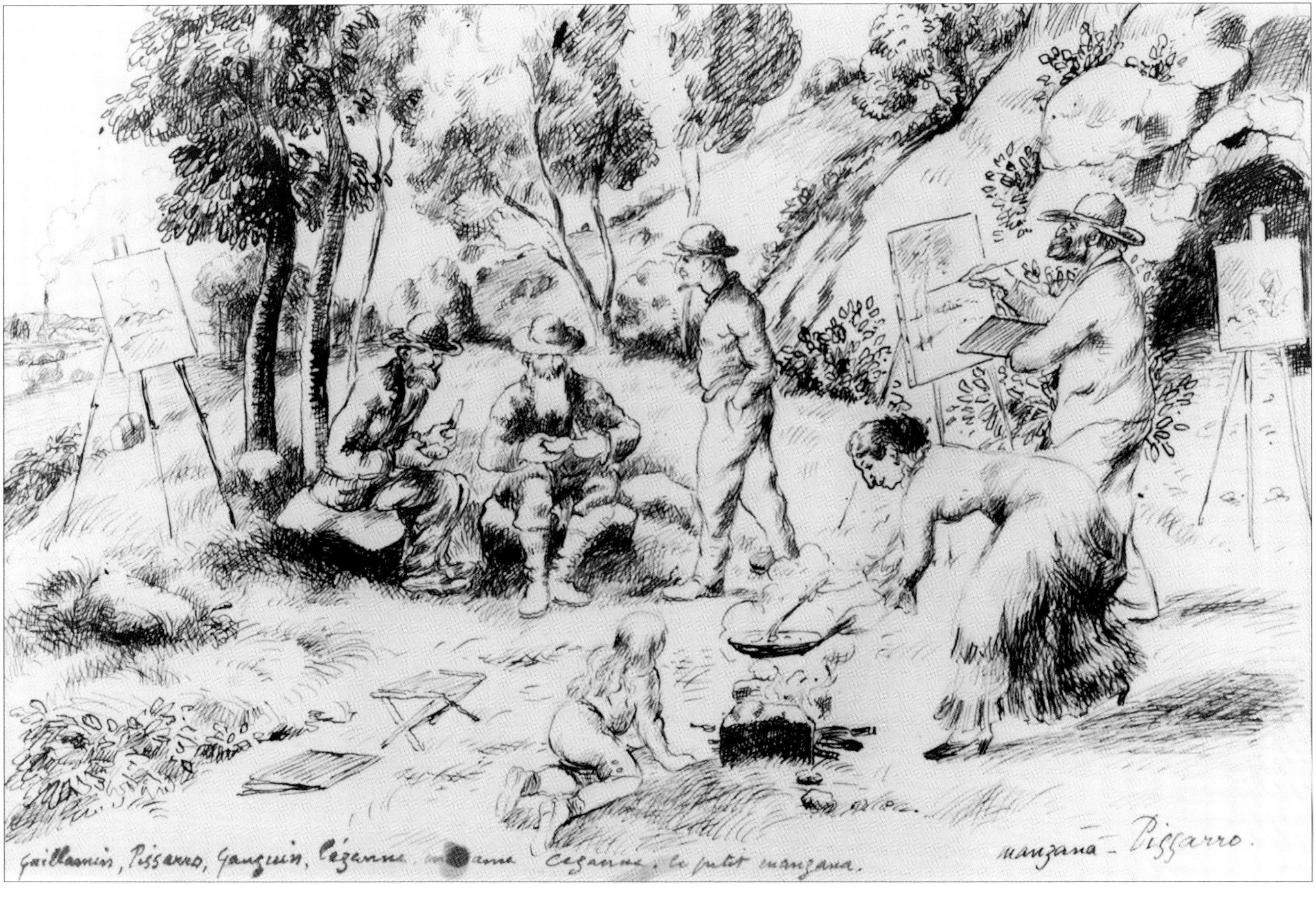
Guillaumin, Pissarro, Gauguin, Cézanne, madame Cézanne, le petit manzana.
manzana - Pissarro.

LEFT: AN IMPRESSIONIST PICNIC, *c.*1881 *A charming pen drawing by Pissarro's young son Georges (known as Manzana) recording one of the painting excursions into the countryside round Pontoise, near Paris, which Gauguin made in the summers between 1877 and 1883, whilst a guest of his friend Pissarro.*

that was hitting France. In 1883 the family moved to Rouen, where he thought life would be cheaper and buyers more plentiful. He was wrong, and on Mette's suggestion they decided to go to her native Denmark. This again was a failure. Gauguin could hardly speak Danish, and presented his most intractable side to her parents; nor were his attempts to earn a living there as a salesman for the French tarpaulin manufacturers Dillies & Co. successful. In June 1885 he returned to Paris on his own with his favourite son, Clovis. His art collection remained in Denmark, and his letters to Mette for the next decade or so were to contain frequent instructions about selling them and forwarding the proceeds to him. He had need of funds as Clovis and he were living in a squalid apartment near the Gare du Nord, and the boy fell ill:

> 'When Clovis came down with smallpox, I had twenty centimes in my pocket and had been eating stale bread on credit for the last three days. In my panic I decided to apply to a firm which displayed railway advertisements as a bill-sticker. My bourgeois apearance made the manager laugh. But I told him very earnestly that I had a sick child, and needed work. So I got a job pasting up advertisements at 5 francs a day. While I did so, Clovis lay sick with fever in our only bed, and in the evening I would come home and look after him.'

Later, he moved up the scale, becoming a clerk in the railway offices.

Whatever his penury, however, Gauguin managed to retain his contacts with Pissarro and the rest of the Impressionists, and through the engraver Félix Bracquemond came to know the ceramicist Ernest Chaplet, from whom he learnt the techniques of that craft which he was to exploit intermittently throughout the rest of his career. He produced works in this medium of remarkable power and originality, and also found employment in a commercial ceramic factory for a short time. But painting remained his main preoccupation, and in June 1886, leaving Clovis in a boarding school, and fortified by a loan of 300 francs from the banker Eugène Mirtil, he made his first excursion to Pont-Aven in Brittany.

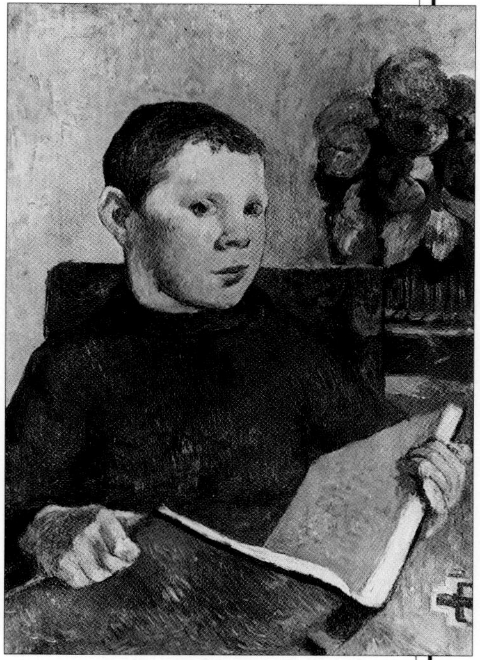

ABOVE: CLOVIS GAUGUIN: PORTRAIT, *c.*1886 *Gauguin took his favourite son Clovis to Paris when he left Copenhagen in 1885.*

CHAPTER 2

Brittany and Martinique

1886–1890

GAUGUIN'S FIRST CHOICE OF BRITTANY as a place in which to contact the primitive and the unspoilt was superficially surprising. It was only a fourteen-hour train journey from Paris, and the main reason he first went there in the spring of 1886 was because he had heard from his Parisian landlord, the Breton painter Félix Jobbé-Duval, that the village of Pont-Aven possessed an inn, the Pension Gloanec, which offered extensive credit. But Brittany was not France, and in spirit and feeling it was more than a railway journey's distance from Paris. A Celtic enclave, superstitiously Catholic and royalist in its attitudes, its roadside calvaries, its contorted churches, its picturesque pilgrimages to certain shrines, and its quaintly dressed people speaking their own bizarre language breathed the last enchantments of the Middle Ages.

There were suggestions everywhere, too, of an even more remote past, in the Stone Age dolmens, menhirs and megaliths that littered the countryside, far-flung progeny of Stonehenge, with their strange drawings and symbols. When Gauguin was living in Pont-Aven, archaeologists at nearby Carnac were uncovering a Gallic temple, with crude statues of Venus, Minerva and a Mother Goddess, symbols of an age utterly alien to the prim niceties of nineteenth-century France.

Gauguin was not the first artist to be inspired by the area. Pont-Aven had been a place of resort for artists since the end of the eighteenth century, and in 1798 the Breton poet Louis Chambry had written of it, 'The neighbourhood of Pont-Aven, and the village itself, offers a hundred picturesque subjects for the painter who wants to make studies.' In 1865 a group of American artists had settled there under the leadership of Robert Wylie of Philadelphia, who had established for himself a reputation as a painter of genre pictures in

BELOW: BRETON GIRL SEATED, 1886 *Gauguin made many studies of young Breton girls at this period, attracted by the dramatic patterns of their dress. Many were used as studies for oils; this girl, done in charcoal, brush and watercolour, appears seated on a wall in 'The Breton Shepherdess'.*

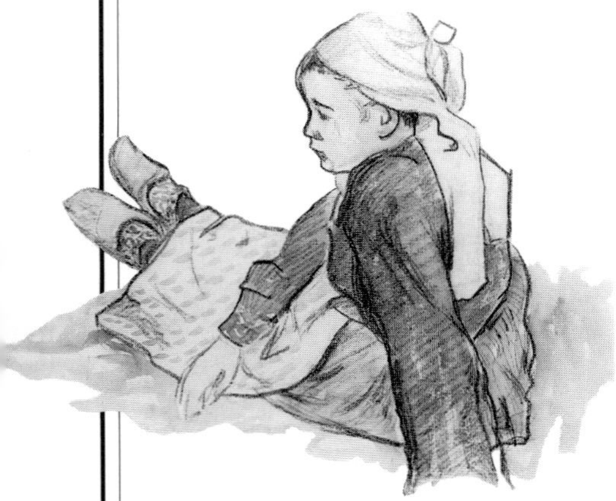

RIGHT: THE ROUND DANCE OF BRETON GIRLS, 1888 *Gauguin described this painting as a 'Gavotte Bretonne' in a letter of June 1888 to Théodore van Gogh (see page 43), who exhibited it in the artist's first one-man show that year, and sold it the following year. The theme of the Round Dance, traditionally performed after haymaking, was popular with many of the Pont-Aven painters. Though he still employs an Impressionist technique Gauguin's use of colour is becoming increasingly less naturalistic.*

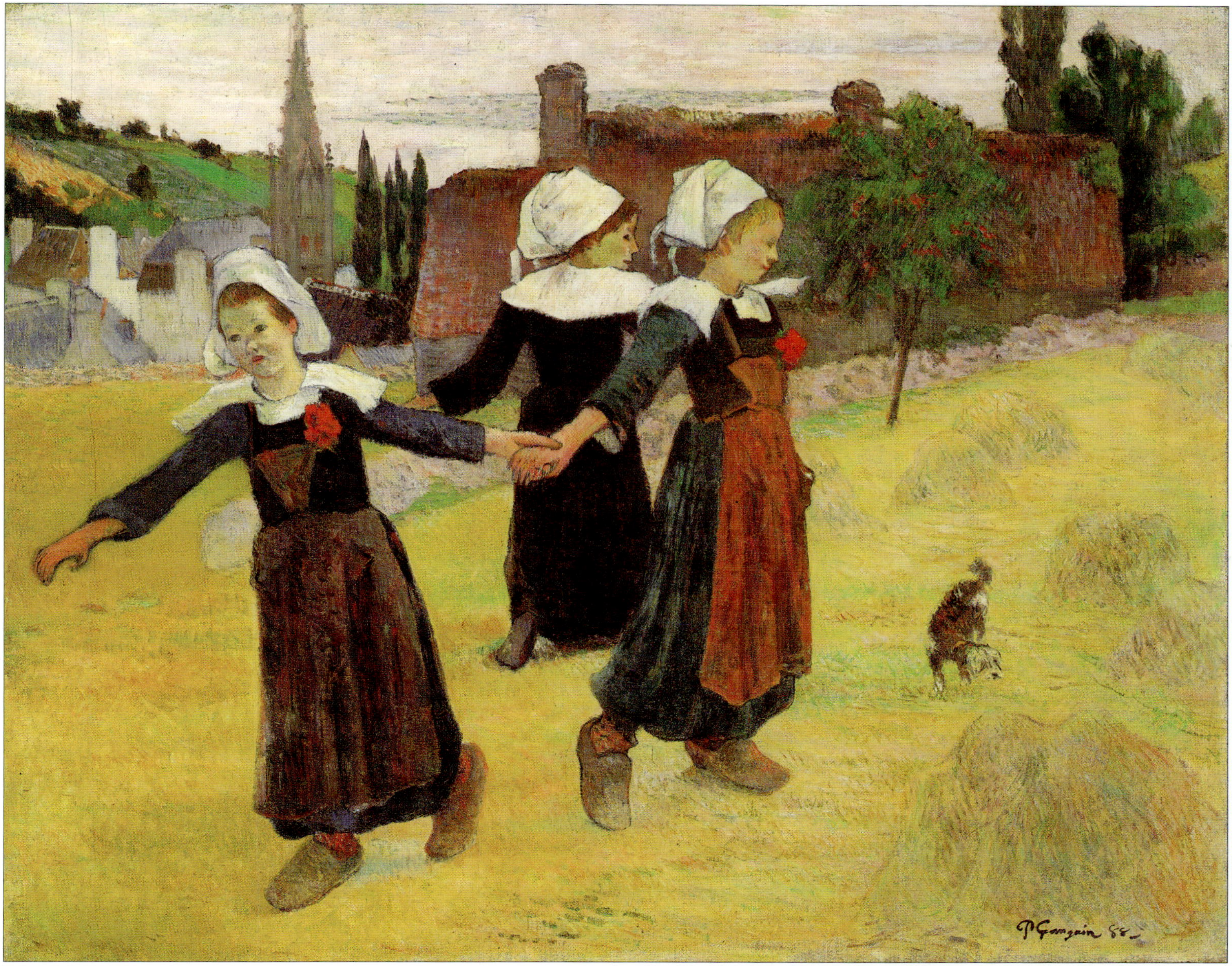
P Gauguin 88

what might roughly be described as a Rembrandtesque style. The number of American and, later, English artists working there had been increased by those reluctant to stay in Paris during the recent war and its aftermath, and they were joined by a number of French painters, the former staying mainly at the more expensive Hôtel des Voyageurs, the latter at the Pension Gloanec, which had an inn sign painted by one of its guests.

Secure in an artistic community, which he strove to dominate, freed from family attachments—his wife and all the children save Clovis, who was at school in Paris, were in Copenhagen—Gauguin found his art flourished, drawing inspiration and subject matter from the peasant life around him as well as from Breton sculpture and the local pottery. During three of his four sojourns in Brittany, in 1886, 1889 and 1890, his painting took on a rugged almost ungainly vitality; it rejected the use of descriptive colour, it assumed mystic dimensions, and, by its vital originality and the fervour of his own convictions, attracted to him followers such as Sérusier, Émile Bernard and others. Despite an occasional complaint, his letters were amiable, boastful, opinionated, confident. He had found a powerful alternative to the sophisticated, the literary and the mechanical, and he revelled in his new-found freedom. A Scottish artist working in Pont-Aven, A. S. Hartrick, recorded Gauguin's appearance at this time:

> 'Tall, dark-haired and swarthy of skin, heavy of eyelid, and with handsome features, all combined with a powerful figure. He dressed like a Breton fisherman, in a blue jersey, and wore a beret jauntily on the side of his head. His general appearance, walk and all, was rather that of a well-to-do Biscayan skipper of a coasting schooner; nothing could be further from madness or decadence.'

Pont-Aven **To Mette Gauguin** ***c.25 July 1886***

I have succeeded in finding some money for my trip to Brittany, and I am living here on credit. There are hardly any French people

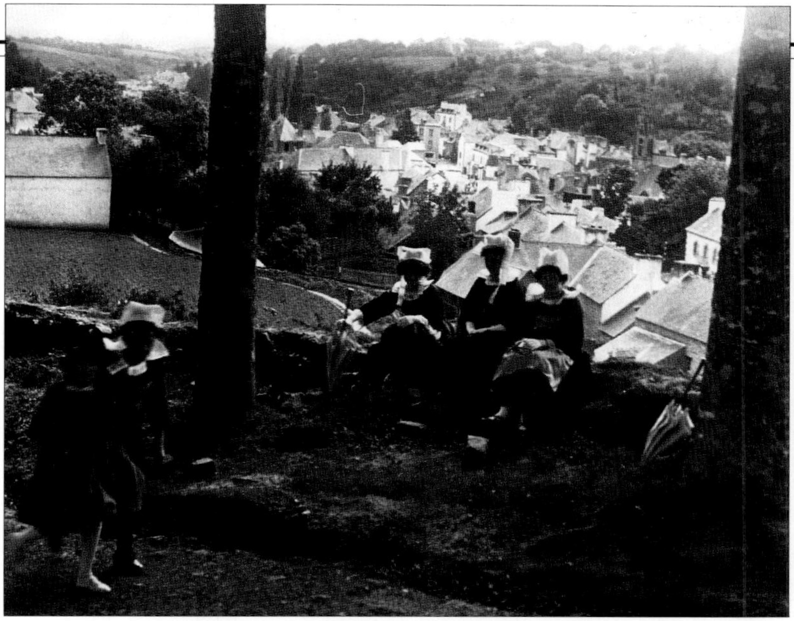

LEFT: *Girls of Pont-Aven, such as these promenading above the village in their Sunday best, were frequent subjects of Gauguin's sketching expeditions. Gauguin carefully distinguished the different headdresses particular to each village and each social occasion; in his Pont-Aven paintings the coiffure is notably different from the dark nun-like coifs of his Le Pouldu women.*

here, but a lot of foreigners—one Dane and two Danish women, Hagborg's brother and a lot of Americans.

My painting provokes a lot of discussion and, I must say, is very well received by the Americans. It is a good sign for the *future*.

It is true that I have made a good deal of progress, and you would hardly be able to recognize my painting. I hope that I shall make something of it this season, and if you can get something out of selling the Manet you must send it to me. What a shame that we did not come to live in Brittany before. At the hotel we pay 75 francs a month for full board and lodging—and the food is enough to make me feel blown out every time I sit down to a meal. There is a house for sale here at 800 francs with a stable converted into a studio, and a garden. I am sure that a family could live very happily here on 300 francs a month.

You may think that life here is isolated and cut off. Not at all. There are painters here in both winter and summer, English, Americans and so on . . . If I can arrange to get a small, certain and regular income from my pictures, I shall come and live here throughout the year . . .

I shall be renting a small studio near the church at Vaugirard,* where I shall be able to work sculpting pots for ceramic production as Aubé used to do. M Bracquemond, who has befriended me because of my talent, obtained this job for me, and says that it could *become* very lucrative.

Let us hope that I have the same talent in sculpture that I have in painting, at which of course I shall continue to work.

Kiss the children for me . . .

If you can take a photograph of little Aline, send it to me.

* In Paris.

Pont-Aven — To Mette Gauguin — **end July 1886**

. . . I am working here a great deal, and successfully too, and am respected as the most redoubtable painter in Pont-Aven, though it is true this does not bring me in a single sou. But perhaps it is laying the foundation for the future. In any case, I have acquired a considerable reputation and everybody here (Americans, English, Swedes and French*) asks me for my advice, which I am stupid enough to give, for in actual fact they take advantage of me without any form of gratitude.

I am not getting any fatter as a result of my work. I weigh 138 pounds—less than you. I am becoming as desiccated as a kipper, but on the other hand I am feeling rejuvenated. The more troubles I have, the greater the strength I seem to possess. I do not know where I am going, and I am living here on credit. Money worries totally discourage me, and I want to see the end of them.

In the long run we must resign ourselves, come what may, and perhaps one day, when my art has opened everybody's eyes, some enthusiastic soul will rescue me from the gutter.

Don't let all this bitterness bother us; since I am going to be here for three months to rehabilitate myself, let us take advantage of the tranquillity . . . Kiss the children for me, and send me news of them.

RIGHT: *The kitchen of the Pension Gloanec in July 1892; Madame Jeanne Gloanec with her chef and other staff in a playful charade. On the dresser above them, the bed-warmers and candle-sticks await to fight the Breton damp and evening darkness.*

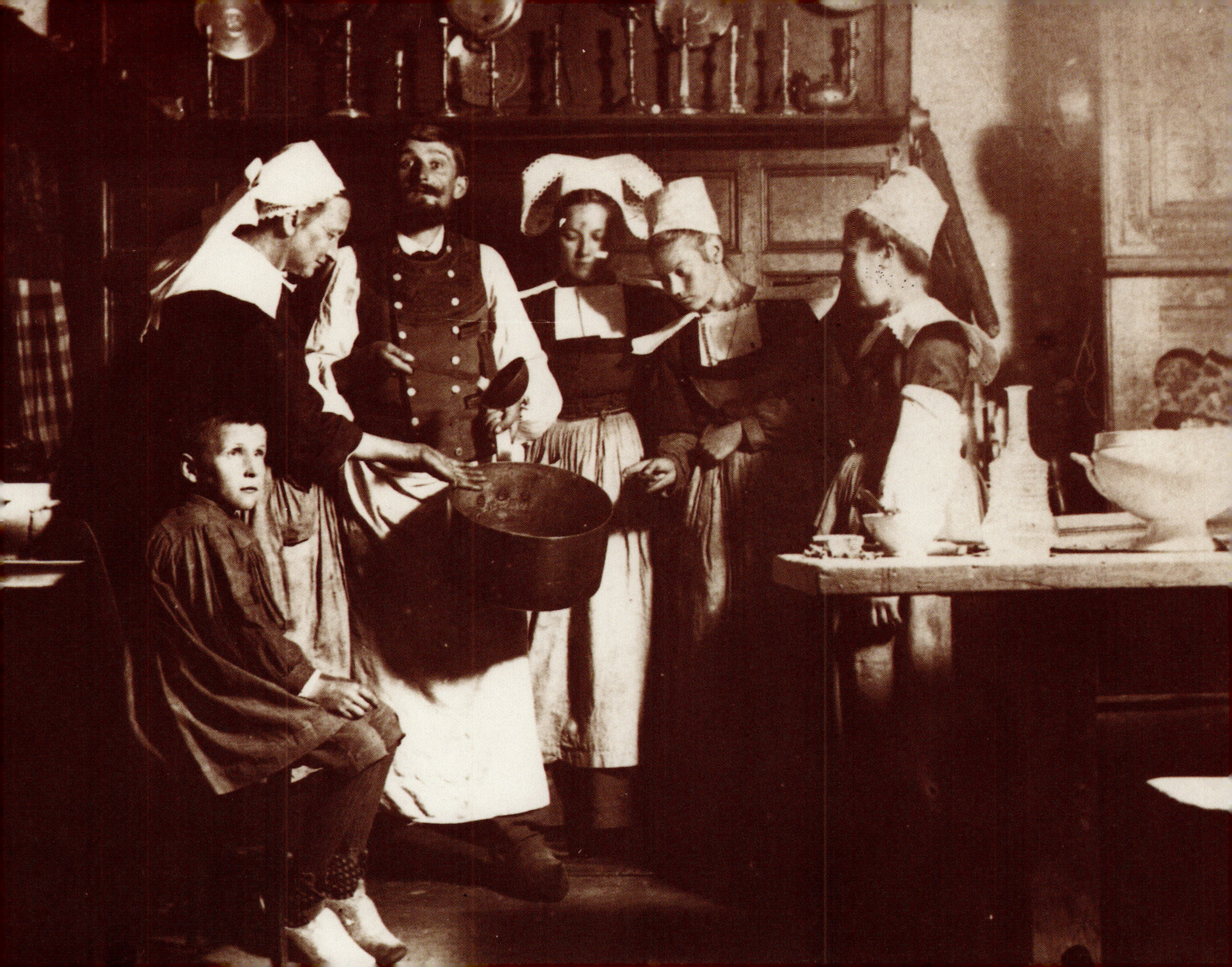

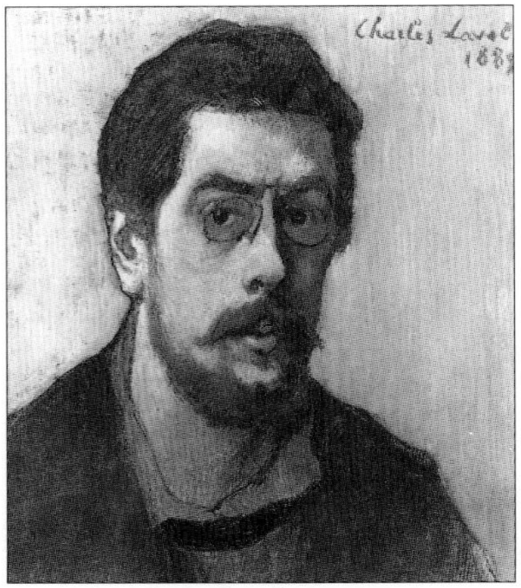

ABOVE: *Charles Laval accompanied Gauguin to Martinique, via Panama, in 1887. Following severe attacks of malaria and dysentery, Gauguin returned by working his passage to France in November, but Laval stayed until the following summer. He painted this self-portrait the following year.*

* In the summer of 1886, amongst the painters in Pont-Aven were: twenty-six year old Charles Laval, who had just left Cormon's studio and became the only close friend Gauguin made in Pont-Aven at this time; the American Presbyterian landscape painter Arthur Wesley Dow; Émile Bernard, who had turned up with a visiting card with 'Impressioniste' after his name, and who later recorded, 'Gauguin paid absolutely no attention to me'; and a handful of older academic painters.

Pont-Aven **To Mette Gauguin** ***mid-September 1886***

. . . The other day I had news of Clovis; he seems to be enjoying the *pension* much more and he is behaving like the old Pont-Neuf. I miss him, and if I had the money I would bring him here. The poor little fellow has never had a holiday, but one can only do what one can in this world. The evenings at Pont-Aven are a bit tedious when one is on one's own and has finished working . . . There is absolute silence all around me; I must admit it's not very stimulating. Days follow each other with such uniformity that I have nothing to tell you that you do not know already.

In a month's time, unfortunately, I shall have to go back to Paris to look for business; let us hope that the sculpture for ceramic production which I am going to undertake will bring in enough to feed me and Clovis . . .

GAUGUIN RETURNED TO PARIS late in 1886, and spent a month in hospital as the result of some kind of heart attack. When he recovered he threw himself vigorously into the production of ceramic ware, many pieces of which were ornamented with Breton themes. Anxious to escape from Paris again, in April 1887, with Charles Laval, a young painter whom he had met at Pont-Aven, he set off for his first island paradise, Taboga in the Pacific. Inadequate funds got them only as far as Panama, where his brother-in-law, Juan Uribe, lived. After spending fifteen days as a navvy on the building of the Panama Canal, Gauguin accumulated enough money to move

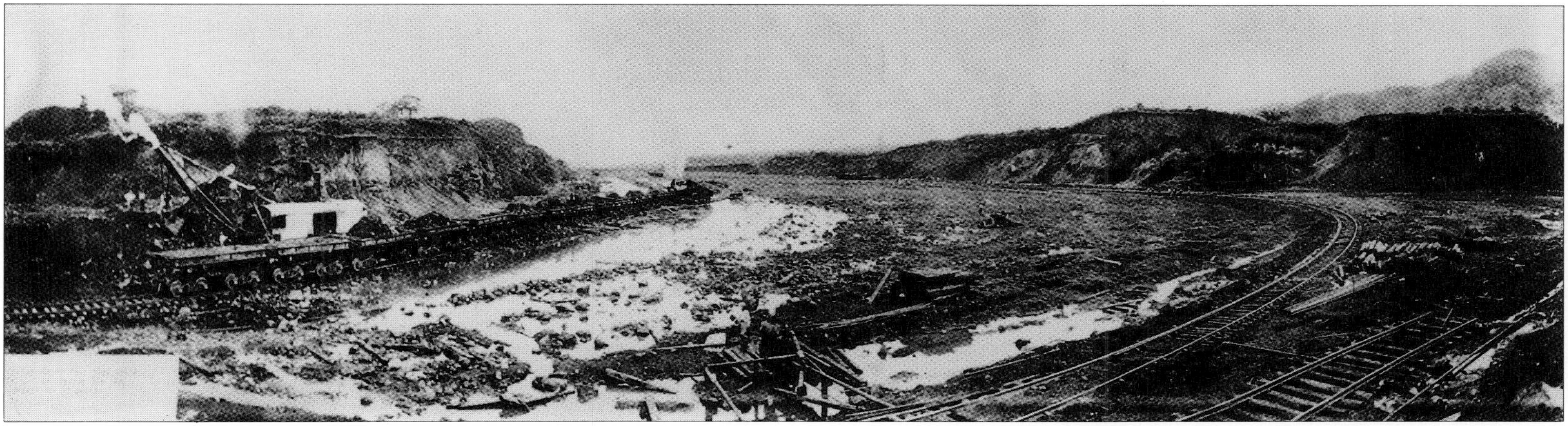

ABOVE: *The Panama Canal in the early days of its construction, at the time of Gauguin's stay in May 1887. He worked for two weeks for the Society of Public Works in Colon, staying with his brother-in-law, Juan Uribe, until he could afford to move on to Martinique.*

on to the Caribbean island of Martinique, where he stayed for four months, living in a hut on a plantation two kilometres from Saint-Pierre, wracked with dysentery—his first experience of a tropical paradise.

Martinique **To Mette Gauguin** ***20 June 1887***

This time I am writing to you from Martinique . . . Laval has just been struck by a bad attack of yellow fever, which I cured with homeopathic medicine. So all's well that ends well.

At the moment we are both living in a native cabin, and it's a paradise on the shore of the isthmus. Below us is the sea, fringed with coconut trees, above, fruit trees of all sorts, and it is only twenty-five minutes away from the town. Negroes and negresses walk about all day with their Creole songs and constant chattering. But don't think that it's monotonous—on the contrary, it's very varied. I can't tell you my enthusiasm for life in the *French* colonies, and I'm sure you would feel the same. Nature is at its most opulent, the climate hot, with cool spells intervening. With a little money you can have all that is needed to be happy. But a certain sum is

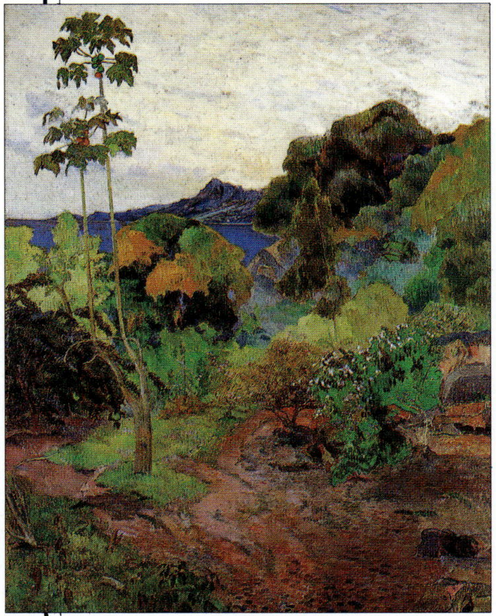

ABOVE: TROPICAL VEGETATION, MARTINIQUE, 1887 *'I had a decisive experience in Martinique. It was only there that I felt my real self,'* Gauguin *said in a letter to Charles Morice at the end of 1890. This painting from Gauguin's first stay in the tropics prefigures his future style in its brilliant warm colours and dense patterns. The volcanic peaks overlook the bay of St Pierre from the south; comparison with the photograph (right) emphasizes how Gauguin has striven to remove practically all trace of habitation.*

necessary. For instance, with *thirty thousand francs* one could have, at this very moment, an estate which would bring in between eight and ten thousand francs a year, and live, that is to say eat, like a gourmet.

And the only work you would have to do would be to supervise some negroes to harvest the fruits and vegetables, which need no cultivation anyway.

We have started to work, and I hope to be able to send back some interesting pictures. In any case, we are going to need some money in a few months; it is the only black cloud on the horizon. I would very much like to have some news from you, and with all this moving about I haven't had a letter. Here is a festival coming along again which I shall pass without *anybody* saying a word to me!

I assure you that here a white person has great difficulty keeping his virtue intact, for the wives of Potiphar are everywhere. Practically all of them are coloured, ranging from ebony black to the tinted white of the black race, and they exercise their spells through fruits, which they give to you after endowing them with powers to seduce you. The day before yesterday, a young negress of sixteen—and my word wasn't she pretty—offered me a guava, which had been split and squeezed at the end. I was about to eat it after the young girl had left when a yellow-skinned notary who happened to be there took the fruit from me and threw it on the ground. 'You are a European and don't know the country,' he said. 'You must never eat a fruit without knowing where it comes from. This fruit possesses a charm; the negress has rubbed it on her stomach, and afterwards you will be at her command.' I thought he was joking.

Not at all—this miserable mulatto (who was, nevertheless, educated) believed what he was saying. Now that I have been warned, I shall not succumb, and you can rest assured about my virtue. I hope to see you here one day with the children. Now don't start bewailing; there are colleges in Martinique, and whites are treated like superior beings.

Write twice a month. I kiss you and the children tenderly. You can't say this is a horrid letter.

Martinique — **To Émile Schuffenecker** — ***early July 1887***

. . . We have been in Martinique, the land of Creole gods, for three weeks . . .

What gives me the greatest pleasure are the human beings, and every day there is a constant coming and going of negresses decked in gaudy brightly-coloured finery, walking with infinitely varied and graceful movements. At the moment, I confine myself to making sketch after sketch to penetrate their character, but I shall get them to pose eventually. Whilst carrying heavy burdens on their heads, they chatter on endlessly. Their gestures are very special to them, and their hands play an important role, in harmony with the movement of their hips . . .

Martinique — **To Mette Gauguin** — ***c.25 August 1887***

Do not be too sad when you receive my letter; every day it is necessary to get more and more used to unhappiness. It seems that ever since I left Copenhagen everything has come collapsing down on us. They are right: no good comes when a family is separated.

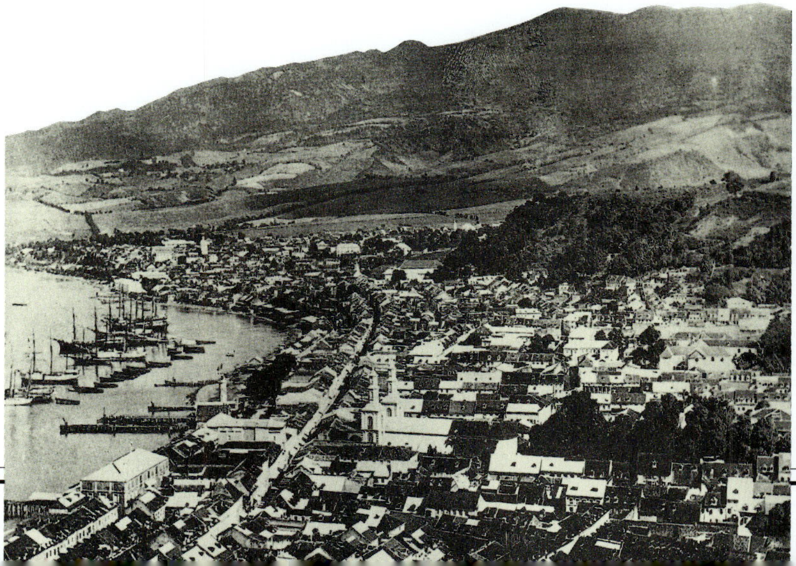

RIGHT: *A photograph of St Pierre, Martinique, taken before the eruption of Mount Pelée in 1902 destroyed the busy port and town.*

The Search for Paradise

I have virtually risen from the grave to write. This is my first news from you; all your letters have gone wandering all over the place.

During my stay at Colon I contracted an illness; I was poisoned by the marshy miasmas that rose from the canal. My vitality gave me enough strength to resist, but once arrived in Martinique, I began to get weaker day by day. Briefly, it is a year since I collapsed with dysentery and marsh fever, without the power to get up. At the moment my body is a skeleton, and my voice has vanished in my throat. Very close to succumbing every night, I finally got the upper hand, but I have suffered agony in the stomach. Even the little I eat gives me atrocious pains in the liver, and I have to make an effort to write to you. I am at the end of my tether. You can understand that my last financial resources have gone on medicine and visits to the doctor. He says that it is absolutely necessary that I return to France, otherwise I shall always be ill with liver troubles and fever.

Ah my poor Mette, how I regret that I am not dead, and then all would be over. Your letters have given me pleasure, but at the same time sorrow, which at the moment overwhelms me.

RIGHT: MARTINIQUE PASTORAL, 1887
This zincograph was one of two inspired by Gauguin's stay in Martinique included in the 'Volpini Suite' exhibited in Paris during the World's Fair in 1889.

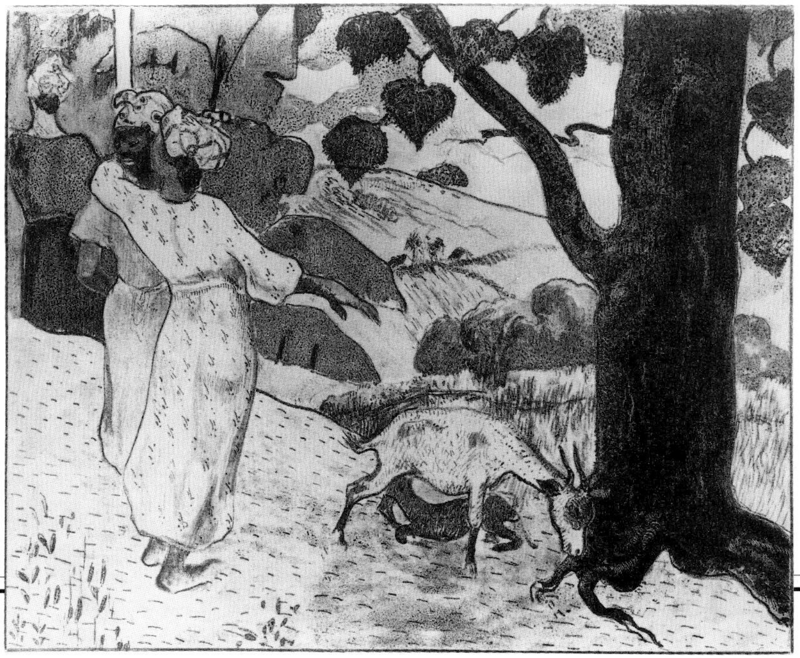

RIGHT: THE MANGO PICKERS, 1887
One of the earliest examples of Gauguin's desire to record the daily lives of the natives of the tropical islands, this canvas still reveals the influence of Cézanne and the Impressionists in its return to looser brushstrokes and less solid areas of colour; the angled perspective suggests a debt to Degas's characteristic bird's-eye view and vanishing horizon.

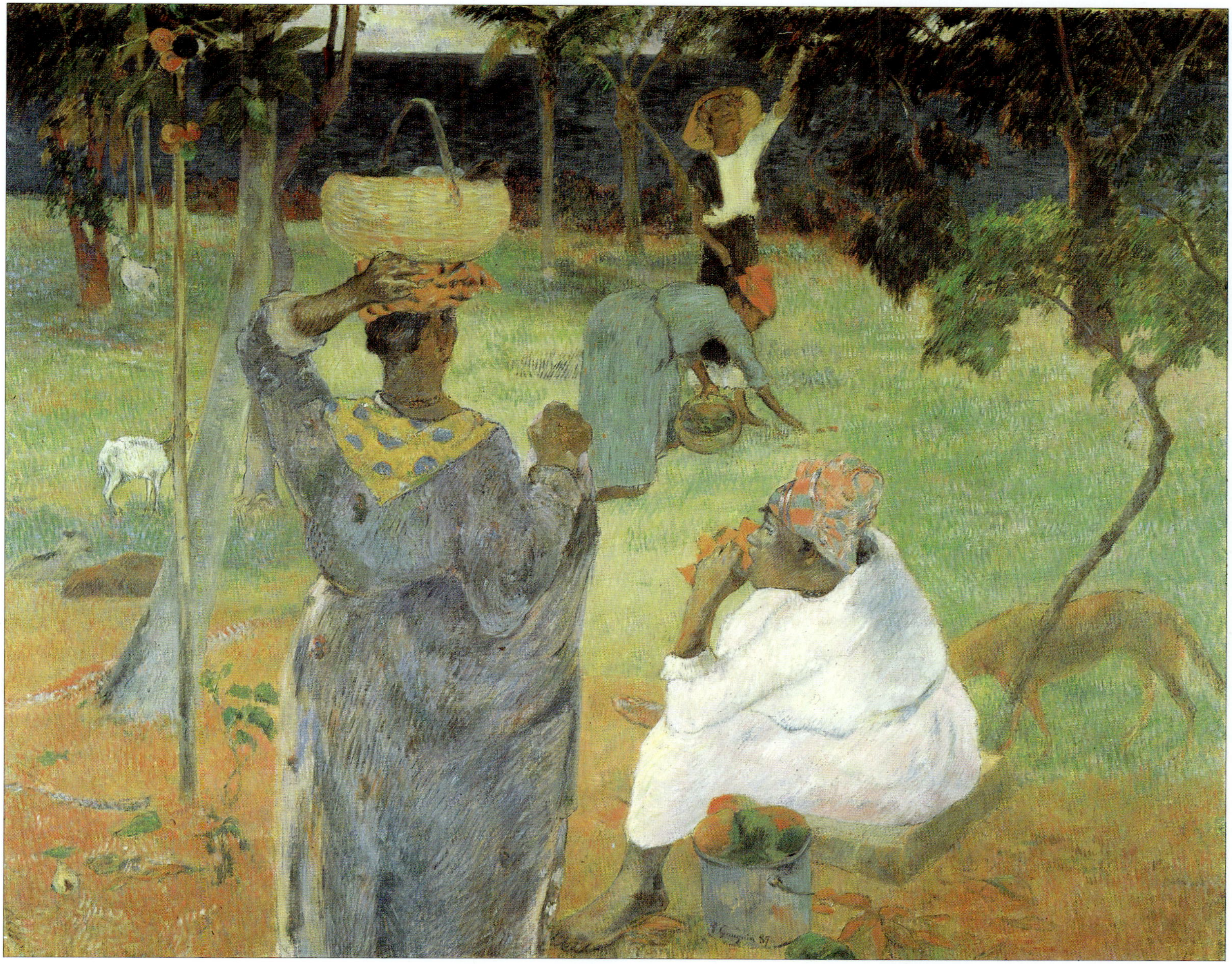

If we detested each other, *hate would give us strength*, but you are beginning to feel the need of a husband just when that is impossible. Overwhelmed with work, you ask me to come to your rescue.

What can I do? At this moment I am in a native cabin, stretched out powerless on a bed of seaweed, and I have nothing to pay for my return to France. I am writing to Schuff so that, for the last time, he can come to my assistance, as he has done in the past. This post brought me good news about my *ceramics*. It seems that they have had some success, and that on my return I shall find a silver lining. When things are going well it is a *good trade* to make money out of—15 to 20 francs a day, in addition to my painting . . .

See you soon, dear wife. I embrace you, and I love you; though I should hate you when I look back and see the evil passions that separated us. From that day onwards, everything has gone from bad to worse. A thousand kisses to the children. Shall I ever see them?

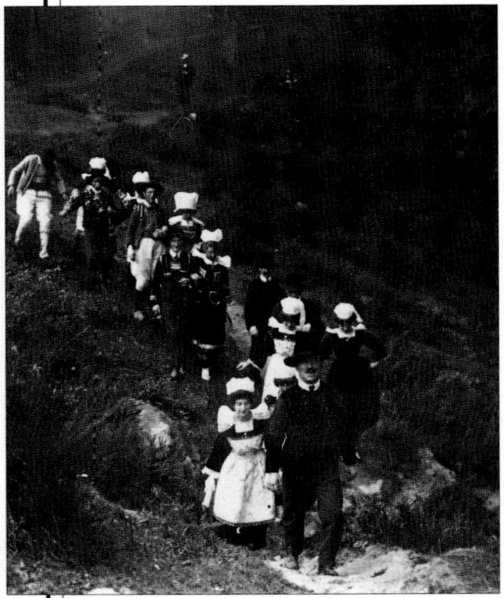

ABOVE: *Inhabitants of Pont-Aven walking in the Bois d'Amour, or Woodland of Love. This was a popular local beauty spot, also much frequented by the community of artists, and its air of mysterious gloom inspired several paintings by the Nabis and Symbolists.*

IN NOVEMBER GAUGUIN RETURNED TO PARIS, bringing back with him a number of paintings and drawings which were exhibited at Arsène Portier's gallery. The response was varied. A friendly critic, Gustave Kahn, later wrote:

'What he exhibited disappointed his admirers and the critics. They expected new conquests of colour, more radiant and more violent effects of sunlight. In his paintings, with their heavy and warm shadows, the forms seemed purplish and black. He simplified the colours, contrasting them violently. Pissarro defended him and explained that in these countries forms were swallowed up by the light, that the nuance did not exist and that one could not therefore think of rendering it, but could proceed only through violent opposition.

Just the same, the exhibition had no success, the few collectors of Gauguin's works were disconcerted. This was neither pointillism nor optical mixture, nor was it exactly an art which broke openly with Impressionist ideas. People did not understand this foretaste of an evolution which did not even assert itself with any vigour.

Nevertheless, this trip had been of great aesthetic benefit to Gauguin. He now began to change visibly.'

He had indeed found himself. The experience of Martinique had enabled him to break away from the conventions of European painting as it was in the late 1880s. He was free from the Impressionists' concern with naturalism, with chromatic accuracy, with nature rather than with man. He had become aware of the emotional dimension of colour, the spiritual qualities of a painting

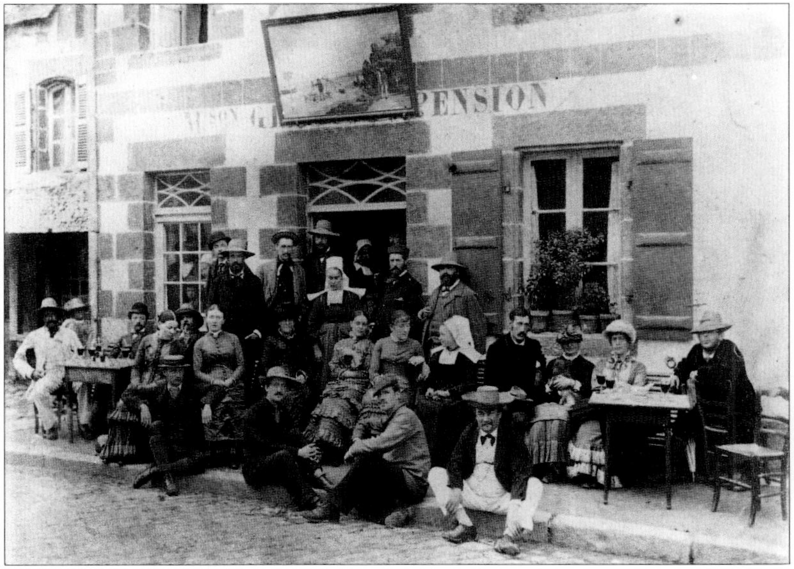

RIGHT: *Painters and local worthies assembled outside the Pension Gloanec, Pont-Aven, in 1888, including Gauguin, seated on the pavement.*

and the turbulent vigour of his own creative imagination which had first been liberated in the rural wildness of Brittany, where he returned early in 1888.

Paris **To Mette Gauguin** ***c.22 January 1888***

On Friday I am setting off for Pont-Aven, and I can reply to your letter when I am more settled.

Apparently the weather in the country during the winter is not very good for my health, but I must get down to work as quickly as possible, and here, without a studio or a model, it is impossible . . .

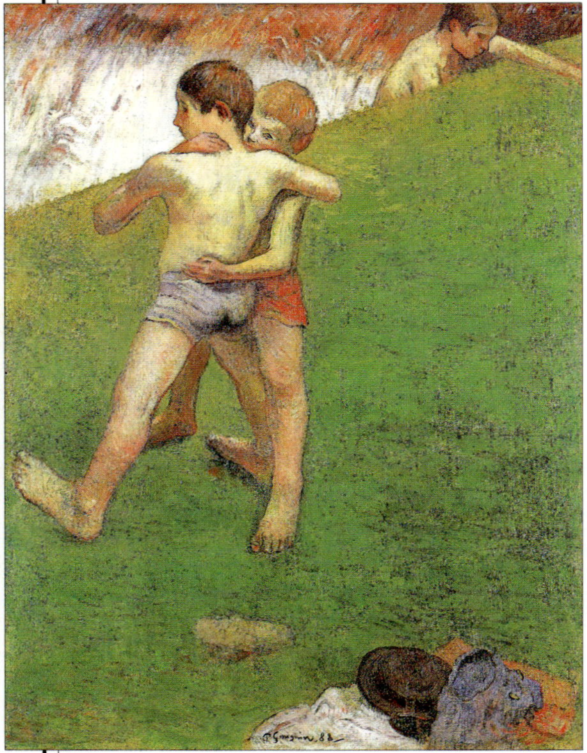

ABOVE: CHILDREN WRESTLING, 1888 *'. . . Two boys wrestling beside the river, thoroughly Japanese, but seen through the eyes of a Peruvian savage,' Gauguin wrote to Schuffenecker. (See also letter to Vincent van Gogh, page 43–4.)*

In Brittany, on the other hand, where I have already been, I can work for seven or eight months without a break, saturated with the character of the peasants and the countryside, something essential for good painting. In this context, I feel from your letter that for you a wall still stands, which makes you like the first bourgeoise ever to have existed.

There are two classes in society. One has inherited wealth, allowing individuals to become landowners, employed in this capacity, or owners of businesses. The other class, which has no capital, exists on what? The fruits of their labours. With the one group, long service in their professional activities (either commercial or administrative) eventually leads to a more or less humdrum goal. With the others, the spirit of initiative (art and literature) creates, after a long time, it is true, a situation of independence and productivity. That is why the children of an artist's family have to suffer more than those whose parents have a salaried position . . .

And what is the finest part of a living nation, nurturing and advancing progress and enriching the nation? It is the artist. For your part, you do not like art.

What then is it that you do like? Money. And when the artist makes money you enjoy it.

In any game, if there is gain, there is loss, and you don't experience the pleasure unless you have also experienced the pain.

Why do you educate your children, since it is for them an immediate torment leading only to an uncertain reward in the future? . . .

Send me two or three flannel vests. I don't have any, which is unpleasant in the winter . . .

RIGHT: BRETON PEASANT WITH PIGS, 1888 *Gauguin seldom painted landscapes of Brittany in sunshine, and this rare example shows the liberating effects of his stay in Martinique on his palette. It shows a view of Pont-Aven looking towards the hill known as Sainte-Marguerite; the piglets are a symbol of fleshly pleasures.*

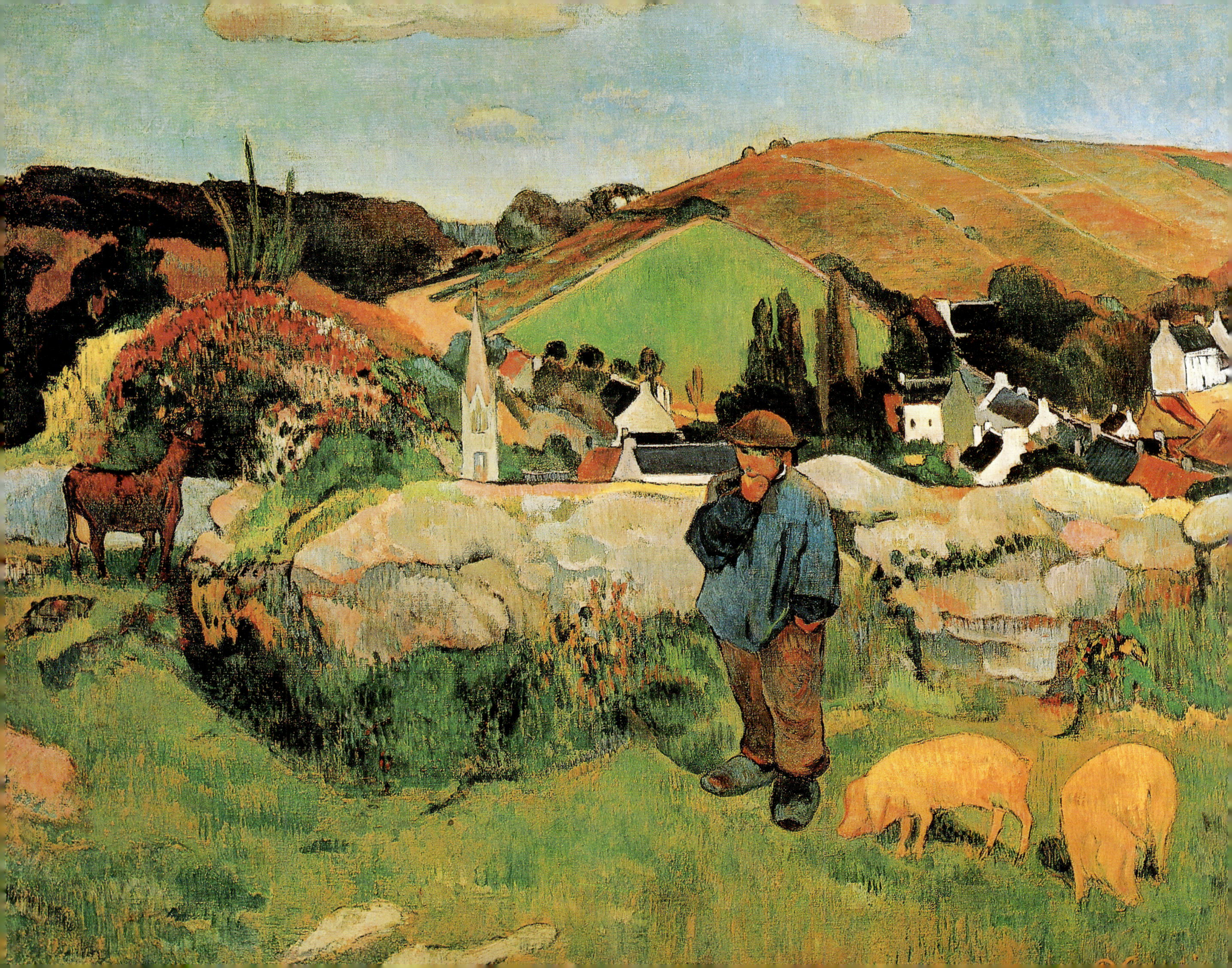

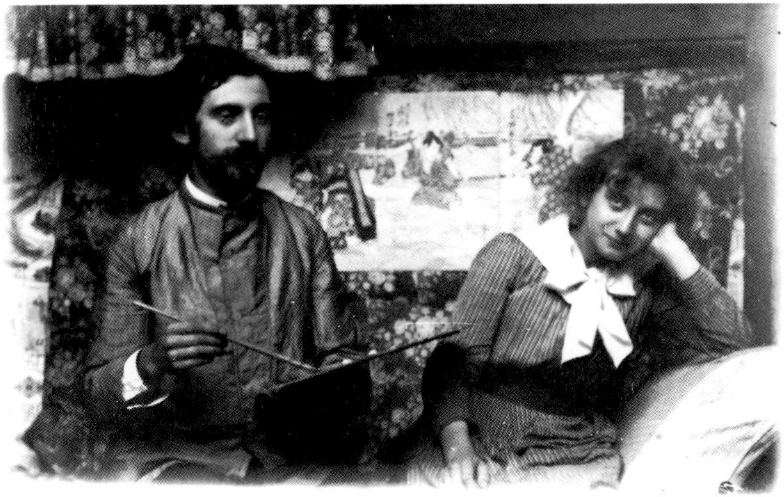

LEFT: *A photograph of Émile Bernard and his sister Madeleine taken in Bernard's Pont-Aven studio c.1888. Madeleine, on holiday there with her mother for the summer, was pretty and captivating, and although she was betrothed to Charles Laval, his friend and companion in Martinique, Gauguin could not resist a flirtation.*

Pont-Aven **To Émile Schuffenecker** ***end February 1888***

. . . I have already been here for a month without letting you have any news. It is true that for three days out of every six I am in bed and little inclined to work, with terrible suffering which gives me no respite. I let myself live in the dumb contemplation of nature which provides the whole of my art. Apart from this, there is no salvation, and in any case it's the best way of keeping physical suffering at bay. In this way, I manage to live without being too much of a nuisance to my fellow beings.

When I am up and about, I have four canvases under way, nearly all finished—two of 50 metres and two of 30.

And what about you? What are you doing? Have you finished 'The Road-Menders'? You are a real Parisianist. But I'm for the country. I love Brittany. I find here the savage and the primitive. When my sabots clang on this granite earth, I hear the dull, muffled tone, flat and powerful, that I try to achieve in painting . . .

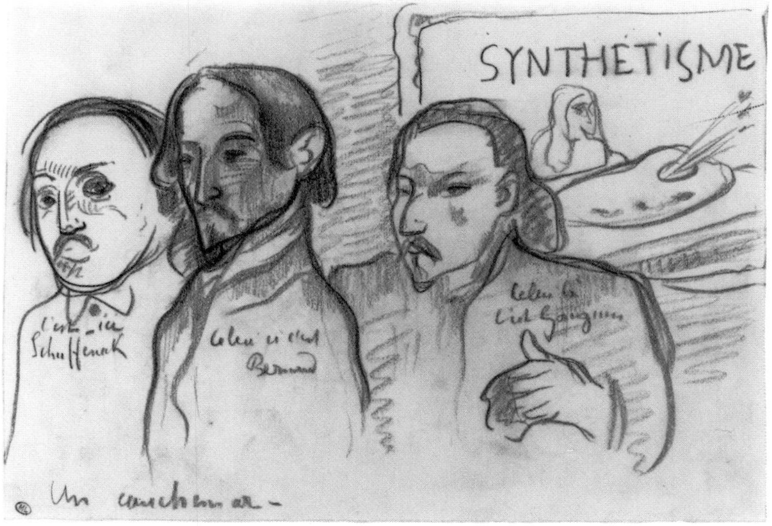

LEFT: SYNTHETISM, A NIGHTMARE, *c.1889 Attributed to Gauguin, the drawing made in Bernard's sketchbook, of Schuffenecker, Bernard and Gauguin around the time of the Volpini Exhibition, refers to the Synthetist style primarily developed by Bernard. Its revolutionary aim was to create a synthesis or abstraction of different elements: from both nature and the imagination, from observation, the art of the past, and diverse cultures and religions.*

BELOW: *Théodore van Gogh, brother of Vincent, was manager of the art gallery, Boussod and Valadon, in Paris, where, in 1888, he gave Gauguin his first show. He became Gauguin's dealer and financed his trip to Arles where he lived and worked with Vincent in the autumn of 1889.*

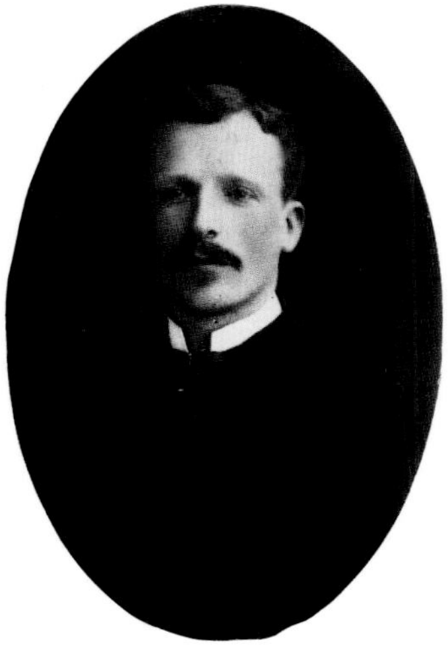

GAUGUIN'S PAINTINGS FROM MARTINIQUE had been much admired by the Van Gogh brothers, Vincent and Théodore. Théodore worked as an art dealer at Goupil's in Paris, and did much to support his brother financially. He now took Gauguin under his wing, organizing his first one-man show in Paris, introducing him to a range of other artists and dealers and initiating a correspondence with his brother.

When Théodore offered Gauguin 150 francs a month to stay with Vincent at Arles and paint, he willingly accepted, but from the start the two men argued. They tried to paint the same subjects, but their different approaches became a source of tension: Gauguin worked from his imagination; Vincent strove to capture the essence of what he saw in front of him. In frustration, Gauguin made up his mind to return to Paris, but was delayed when on the evening of 23 December 1888, after he had moved out of their shared Yellow House to a hotel, Vincent's unstable condition led him to cut off part of his ear lobe.

RIGHT: THE LOSS OF VIRGINITY, 1890 *This haunting image belongs to the final period of Gauguin's stay in France before he left for Tahiti, and was painted in Paris after his return from Le Pouldu in 1890. The model was a Parisian seamstress called Juliette Huet, whom he left pregnant on his departure for Tahiti in 1891; she subsequently destroyed all mementos of him. The knowing fox, Breton symbol of the power of the sexual urge, was described in a letter to Bernard as 'The Indian symbol of Perversity'.*

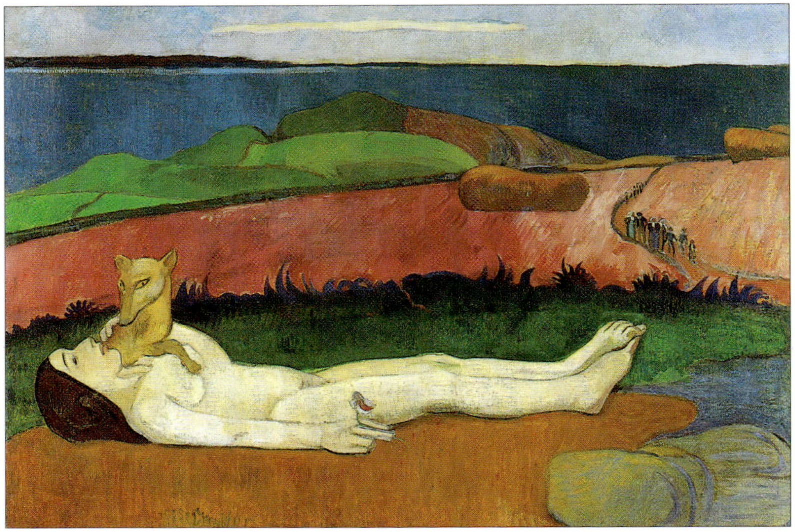

RIGHT: THE VISION AFTER THE SERMON, 1888 *This, Gauguin's first religious painting, marks his break with the Impressionists and his adoption of the new Synthetist style to reveal the mysteries beneath surface realities. His new technique largely dispensed with modelling and used line and flat planes of intense colour. Meaning was suggested by the arrangement of forms on the page; here the diagonal of the tree separates the real world of the women from the imaginary world of their vision. The painting was rejected by the church at Pont-Aven to which he offered it. The subject, from Genesis, of Jacob wrestling with the Angel no doubt signified for Gauguin the spiritual – and indeed material – struggles in which he found himself increasingly engaged. (See also letters page 44–7.)*

Pont-Aven **To Vincent van Gogh** ***29 February 1888***

I have been wanting to write to your brother, but I know that you see each other every day and he is always so busy. I have come to work in Brittany (always a rage for painting!) and I had every reason to believe that I had enough money for it. The little I have from what I have sold has gone to settle some pressing debts and in a month I shall have nothing—Zero is a very negative force.

I don't want to press your brother, but a little word from you on the subject would set my mind at rest, or at least give me patience. My God how terrible these money matters are for an artist!

And if it's necessary to make some *reductions in price* do not hesitate to do so, as long as I am provided with some money. I have recently spent fifteen days in bed struck down with a fever and I am just starting to work again. If I can manage to survive five or six months I think that I shall bring back some good canvases.

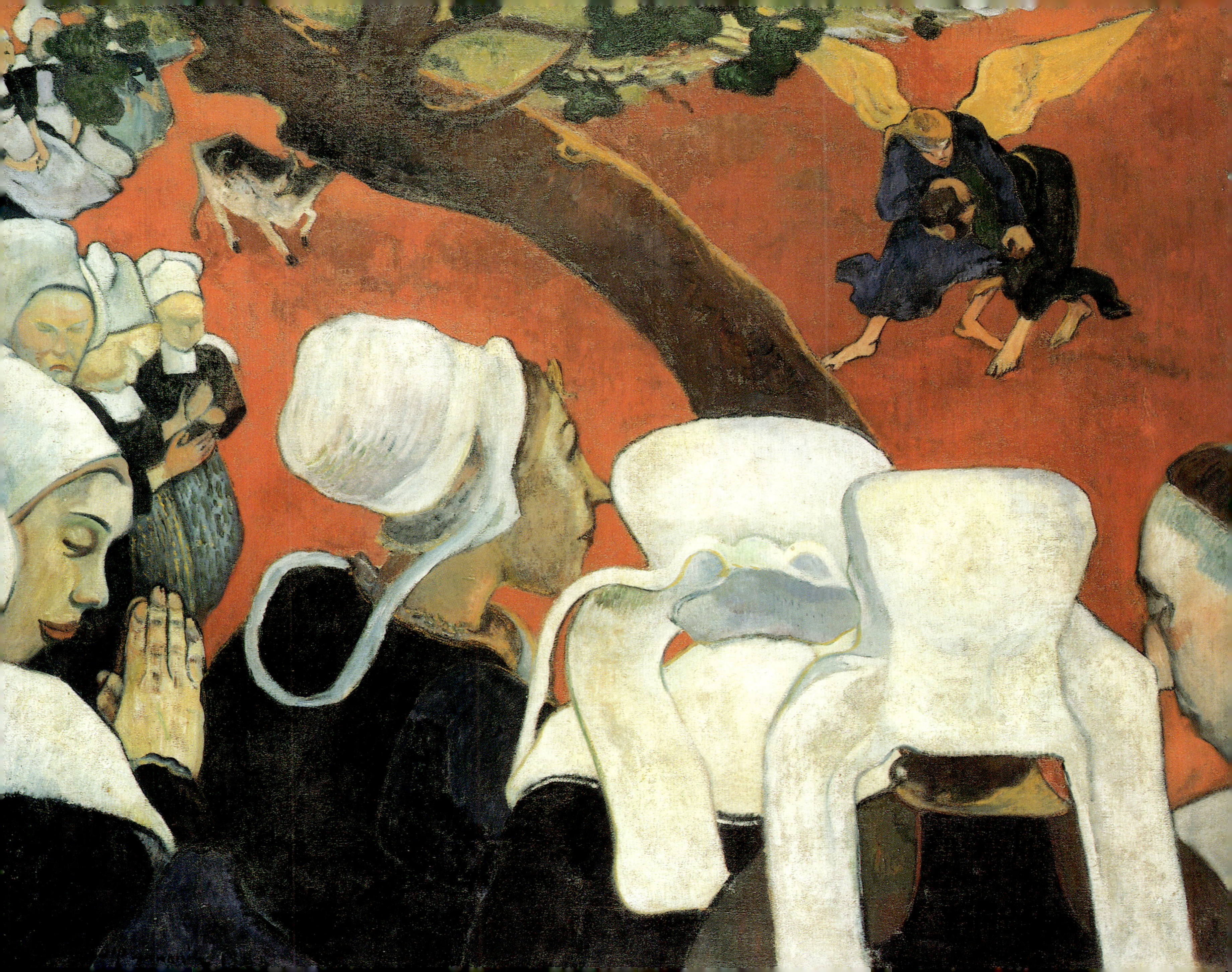

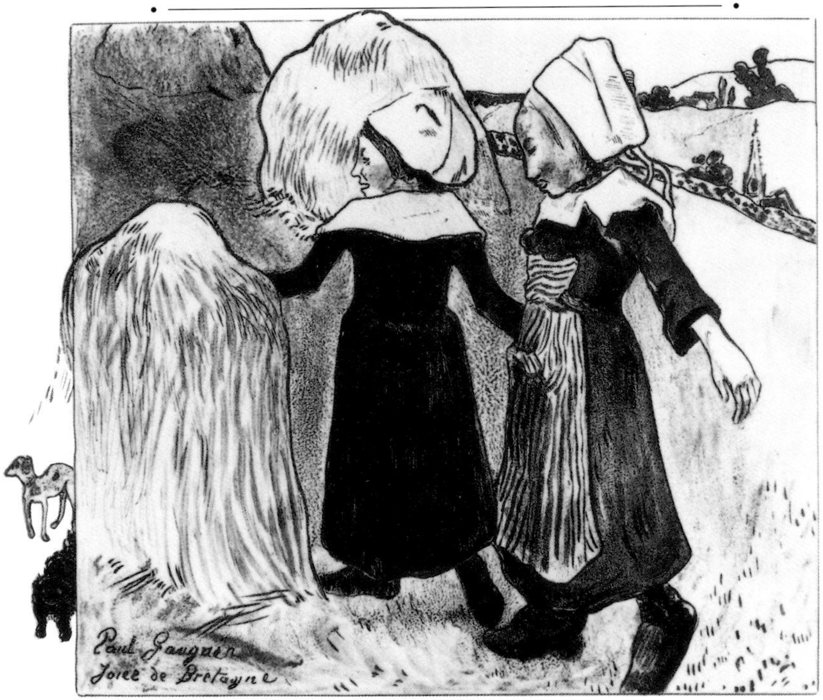

LEFT: THE JOYS OF BRITTANY, 1889
'Drawing: that's all there is,' wrote Gauguin, demonstrating his mastery of printing in this zincograph of a Round Dance.

Pont-Aven **To Vincent van Gogh** ***c.15 March 1888***

Thank you for replying to me. I see that you are in a fine place* for studying the sunshine which so entrances you and that you are working so much better when the subject grips you. Thank you very much for your good offices on my behalf; the sale of pictures is such a hard thing in these times.

Despite this, I am in a state of perpetual apprehension. Money worries are the only ones that have any effect on me, and unfortunately I feel that I shall always be subject to them.

At the moment, Pont-Aven is a very dreary place as a result of the bad weather, wind and continual rain, and I am awaiting the fine

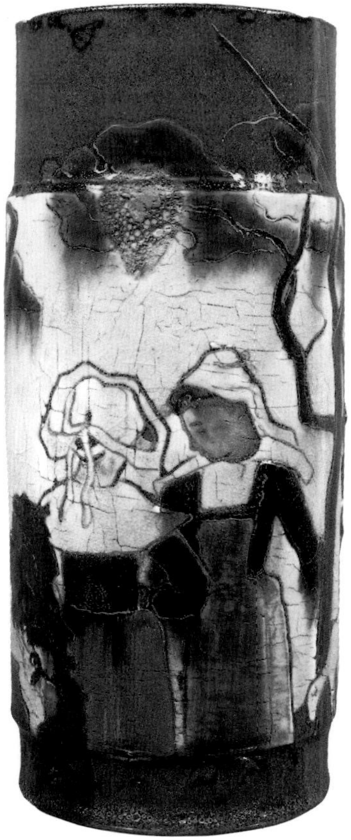

ABOVE: *In luminous blue and gold on white, this vase brings out the influence of cloisonné enamel work on the Synthetists which gave them their alternative name (Cloisonnists).*

weather to start work again, having abandoned it a little because of my illness.

A cordial handshake.

* Arles.

Pont-Aven To Théodore van Gogh *c.15–18 June 1888*

I have received with pleasure your draft for 39 francs 60 . . . I am in the process of painting a picture of a Breton gavotte danced by three little girls in a hayfield. I am sure that you will like it. I think it is really original and I am very pleased with the drawing.

Looking forward to hearing from you.

Pont-Aven To Théodore van Gogh *c.7 July 1888*

Some time ago I sent you a letter responding in a categorical and affirmative way to your suggestion that you would pay for my going to Arles. Have your intentions about this altered?

I am perplexed at not having had a reassuring word from you. I have just heard that the lady buying my negresses cannot pay for them till *January*: another let-down.

Be kind enough to send me a few reassuring words.

Pont-Aven To Vincent van Gogh *c.24 July 1888*

I have just read your interesting letter and agree completely with what you say about the small importance of accuracy in art.

Art is an abstraction which unfortunately means one becomes less understood. I hope that we soon reach our aim, that is, my journey to Provence. I have always had a craze to interpret the bull-fights in my own style, as I understand them. I am beginning to achieve physical freedom again. My illness had weakened me, but in my most recent studies I have surpassed what I did before.

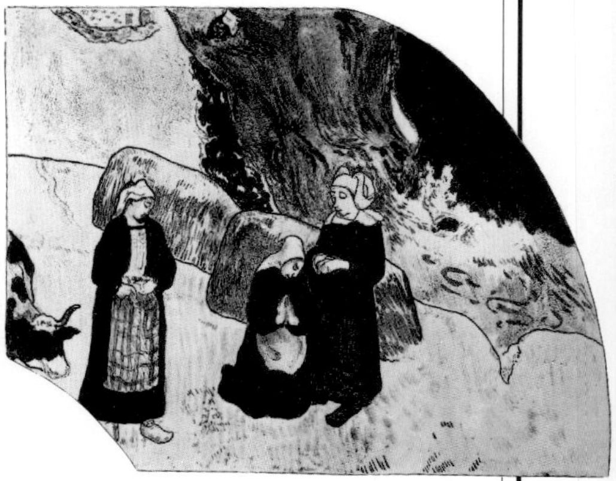

ABOVE: THE DRAMA OF THE SEA, 1889 *Both these prints (above and far left) formed part of the 'Volpini Suite' which could be seen at the epoch-making exhibition in the Volpini Café at the entrance to the World's Fair in early summer 1889.*

Naturally, the band of boors who are here think that I am completely mad, which I find most gratifying, for it proves to me that I am not. I am on the point of finishing a Breton wrestling match, which I am sure you will like.*

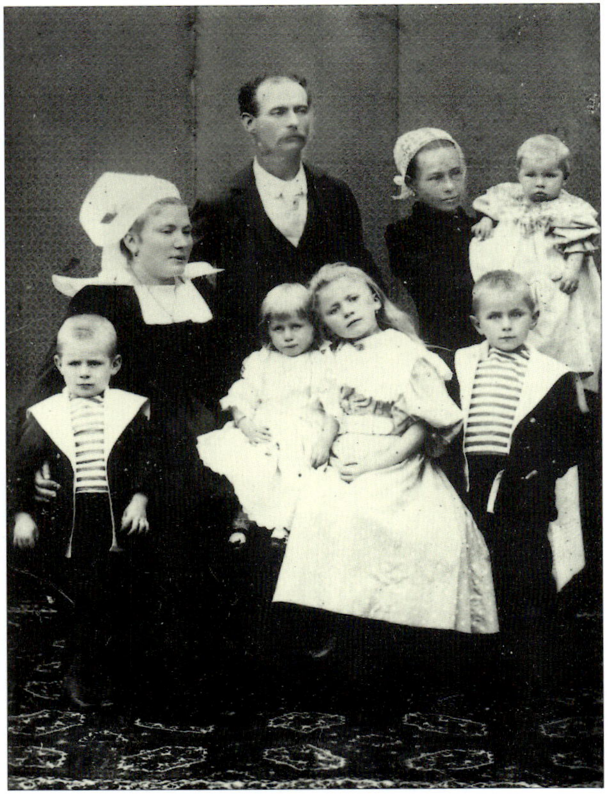

Two boys, one in a blue the other in a vermilion shirt. Another one at the top, just climbing out of the water. A green sward—a pure second-class Veronese even in its *untouched* chrome yellow, like thick Japanese crepe.

At the top, a cascade of foaming water in a rosy white, with a rainbow at the edge near the frame.

At the bottom, a splash of white, a black hat and a blue shirt . . .

If it weren't for this bloody money business my trunks would be already packed. I don't know why, but for the last ten days or so I have had in my mind a mass of painted fantasies that I want to execute in the Midi. I think that this is why my state of health has become so flourishing. I seem to have a need for *struggle*, to hew things out with blows like a mason. After all the experiments that I intend to make here, I believe that I have the power to progress easily in the future.

Hoping that we shall soon be reunited.

* A drawing is enclosed showing the rough outline of the painting.

LEFT: *Marie-Angelique Satre and her family. An acknowledged beauty of the area, she ran a pension not far from the Gloanec Inn in Pont-Aven. Her husband, Frédéric-Joseph, a builder, was mayor of the village.*

Pont-Aven **To Vincent van Gogh** ***c.27 September 1888***

. . . I have just finished a religious painting, very badly done, but which has interested me a good deal, and which pleases me. I wanted

RIGHT: THE BEAUTIFUL ANGEL, 1889 *Marie-Angelique was horrified by this portrait, which she considered unflattering. She sits in feast-day finery separated from the background by an enclosing circle in the manner of Japanese prints by Hokusai and Hiroshige. Gauguin had recently seen examples at the World's Fair in Paris and showed an intense interest in the decorative qualities of Japanese art. Interestingly, he includes a Peruvian-inspired pot in the assembly.*

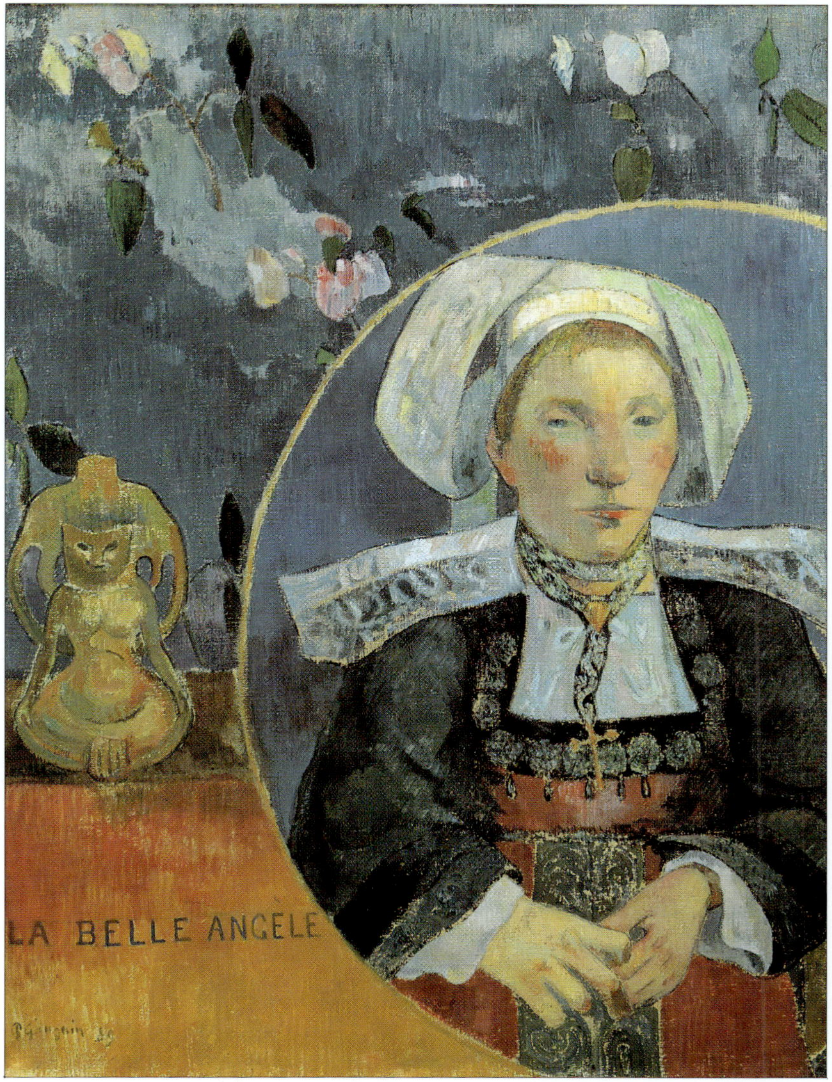

to give it to the church of Pont-Aven. Naturally, they weren't interested in the slightest.

Two groups of Breton women are at prayer, dressed in intensely black clothes, their yellow-white bonnets very luminous. An *apple tree* cuts across the sombre violet canvas, and the leaves painted in great clumps, like clouds, are *emerald* green, with the *spaces in between* coloured greenish yellow by the light of the sun. The earth is *pure vermilion*. In the church it drops in tone and becomes a reddish brown.

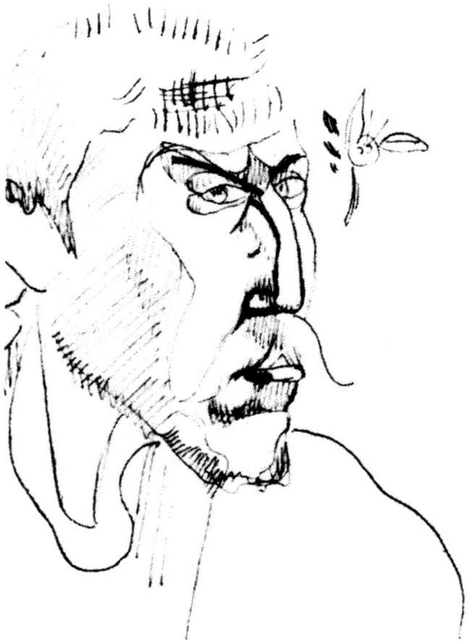

The angel is dressed in violent ultramarine and Jacob in bottle green. The angel's wings are pure chrome-yellow, and its hair a different shade of chrome; its feet orange. I feel that I have achieved in these figures a great rustic and *superstitious* simplicity. The whole composition is very austere. The cow under the tree is small in comparison with its real size and is rearing its leg. To me, in this painting the landscape and the struggle exist only in the imagination of the people who are praying as a result of the sermon, and that is why there is such a contrast between the people themselves and the struggle in the landscape, which is not realistic and is out of proportion . . .

LEFT: *A sketch of the self-portrait known as 'Les Miserables', which Gauguin made for Vincent van Gogh, from a letter to Schuffenecker, 8 October 1888. Pleased with the pose, he re-used the image in the ironic 'Self-portrait with Halo' (which decorated Marie Henry's inn at Le Pouldu) and 'Self-portrait with Yellow Christ', both painted the following year.*

There is no question of my settling in a studio up here in the North, since I daily expect to effect a sale which will allow me to escape from Pont-Aven. The people who feed me here, the doctor who looks after me, have given me credit, and do not take a painting or any of my clothes as a guarantee. Their behaviour to me is perfect. I cannot take advantage of them without committing *an evil deed* which would trouble me greatly. If they were rich or thieves, I would have no scruple. I shall wait, therefore. If, by any chance, the day arrived when you felt differently* and you felt that you should say to me 'Too late' . . . I would like you to do it straightaway . . .

Well there it is! I want to think of the promised fruit as little as possible—to wait for better days at least, so that I can escape from this miserable squalid existence which, my work apart, weighs on me so horribly.

About Gauguin's proposed excursion to join Van Gogh at Arles.

Quimperlé **To Émile Schuffenecker** ***8 October 1888***

. . . I have painted a picture for a church, which, naturally, has been rejected, so I am sending it to Van Gog.* There is no point in describing it to you, as you will be seeing it. This year I have entirely sacrificed execution and colour in favour of style, wishing to impose on myself something other than what I can already do. I have done a self-portrait for Vincent, who asked me to. I think that it is one of my best things; it is so abstract (for example) as to be totally incomprehensible. First of all, it is the head of a bandit, a Jean Valjean,† which also personifies an Impressionist painter, despised and yet always chained to the world. The drawing involved is quite special (complete abstraction). The mouth, the eyes and the nose are like the flowers you find on a Persian carpet, also personifying the symbolic aspect. The colour is far removed from nature: imagine a vague echo of my pottery moulded by the intense heat of the kiln. All the reds and violets burnt on to the surface by the great sheets of flame are like a furnace glowing in the eyes, the seat of the painter's thought—all against a background of pure chrome over which childish bunches of flowers are scattered—like a young girl's bedroom.

The Impressionist is a pure being, unsullied still by the putrid kiss of the École des Beaux-Arts. I am sending you a letter from Vincent to let you see how I stand with him and all that we are planning at the moment. Show it to Madame Poujin‡ to let her see that you are not the only one who has a high opinion of me. It will also make her see that artists are a people apart, who have no idea of the kind of commercial considerations which she holds.

Van Gog has sold some of my pottery for 300 francs. And so I shall be leaving *at the end of the month* for Arles where I shall stay for quite a while, provided that I am able to work without money worries until I am *ready to launch myself.* In any case, the venture will

RIGHT: *The words used by Gauguin to describe 'Les Miserables' could also refer to this jug made a few months later, the dark brown clay of which is streaked with blood-like red and crimson glazes: 'The colour is far removed from nature: imagine a vague echo of my pottery moulded by the intense heat of the kiln. All the reds and violets burnt on to the surface by the great sheets of flame are like a furnace glowing in the eyes, the seat of the painter's thought.'*

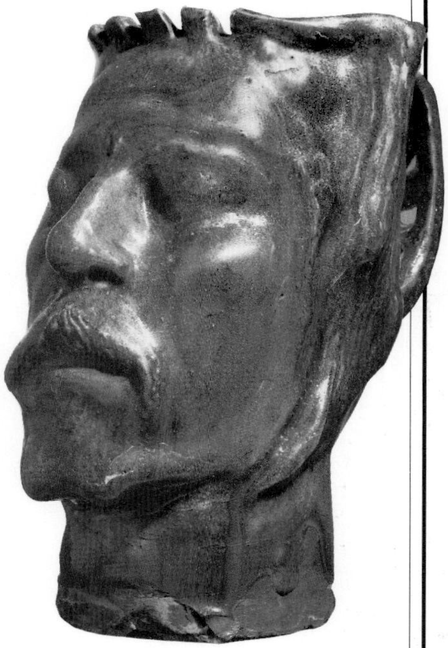

BELOW: BONJOUR MONSIEUR GAUGUIN, 1889 *The title of this canvas recalls Courbet's 'Bonjour Monsieur Courbet' which Gauguin and Van Gogh had seen in Montpellier a year earlier.*

furnish me with a small allowance each month. Do not forget me when I am away. I shall write to you and think about you.

* Gauguin nearly always spelt the name like this.
† A character in *Les Misérables* by Victor Hugo.
‡ A prospective patron.

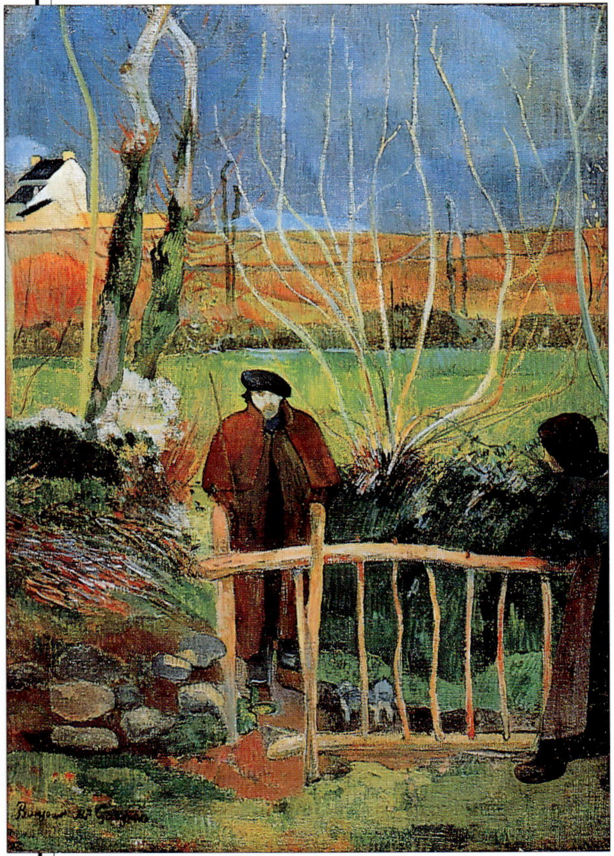

Quimperlé **To Émile Schuffenecker** ***16 October 1888***

. . . Another thing. You know my fixation about paying my debts as soon as I have any money. So I paid the doctor what I owed him, and also a little to Marie-Jeanne, without working it out properly, with the result that I now don't have enough to pay for my journey.

Will you be kind enough, therefore, to go *immediately* to Van Gog and arrange with him to send me 50 francs. And send me a telegram.

Just at the time I wanted to go to the Midi I ran up a fever. But since then I have recovered, and am on the verge of producing some good work.

I believe that in a year's time I shall be free of all this and that I shall have been able to liberate myself in your company. In any case, I shall not cease to be your grateful and devoted friend.

If you see Guillaumin ask him why he hasn't written to me. This summer I sent him my portrait and I haven't heard a word. Is he upset that Van Gog has become so impressed by me? In any case, what's good for the one will do no harm to the other.

I notice that you speak of my *terrible* mysticism. Keep on being an Impressionist till the bitter end and you will have need to fear nothing. Obviously this Symbolist way is full of pitfalls and I have only dipped my toe into it, but it is basic to my nature and one should always

RIGHT: VAN GOGH PAINTING SUNFLOWERS IN ARLES, 1888
The close collaboration with Van Gogh which Gauguin enjoyed during their months together in Arles is recalled by this affectionate portrait.

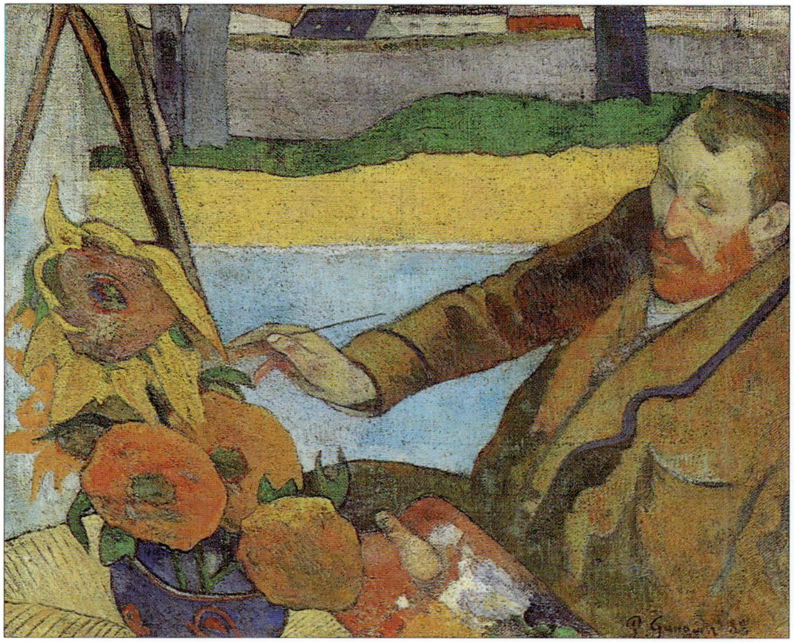

follow one's temperament. I realize that people will understand me *less and less.* What does it matter if I distance myself from others? For the majority I shall always be an enigma, for others a poet, and sooner or later good will prevail. No matter what happens, I assure you that I shall achieve *things of the first order*; I can feel it, and we shall see. You know that in matters concerning art I am always fundamentally right. Pay attention to this: there is circulating at this moment among *artists* a very strong reaction in *my* favour. I know about it from certain indiscretions, so for your part remain tranquilly fond of me as much as Van Gog is—he is not prepared to maintain me in the Midi just because he likes me. He has studied the lay of the land like the calculating Dutchman he is, and clearly intends to pursue his policy as far as it will go, and keep exclusive rights. I have asked him to lower his prices to tempt buyers, but he replied that, on the contrary, his intention was to raise them. Optimist though I am, this time I have got my feet firmly on the ground . . .

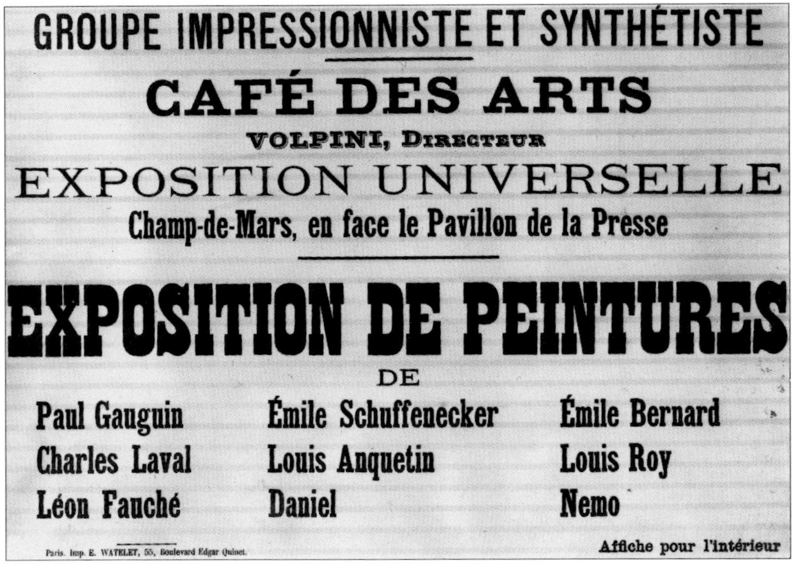

LEFT: *The poster for the Volpini Exhibition, 1889. This epoch-making show, organized by Schuffenecker, was held in the Volpini Café at the entrance to the Paris World's Fair. Gauguin showed seventeen paintings and the folio of prints known as the 'Volpini Suite', which would not however have been seen by many people as one had to ask to be shown them. It was here that the Nabis group first encountered Gauguin's work, and was greatly influenced by it.*

VAN GOGH

. . . It was to Arles that I went to see Van Gogh, after many solicitations on his part.

He wished, he said, to found the Atelier of the Midi, of which I was to be the director. This poor Dutchman was all ardour, all enthusiasm. Reading *Tartarin de Tarascon* had made him believe in an extraordinary Midi, to be expressed in jets of fire.

And on the canvas chrome colours blazed forth, drowning in sunshine the *mas* and the whole plain of the Camargue . . .

In my yellow room, sunflowers with purple eyes stood out against a yellow background. They were standing in a yellow vase, on a yellow table. In a corner of the painting, the signature of the painter: Vincent. And the yellow sun that shone through the yellow curtains of my room inundated all this magnificent efflorescence with gold so that when I woke in the morning I should feel how good all this was. Oh yes, the good Vincent loved yellow. This Dutchman loved the light; it warmed his soul, horrified by the fog. A need for warmth.

When we were both together at Arles, both of us crazy, in constant battle for the good colours—myself I adored red, where could I find a perfect vermilion?—he painted on the wall with his yellow-charged brush: Je suis sain d'esprit, Je suis Saint-Ésprit.*

In my yellow room, a little violet still-life. Two enormous sabots, worn and misshapen, the shoes of Vincent. He had put these on one fine morning some nine years before, when they were new, to walk from Holland to Belgium. The young clergyman (he had just finished his theological studies, intending to become a pastor, like his father) was going to the coalmines to meet those whom he called his brothers. He had heard of them in the Bible, the oppressed, simple people, working to provide luxury for the great ones . . .

Avant et Après

* I am sane in spirit, I am the Holy Spirit (In French a pun).

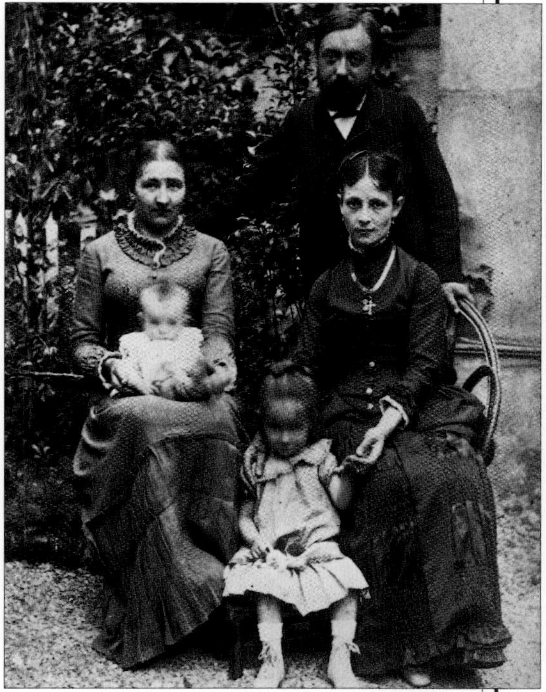

ABOVE: *Émile Schuffenecker and his family. Gauguin rather cruelly depicted his long-suffering friend cowering in the implacable presence of his wife Louise, whom Gauguin regarded as a shrew, in a painting of 1889. Perhaps she resented Gauguin's constant demands on the pocket of the family, or his persistent advances towards her, but the portrait, given somewhat tactlessly to the couple, was never exhibited in Gauguin's lifetime.*

LIVING WITH VAN GOGH

I was at Arles and around it for some time before beginning to savour its harsh atmosphere. No matter that one worked hard, especially Vincent. Between two human beings, he and I, the one all a volcano, the other boiling also, but within himself, a battle of some sort was being prepared.

First of all, I found in everything and for everything a disorder that appalled me. The paint box was hardly large enough to contain all the squeezed tubes of colour, never closed, and yet, despite all this disorder, all this mess and muddle, a unity glowed on the canvas. It was the same with words. Daudet, De Goncourt, the Bible burned this Dutch skull. At Arles, the quays, the bridges and the boats, all

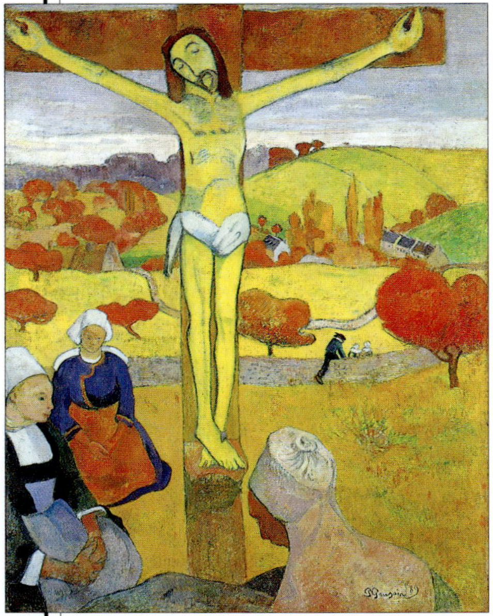

ABOVE: THE YELLOW CHRIST, 1888
The Christ figure, brilliantly painted in Van Gogh's singing yellow, is based on exact observation of the crucifix in the nearby church of Trémalo (in which the face is a whitish wax).

the Midi became his Holland. He even forgot to write in Dutch, and as one can see from the publication of his letters to his brother, he never wrote but in French, and that admirably, with phrases such as 'in as much as' or 'as far as'.

Despite all my attempts to instil in this disordered head some reasonable logic into his critical opinions, I could not bring him to realize the contradiction between his opinions and his painting. Thus, for example, he had a limitless admiration for Meissonier, and a profound hatred for Ingres. Degas made him despair, and Cézanne was no more than a joker. Thinking of Monticelli he used to cry.

One of the great causes of his anger was in being forced to recognize a great intelligence in me, when I had too small a forehead, a sign of imbecility. Yet, in all this there was a great tenderness, an evangelical altruism.

In the first month there I saw our common finances take on the same characteristics of disorder. What could one do? The situation was delicate, our funds being modestly replenished by his brother who was employed by the firm of Goupil, for my part in return for paintings. Speak to him—it was necessary, but it meant clashing with a very great susceptibility. It was not, therefore, without a great deal of caution, and in a wheedling manner, completely incompatible with my character, that I broached the question. I must confess that I was far more successful than I had expected.

We put in a box, so much for our nightly excursions, so much for tobacco, so much for unexpected expenses and the rent. On top of this was a piece of paper and a pencil to write down honestly what each one took from this cash-box. In another box, the rest of the money divided into four parts for our eating expenses each week. We gave up our little restaurant, and with the help of a small gas stove I did the cooking while Vincent did the shopping. Vincent would sometimes wish to make a soup. I

BELOW: *The calvary at Plougastel. The sight of women visiting the numerous wayside shrines, calvaries, and chapels of the area was very familiar to Gauguin and was a potent source of inspiration.*

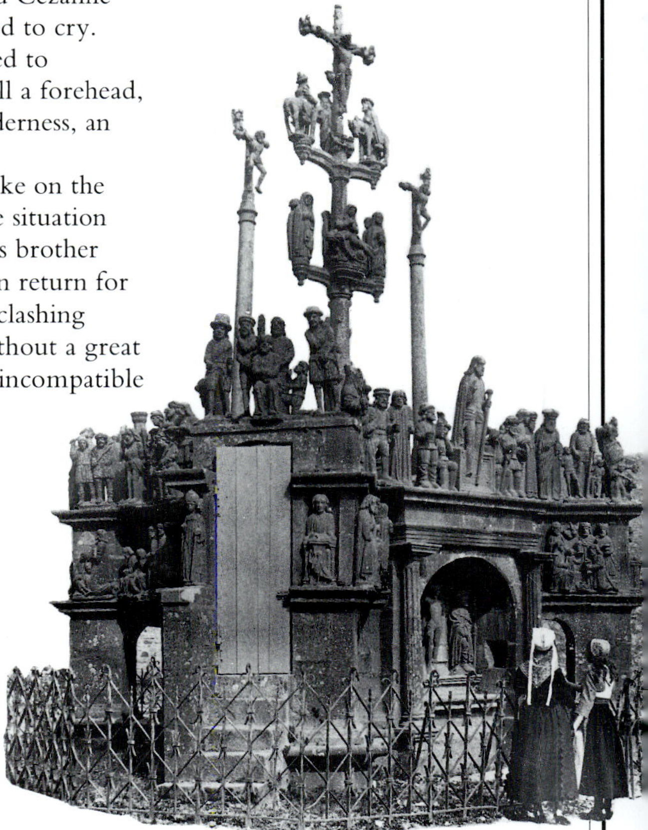

RIGHT: THE GREEN CHRIST, 1888 *The painting combines the dramatic coastline near Le Pouldu, which Gauguin often painted, with the much-weathered calvary in the church at Nizon, near Pont-Aven. Both this and 'The Yellow Christ' were made late in 1888 and reflect Gauguin's horror at the tragedies that had recently befallen Vincent. Though not a Christian, Gauguin was profoundly aware of human suffering and was fascinated by the simple faith of the Bretons – particularly the women.*

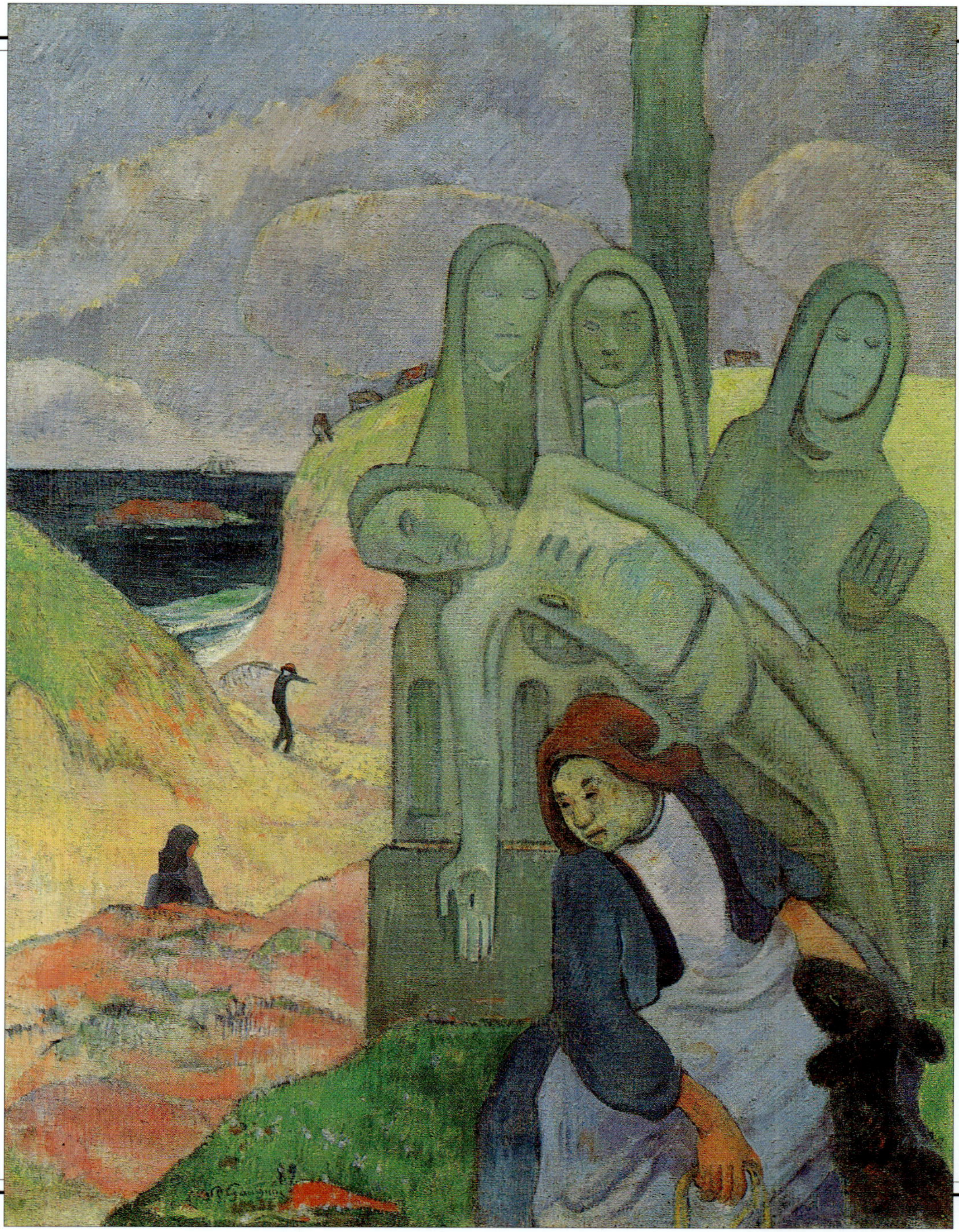

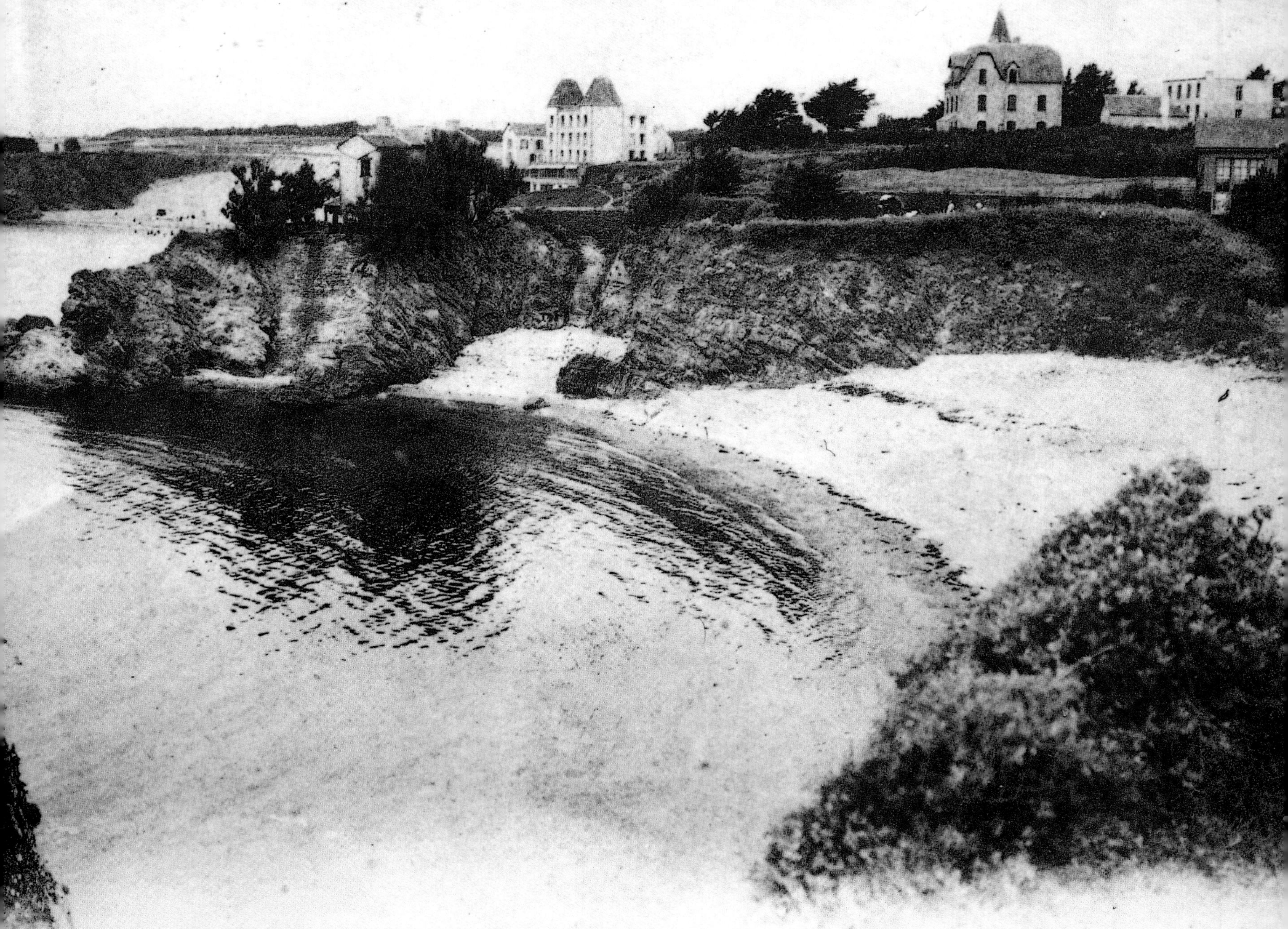

15. LE POULDU (Finistère) — Le Port Guirec

have no idea what mixtures he used—they seemed like those of the colours on his canvases—but it always happened that we could never eat it . . .

How long did we stay together? I couldn't say, having totally forgotten. Despite the rapidity with which the catastrophe happened,* despite the fever for work which possessed me, the whole period seemed like a century.

Without the public having to doubt it, both men did colossal work there, useful for both of them. Perhaps for others? Certain things bear fruit . . .

Avant et Après

* Vincent's suicide in 1890.

AFTER A SHORT SPELL IN PARIS, Gauguin made his third, longest and most decisive stay in Brittany, seeking out the company of his friend Sérusier and the wealthy Dutch painter Meyer de Haan, to whom he had been introduced by Théodore van Gogh and with whom he had worked before the Vincent episode. This time, he stayed at Le Pouldu, a small village on a rocky peninsula fifteen kilometres from Pont-Aven. Towards the end of 1890, a few months after Van Gogh's suicide, Gauguin returned to Paris, where he stayed with his friend Schuffenecker and his young family.

LEFT: *A postcard of the bay at Le Pouldu which lies fifteen kilometres along the coast from Pont-Aven. Gauguin moved there on his return from Paris in the autumn of 1889 to avoid the growing crush of artists and tourists; there were just two inns and two farms. For company he had Paul Sérusier and the Dutchman Meyer de Haan, and the area's dramatically indented coastline inspired some remarkable works in the new 'Cloisonniste' style they evolved together.*

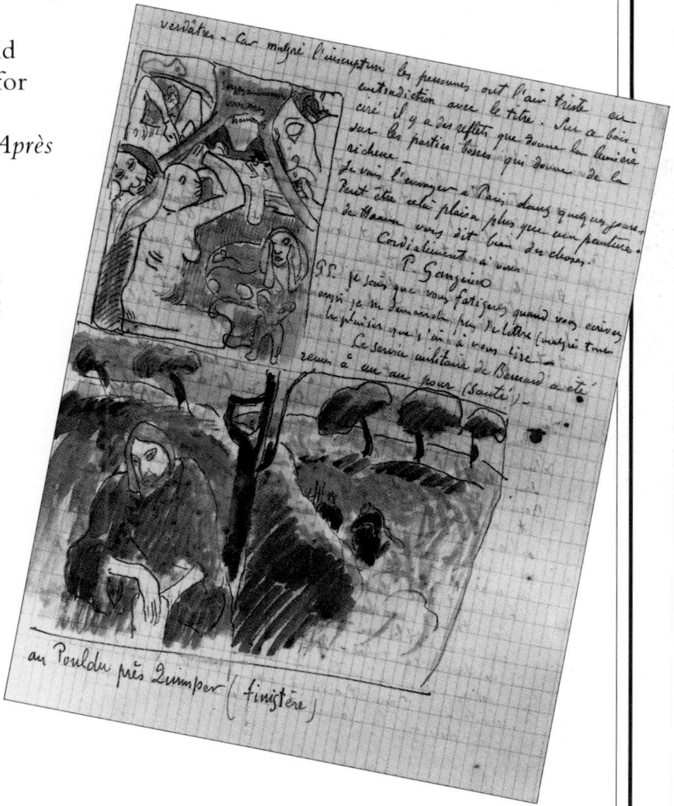

BELOW: *Letter to Vincent van Gogh, November 1889, with sketches of two Le Pouldu works: 'Be in Love and You Will Be Happy' (top), and 'Christ in the Garden of Olives' (bottom).*

CHAPTER 3

The Fragrant Land

1891–1892

INSPIRED BY THE COLONIAL PAVILIONS at the Paris World's Fair of 1889, with their displays of native artefacts, music and dancing, Gauguin was especially attracted by Tahiti, which he had first seen on his naval excursion around the world in 1866 and which had become a French colony in 1880. However, his interest was deflected by the painter Odilon Redon's wife, who spoke enthusiastically about Madagascar and its many charms. Spurred on by the possibility of selling a large number of works to an inventor and collector, Dr Charlopin, he attempted to get his three friends, Schuffenecker, Bernard and Meyer de Haan, to join with him in

RIGHT: TAHITIAN WOMEN ON THE BEACH, 1891 *This painting, with its somewhat misleading title – Gauguin's young native wife Tehemana posed for both figures – displays some of the tensions the artist felt existed between the islanders and the colonial infiltrators. The right-hand figure is wearing the 'missionary style' dress introduced by the Church; in a second version (which Gauguin painted soon afterwards, having sold this canvas to a French settler) she wears a native* pareu *and her arms lie relaxed at her side.*

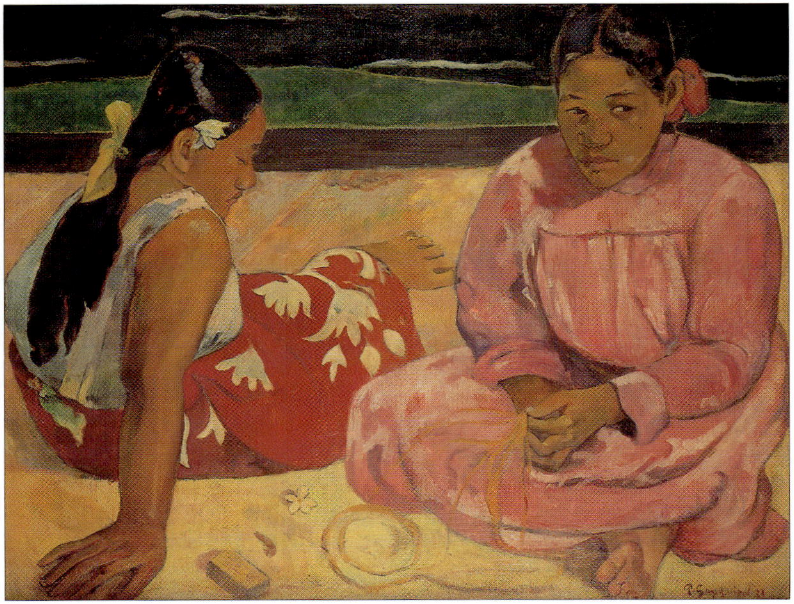

RIGHT: JOYOUSNESS (AREAREA), 1892 *This painting is a representative example of Gauguin's image of Tahiti, halfway between ideal and actual: a land of still and statuesque women unsullied by Western civilization set in a landscape of abstracted natural forms and symbolic colours.*

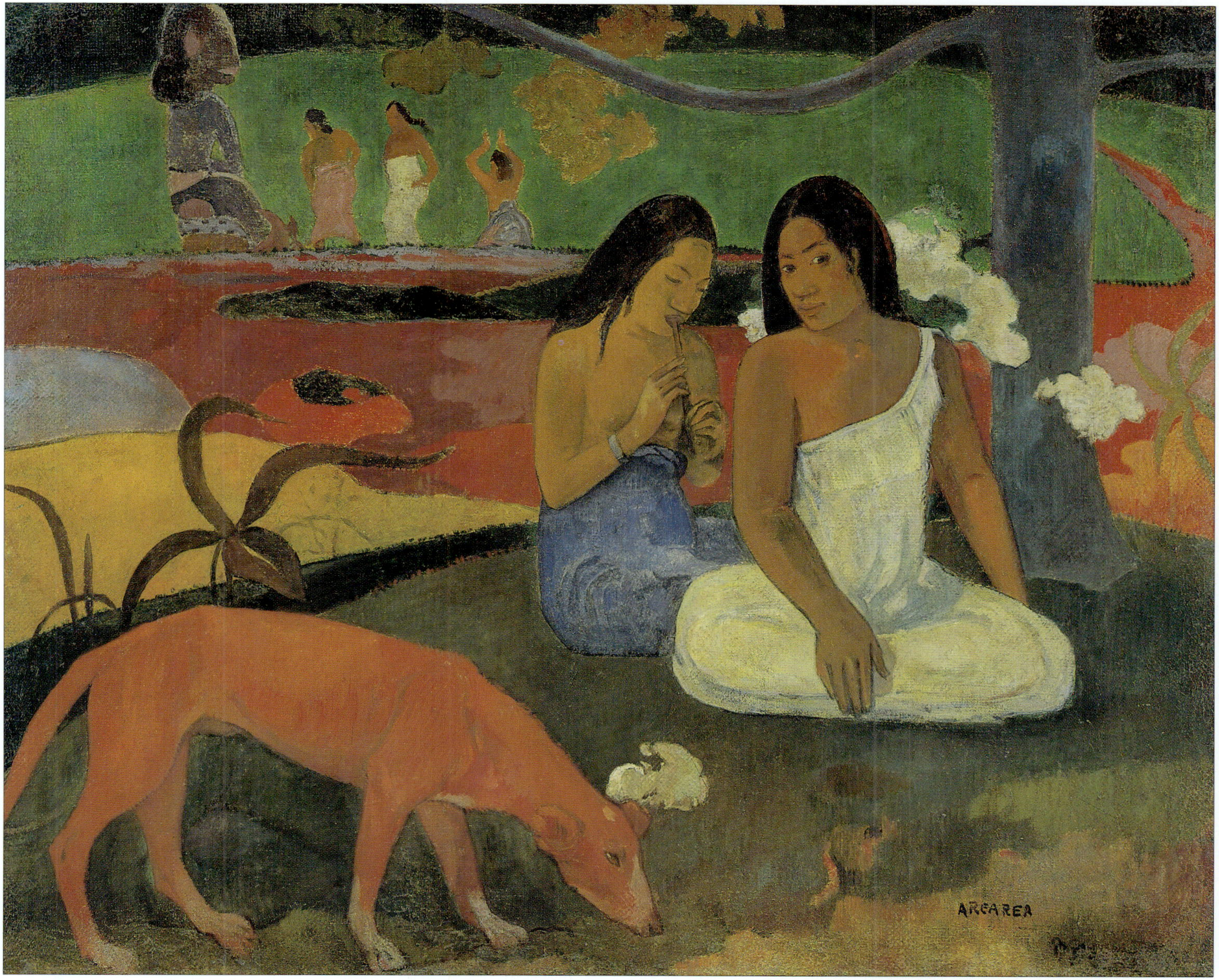
AREAREA

going to Madagascar. Only Bernard was enthusiastic, but complicated matters by suggesting Tahiti as a more suitable refuge from the rigours of Parisian life, largely as a consequence of his having just read the immensely successful novel by Pierre Loti, *The Marriage of Loti*, which described the island in glowing terms.

Gauguin was impressed, but asked for less fictional information, so Bernard sent him the official handbook to the island, published by the French government in an attempt to attract settlers there. To say that it was laudatory would be an understatement. The tone was dithyrambic throughout: 'The lucky inhabitants of this remote South Sea paradise know life only at its brightest. For them, to live is to sing and love.' Particular attention was paid to the charms of the Tahitian woman: 'With her large, dark eyes, so wonderfully fine and clear, her almost excessively full lips and her marvellously white and regular teeth, she looks so sweet and innocently voluptuous.' Gauguin needed no more persuading, writing to Odilon Redon in his customary plangent style:

> 'I am leaving for Tahiti, where I shall hope to end my days. My art, which I know you like, I regard as no more than a tender shoot, though one which I hope to develop into a wild and primitive growth, entirely for my own pleasure. What I need to obtain this end is peace and quiet. The honour and respect of other people are now of no concern to me. The European Gauguin has ceased to exist and no one will ever see any of his works here again.'

In March 1891 he paid a fleeting visit to Copenhagen where he saw Mette and the children. The meeting was very friendly, and though Mette would not agree to accompany him to Tahiti, they resolved to restart their married life on his return—a curious contradiction of his statement to Redon. In the event, it was the last time he was to see them. On his return to Paris, he penned a letter to the Minister of Education and the Fine Arts:

> 'I desire to proceed to Tahiti in order to execute a series of pictures of that country, the character and lighting of which I have set myself to depict. Accordingly, Monsieur le Ministre, I request that

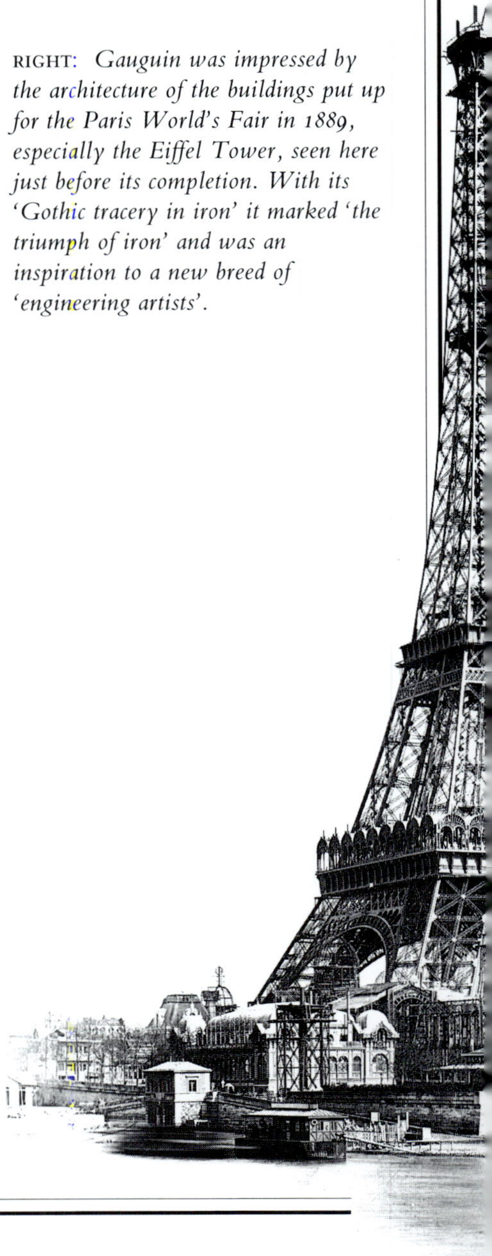

RIGHT: *Gauguin was impressed by the architecture of the buildings put up for the Paris World's Fair in 1889, especially the Eiffel Tower, seen here just before its completion. With its 'Gothic tracery in iron' it marked 'the triumph of iron' and was an inspiration to a new breed of 'engineering artists'.*

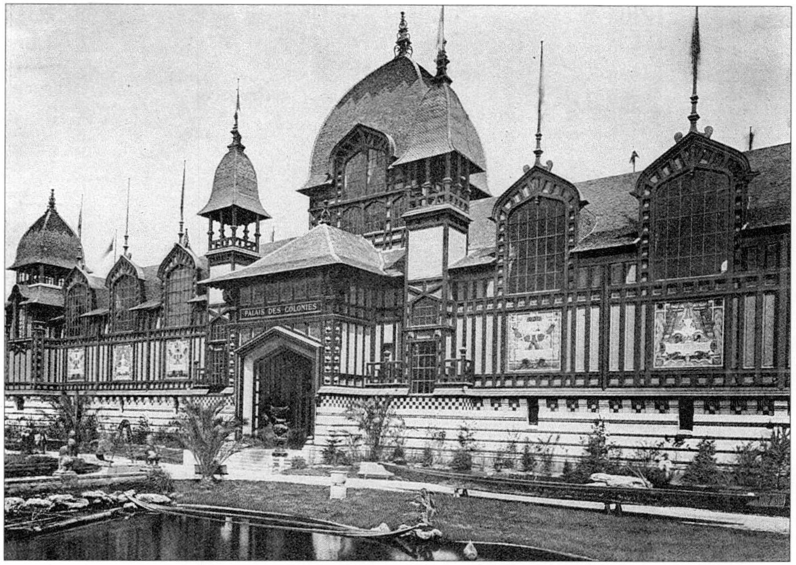

LEFT: *The World's Fair, or Exposition Universelle, provided many experiences for Gauguin, including some which inspired him to search for a tropical paradise. In the Palais des Colonies, Gauguin saw exhibitions and dances, and had direct contact with natives of several cultures in French colonial lands, including Tahiti, Martinique, Madagascar, and Indo-China.*

you grant me an official mission, which, while unremunerated, will, in the light of other benefits which it will confer, nevertheless facilitate my studies and my voyage.'

The application, endorsed by Georges Clemenceau, was granted, its most fruitful result being a reduction of 30 per cent on the second-class fare from Marseille to Tahiti. As he started to fall out with the officials in Tahiti almost as soon as he got there, the recommendation he carried out with him from the French Colonial Office was of very limited utility.

His friends gave him a farewell banquet at the Café Voltaire, a meeting place popular amongst Symbolist artists and writers, at which, to the accompaniment of numerous bottles of Bordeaux, they ate soup, hors d'œuvres, brill, ragoût of pheasant, roast lamb, Brie and petits fours. Stéphane Mallarmé proposed an admirably brief toast:

'To cut short the preliminaries, let us drink a toast and wish Paul Gauguin a welcome return, while declaring our admiration for the

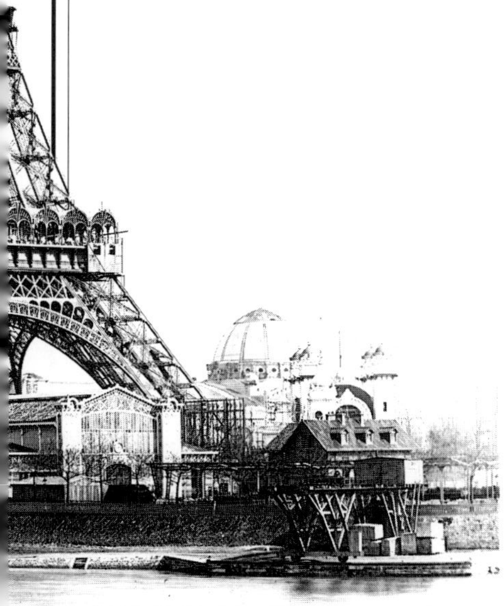

superb dedication with which, at the zenith of his powers, he looks for renewal in distant lands and deep down into his own soul.'

On 1 April, he left Marseille aboard a comfortable and fairly fast steamer, the *Océanien*, bound eventually for Tahiti.

250 miles from Sydney **To Mette Gauguin** ***4 May 1891***

In two days I shall be at Noumea where the boat for Tahiti will pick me up and take me there. It was a speedy and pleasant journey, and the weather was magnificent, designed especially for me. But what extraordinary passengers there were on the voyage! I was the only paying one. All the rest were government employees of that beneficent government which pays everybody to go on expensive little pleasure trips with travel costs paid for wives and families. They're nice people who have only one fault: mediocrity.

There were plenty of ports of call on the journey. The last two we made were absolutely astonishing to see: Melbourne and Sydney. Imagine two cities, hardly fifty years old, with half a million inhabitants, houses twelve storeys high, steam-driven trams and cars, just like in London. And their clothes, there are signs of wealth everywhere. It is worth coming 4,000 leagues to see.

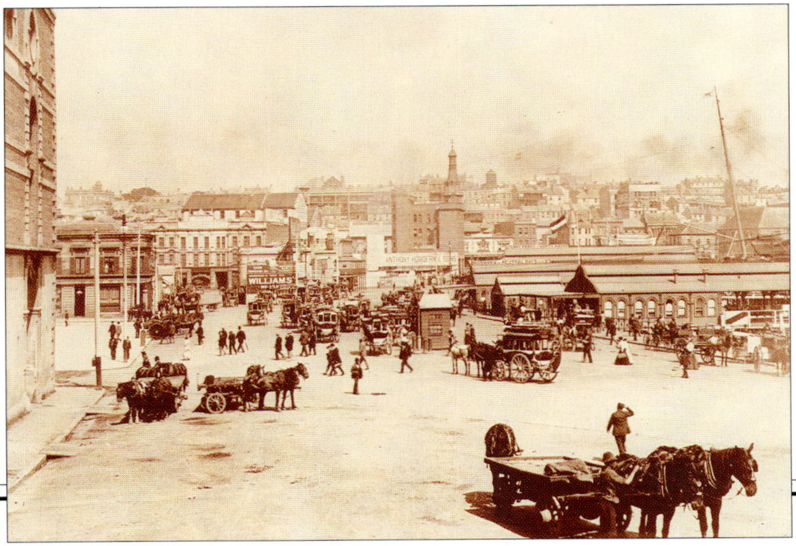

LEFT: *The Circular Quay, Sydney, 1892 Gauguin's first sight of Sydney, a year before this photograph was taken, must have been very similar: crowded quays, closely-packed houses and a busy town centre.*

In Sydney, a dock-labourer gets betweeen 20 and 25 francs a day, and meat costs 4 sous a pound. It is very easy to make money in Australia, but it costs at least 25,000 francs a year to live, and that not very extravagantly. Despite all these bitter remarks, I must confess that the English are an extraordinary people in their colonizing activities and in their creation of great ports, which are grandiose in an almost burlesque way . . .

Tahiti To Mette Gauguin *29 June 1891*

. . . I have now been here for twenty days, and I have already seen so many new things that I am totally disorientated. It will be some considerable time before I can produce a good painting, but little by little I am settling down to do so by studying a little every day. The King* died a few days after my arrival, and everybody on Tahiti and the neighbouring island was expected to attend his funeral service, about which they had all been informed. You can't imagine what the burial was like. In the evening, each village in turn, seated on the grass, sang their special choral hymns in unison, and went on like that all night. For anyone who likes music it was a real pleasure, for these people have an extraordinary gift for it. Two songs are inter-

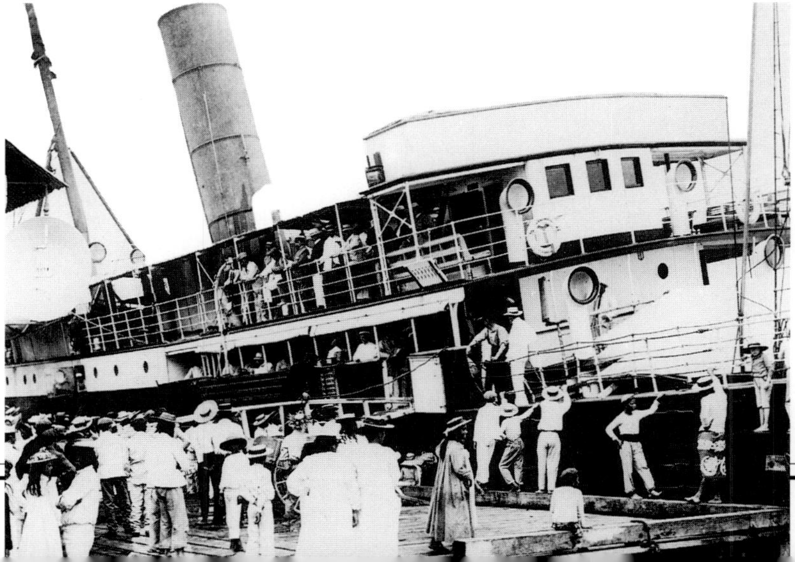

RIGHT: *The arrival of the* Croix de Sud *steamship at the port of Papeete must have been a perennial excitement: the European men on deck in Panamas and boaters, the natives and Europeans on the quay wearing their Sunday clothes and flowered hats, awaiting the lowering of the gang-plank.*

woven on a high register by both men and women, and then there are several accompanied portions which create bizarre chords. A group of male basses imitating the sound of the drum provides the cadence—a very special one. It is absolutely impossible to imagine anything more harmonious and abstract. There is not a false note to be heard.

The hearse, all covered with flowers, was pulled by mules, which the artillery had festooned with black ribbons. Arriving at the tomb, the priests and the chiefs delivered orations in Tahitian. It would take too long to describe the whole event.

BELOW: *The coast of Mataiea, where Gauguin settled in 1891, showing the River Tasutira flowing down between the mountains. This landscape was memorably described by Gauguin in his* Noa Noa *manuscripts.*

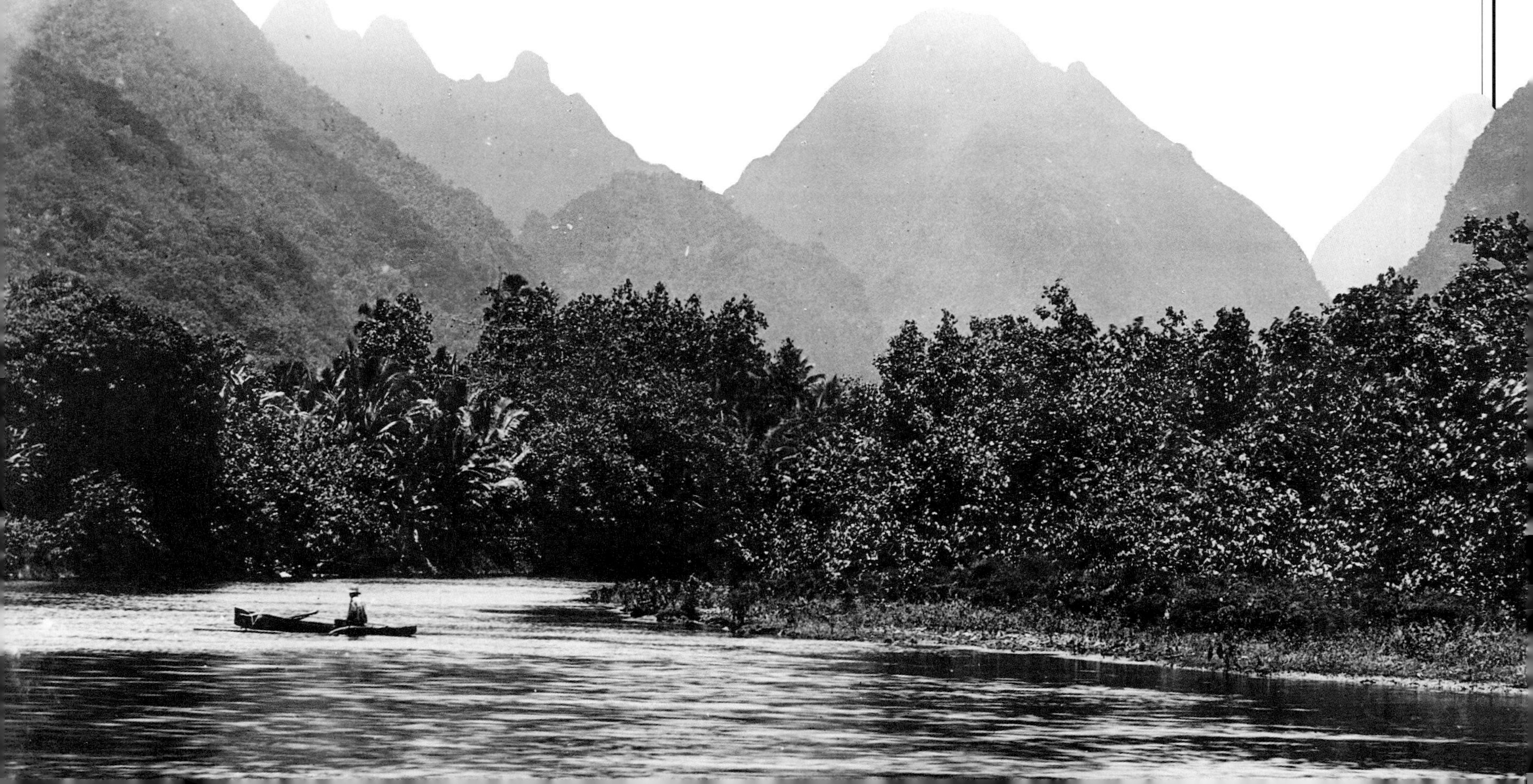

I am writing this in the evening. The silence of the night in Tahiti is something stranger than anything else about it. It is absolute. Nothing else exists; there is not even the cry of a bird to break the quiet. Here and there a large dried leaf falls, but it gives no impression of noise. It is more like a rustling of the spirit. The natives often walk about at night, but silently, with bare feet. Always this silence. I can understand why these people can stay for hours on end—even for days—sitting down without saying a word, just looking melancholically at the sky. I can feel all this permeating me, and at this moment I feel a sense of total repose.

It seems to me that all the things that make life in Europe so troublesome do not exist anymore, and tomorrow will be just the same as today, and so on, until the end. Don't think that because I say this I am an egoist and that I am abandoning you. But give me some time to live like this. Those who are always reproaching me have no idea what makes up an artist's nature, and why should they impose on us responsibilities like their own? We do not impose ours on them.

What a wonderful night it is. Thousands of other individuals are doing what I am doing; they are allowing themselves to live, and their children bring themselves up on their own. All these people go into any village, by no matter what road, sleep and eat in somebody else's house, etc., without as much as a 'thank you', on the principle that one good turn deserves another. And yet one calls them savages! . . . They sing, they never steal—my door is never closed—they don't murder people. Two words characterize them: *Iorama* (good day, goodbye, thank you, etc.; and *Onatu* (I don't care—what does it matter?)—and yet one calls them savages! I look on the death of King Pomaré as something tragic. The land of Tahiti is becoming entirely French, and little by little all that old order of things will give place to new.

Our missionaries have already introduced a new element of Protestant hypocrisy and are destroying the sense of poetry—quite apart from syphilis, which has taken hold of the whole race without,

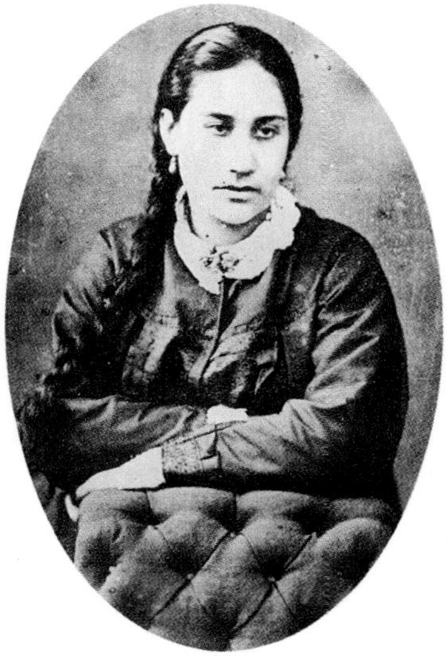

ABOVE: *Queen Marau, widow of Pomaré V, impressed Gauguin with her comprehensive knowledge of the culture and folk-lore of the island. It has been suggested that Gauguin's oil known as 'The Queen' or 'The Noble Woman' (see page 109) was based on her.*

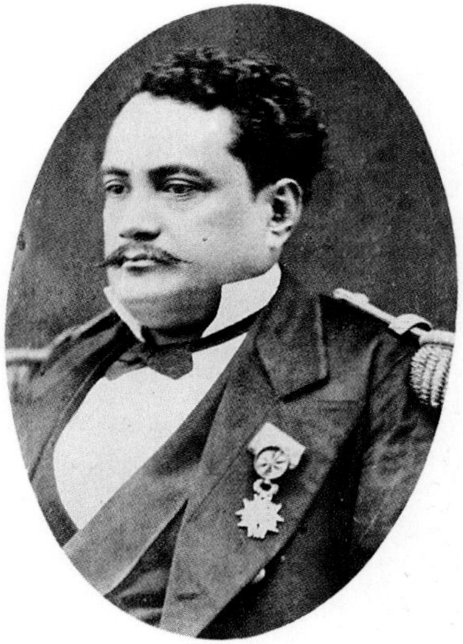

ABOVE: *King Pomaré V, whose death coincided with Gauguin's arrival on Tahiti, and whose funeral he described in an early letter home (see page 61–5). Both portraits, of husband and wife (above and left), were pasted into the* Noa Noa *manuscript.*

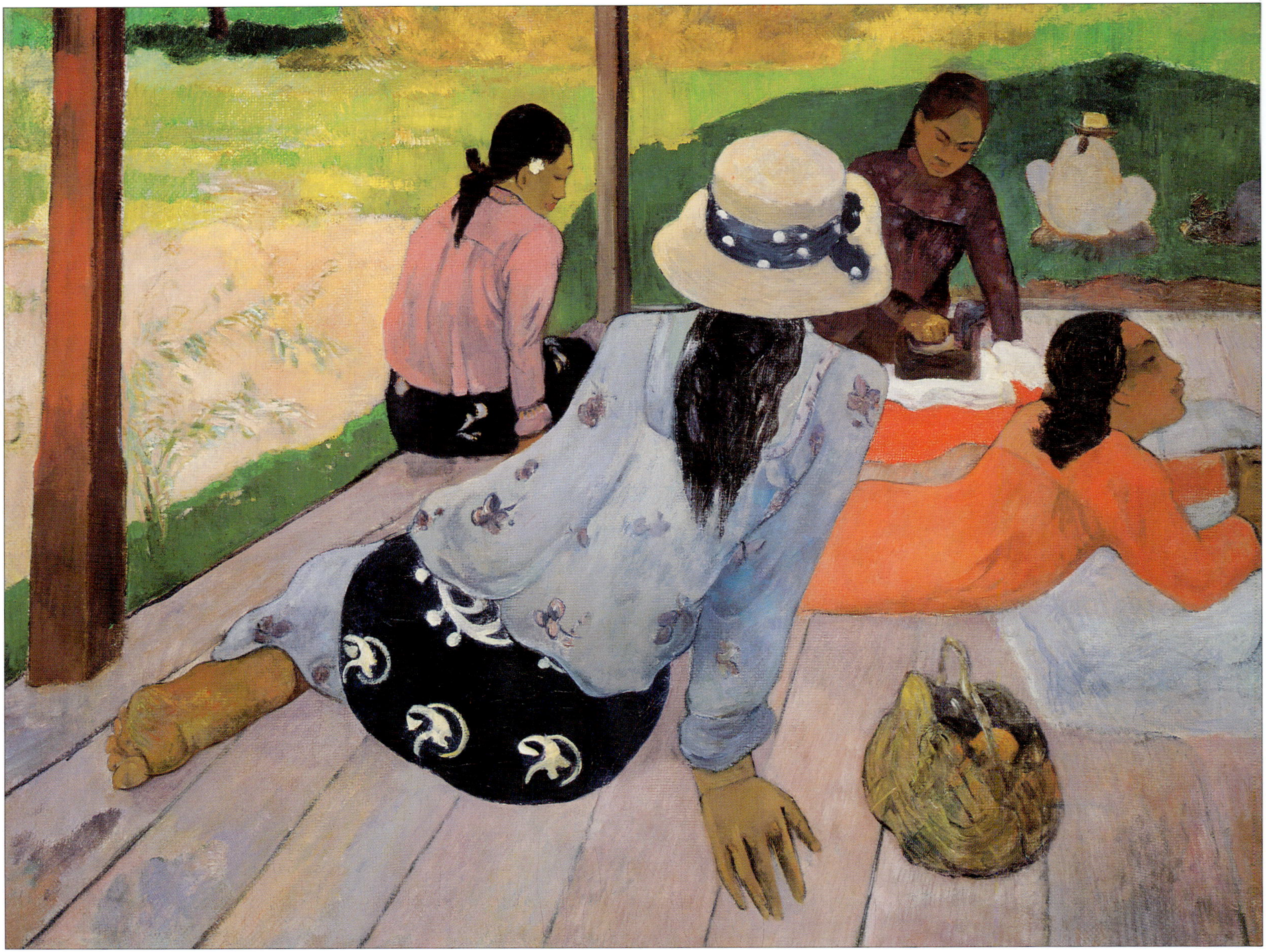

LEFT: THE SIESTA, *c.*1891–2
This painting, considered unfinished, hints at ways in which the way of life of the islanders was being changed by the presence of colonial settlers, with its newfangled verandah and style of dress. The women of the island increasingly adopted Western garments, including the voluminous 'missionary style' dress. These clothes needed ironing, a task carried out in the painting by one of the girls, who wear both Western dress and traditional pareus *made of European printed material.*

thank God, debasing it. You who like handsome men would find no shortage of them here; they are taller than I, and have limbs like Hercules . . .

I am putting out my lamp as I embrace you and say good-night . . .

* Pomaré V, the last king of Tahiti.

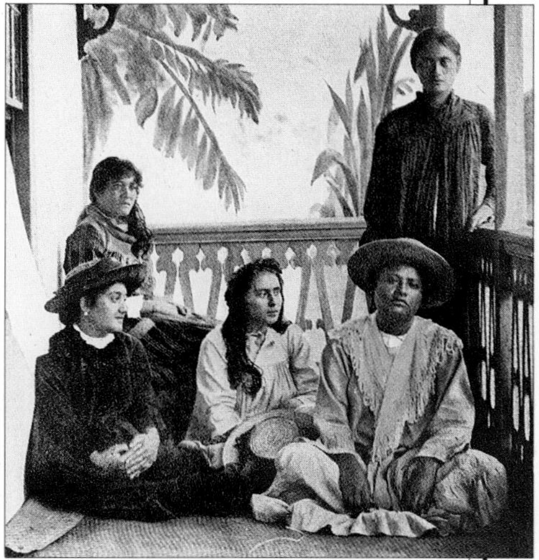

ABOVE: *A group portrait of Tahitian women, possibly servants of a well-off settler family.*

Tahiti — To Mette Gauguin — *March 1892*

. . . I am indeed a great artist; you are right, you are not mad. I am a great artist, and I know it. It is because I am what I am that I have to endure so much suffering. If I did not pursue my own road, I would be a brigand, which indeed I am to a lot of people. But what does it matter in the long run? What annoys me most is not so much the misery, but the fact that constant obstacles are put in the way of my art so that I cannot do what I feel and that I should be able to do it

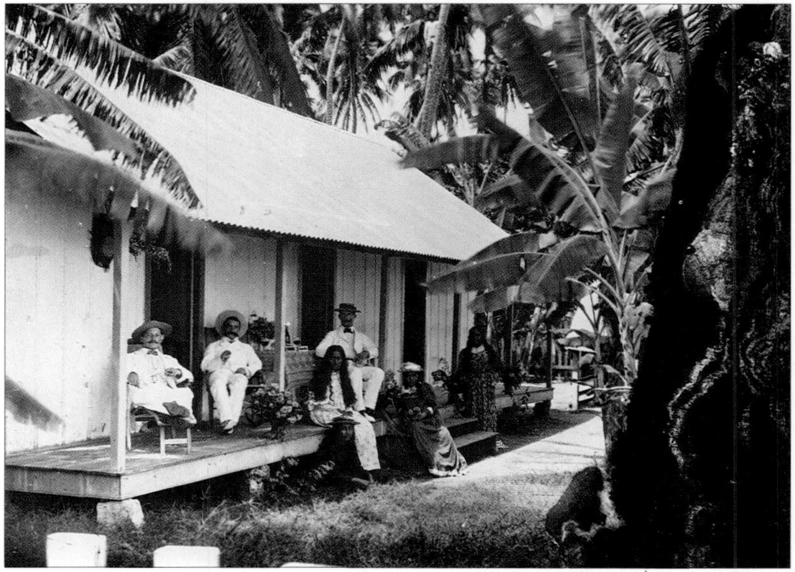

RIGHT: *Western men and Tahitian women taking their siesta. The traditional afternoon rest from the heat of the sun was increasingly taken on the verandah, a European import which in the houses of the settlers had a carved wood balustrade.*

without the misery which is always tying my hands. You say that I am wrong in staying away for so long from the centre of the art world. The centre of my art world is in my head, not anywhere else, and I am strong because I am never sidetracked by others and I do what is inside me.

Beethoven was deaf and blind, he was isolated from everything, and so his works reflect the living artist who lives in the world within him. Look what happened to Pissarro as a result of his constant quest to keep up with things and always be in the swim. He lost every shred of personality and his work lacks any kind of unity. He followed every movement from Courbet and Millet to these young chemists who build up pictures from little spots.*

No, I have only one goal, and I pursue it, collecting pieces of evidence on the way. It is true that every year there are changes, but they all follow the same path. I am uniquely logical, that is why I have so few followers.

Poor Schuffenecker is always reproaching me for being pig-headed in my intentions. But if I did not act like this how could I have sustained, even for a year, the single-minded struggle that I have undertaken? At the time when I am doing them, my actions, my paintings, etc., are always condemned, until, finally, people admit that I am right. I am always having to begin again. I believe that I am doing my duty, and fortified by that realization, I accept neither advice nor criticism.

The conditions under which I work are unfavourable, and one has to be a colossus to do what I am doing under these circumstances . . .

* Referring to Georges Seurat (1859–91), the pioneer of Pointillism, and his followers. This technique, in which dots of unmixed colour are juxtaposed on a white background, was an off-shoot of Impressionism.

RIGHT: THE BLESSED MARY (IA ORANA MARIA), 1891–2
A joyous and colourful fusion of Christian and Eastern symbolism, the painting shows the infant Jesus and Mary (daringly depicted as Tahitians) sharing a warmth often absent in Western art.

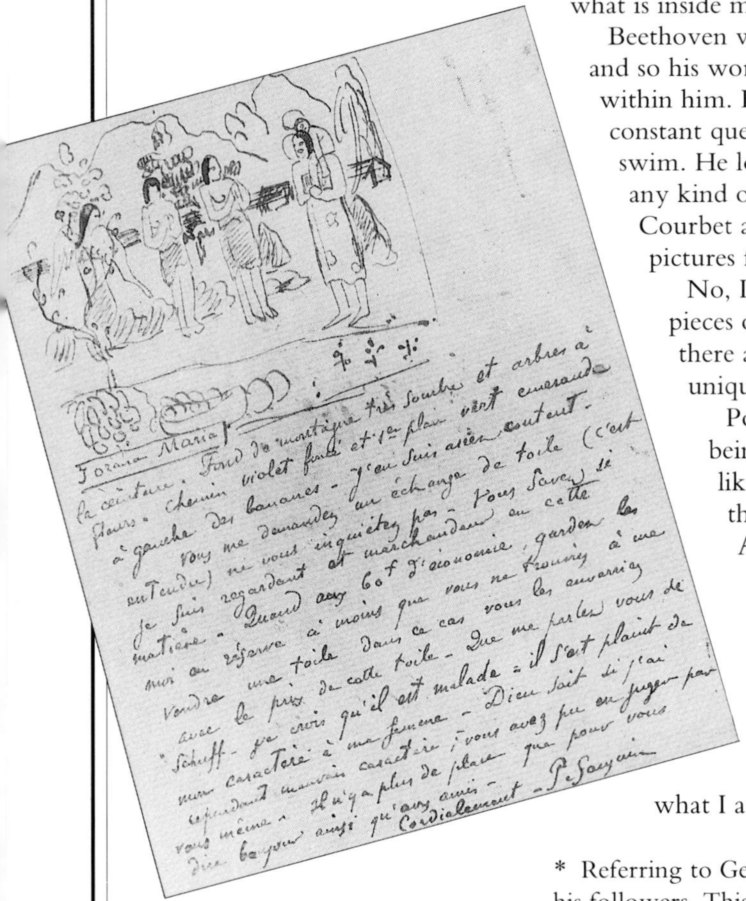

I orana Maria. Fond de montagne très sombre et arbres à fleurs. Chemin violet foncé et 1er plan vert émeraude à gauche des bananes - J'en suis assez content.
Vous me demandez un échange de toile (c'est entendu) ne vous inquiétez pas - vous savez si je suis regardant et marchandeur en cette matière. Quand aux 60 f d'économie, gardez les moi en réserve à moins que vous ne trouviez à me vendre une toile dans ce cas vous les enverriez avec le prix de cette toile. Que me parlez vous de Schuff - je crois qu'il est malade : il s'est plaint de son caractère à ma femme - Dieu sait si j'ai cependant mauvais caractère ; vous avez pu en juger par vous même. Il n'y a plus de place que pour vous dire bonjour ainsi qu'aux amis -
Cordialement - P Gauguin

LEFT: *In this letter to De Monfreid dated 11 March 1892, Gauguin expresses great pride in his painting 'Ia Orana Maria'.*

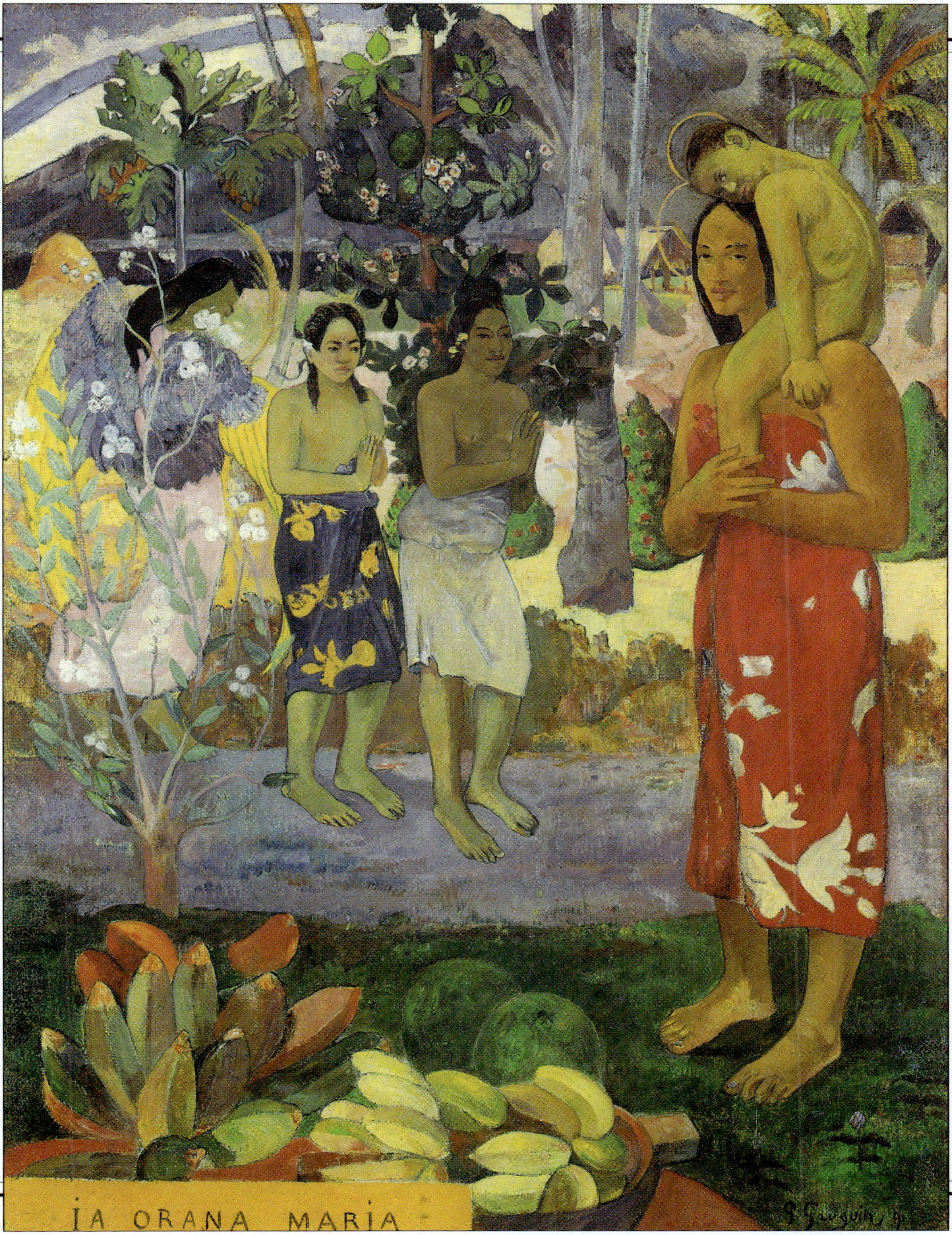
IA ORANA MARIA
P. Gauguin, 91

Tahiti — **To Mette Gauguin** — ***5 November 1892***

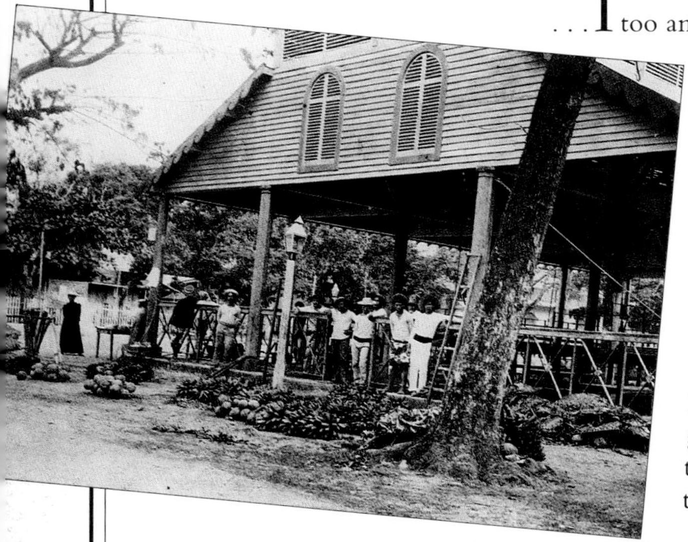

. . . I too am beginning to feel aged, and it's happening very quickly. As a result of being deprived of nourishment, my stomach is getting atrociously ruined, and I am getting thinner every day. But I must keep on with the fight for ever and ever. The fault rests on the shoulders of Society. You do not seem to have any confidence in the future; but I do have confidence *because I will myself to have it*. Were it not for that, I would long ago have blown my brains out. To have hope is almost as important as to live. I must live to do my duty to the very end, and I can only do that by fostering my illusions, making myself live in a dream of hope. When every day here I eat my *dry bread* with a glass of water, I come to believe that it is a beefsteak through sheer will to believe that it is so. Do not, therefore, my dear Mette, speak to me of false hopes . . .

LEFT: *The market-place in Papeete, where Gauguin, along with native and colonial residents, bought his food.*

Tahiti — **To Mette Gauguin** — ***8 December 1892***

. . . Naturally, many of the pictures I am going to send you will be incomprehensible, and will give you something to amuse yourself with. So that you will understand them and, as they say, kid people along, I shall give you an explanation of the sauciest one, 'Le Manau tupapau'. I did a nude of a young girl. In this position, though it isn't important, she is indecent. Still, that's how I wanted it; the lines and the movement interest me. And she is rather frightened. This fear must be implied if not explained, existing as it does in the head of the subject, a Maori girl. Traditionally, these people have a great fear of the spirits of the dead. A young girl in our country would be frightened to have been caught in this position, not so the woman in this picture. I have to explain this fear with the least possible use of literary means—as artists are bound to do. Therefore, I am doing this. A general harmony, sombre, sad, frightening, striking the eye like a funeral knell; violet, a sombre blue and orange-coloured yellow. I have made her shift a greenish yellow because: 1, the clothes of this savage are very different from ours, patterned from the bark of fallen trees; 2, because it creates a feeling of artificial light—Kanaka women never sleep in the dark—and I didn't want the clichéd effect of lamplight; 3, this yellow, linking the orange-yellow and the blue, completes the musical harmony. There are some flowers in the background, but they should not be seen as real but imaginary, so I have made them look like stars. To the Kanaka the fireflies of the night are the spirits of the dead, and they fear them. Finally, to conclude, I have done the ghost very simply, a good homely little woman, because the young girl, not being conversant with what ghosts look like on the French stage, cannot do otherwise than see in the spirit of death, death itself—that is, a human being like death. So here is a little disquisition that will help you show the critics, when they bombard you with their malicious questions, how knowledgeable you are . . .

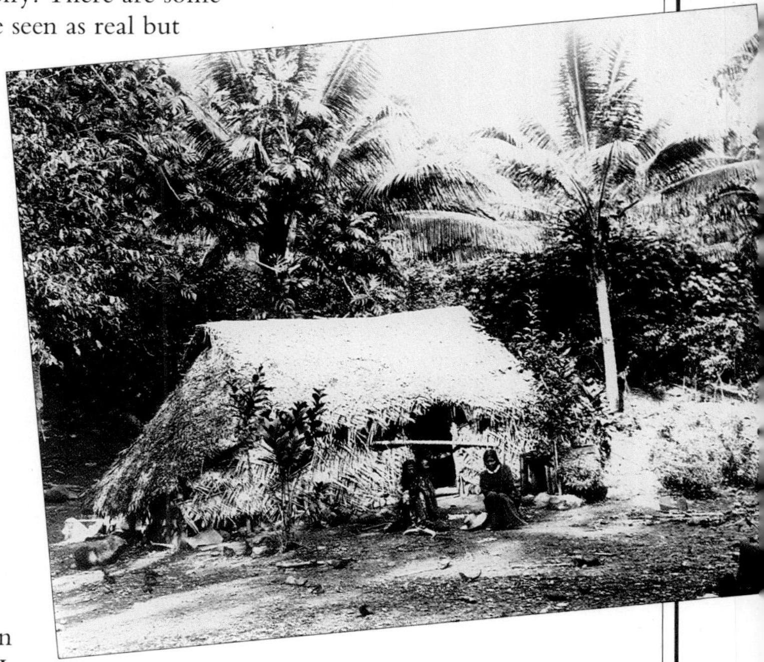

RIGHT: *A thatched hut of a type seen all over the island, often appearing as the subject of Gauguin's paintings as well as in the background landscape of many more. The artist rented such huts as temporary shelters when forced to move from houses he had built himself, and his first home at Mataiea was of this construction.*

INTERSPERSED WITH CONSTANT COMPLAINTS about money, about his health and about other people, Gauguin's letters present only part of his life and preoccupations. He had other concerns, deeper sensitivities, affected though these often were when written down by his own insecure braggadocio. He needed constantly to persuade himself, as well as others, that paradise did indeed exist on this remote, bureaucrat-ridden outpost of the French colonial empire. When he returned to Paris in 1893, he felt a need for some justification of the last two years of his life, more explicit than his paintings of the island which, when exhibited at

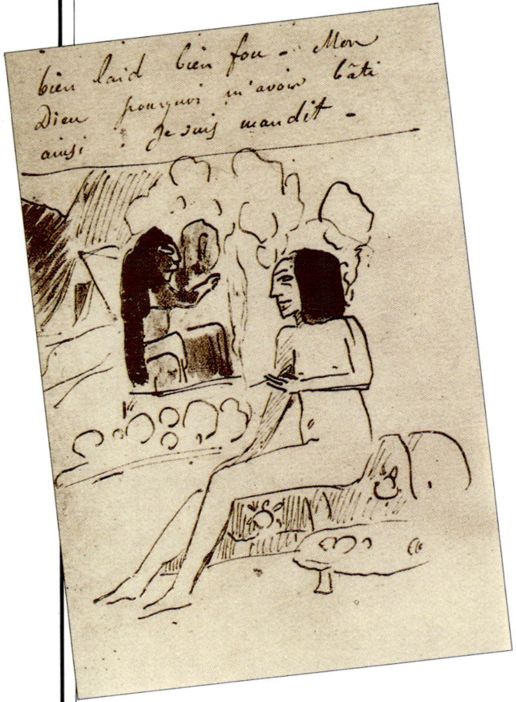

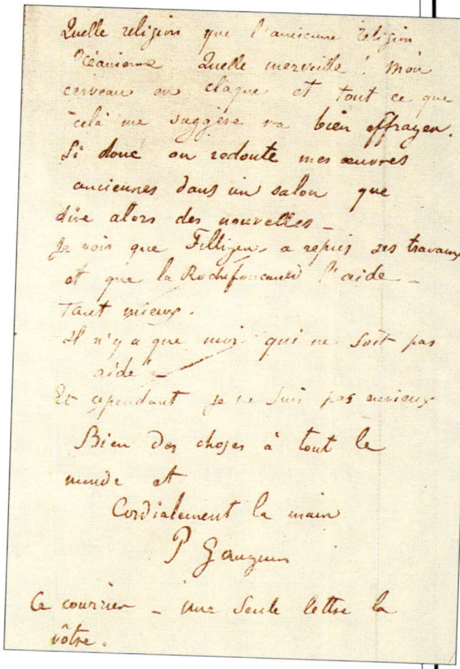

Quelle religion que l'ancienne religion
Océanienne. Quelle merveille ! mon
cerveau en claque et tout ce que
cela me suggère va bien effrayer.
Si donc on redoute mes œuvres
anciennes dans un salon que
dire alors des nouvelles –
Je vois que Filliger a repris ses travaux
et que la Rochefoucauld l'aide –
Tant mieux.
Il n'y a que moi qui ne soit pas
aidé –
Et cependant je ne suis pas sérieux.

Bien des choses à tout le
monde et
Cordialement la main
P Gauguin

Ce courrier – une seule lettre la
vôtre.

ABOVE AND RIGHT: *In this letter to Sérusier of 25 March 1892 Gauguin exclaims, 'What a religion the ancient Oceanic religion is! . . . All the ideas it suggests to me are really going to scare people off.' He had begun the process of collecting Tahitian legends into a notebook which suggested many themes for paintings.*

Durand-Ruel's between November and December 1893, had what can only be described as a modest success—eleven out of forty-four being sold, including one to Degas. Although he himself claimed, in a letter to Mette, 'For the moment, I am considered by many people to be the greatest modern painter,' his works were, on the whole, condemned by artists such as Renoir, Monet and Pissarro, though admired by Symbolist writers such as Mallarmé, who helped to promote the exhibition.

The main intermediary between Mallarmé and Gauguin was Charles Morice, a poet of mediocre ability, who in 1889 had written a provocative book on modern French literature, and whose energy in promoting himself was equalled only by its customary lack of success. It was he who claimed the initiative in the creation of the book of recollections of Tahiti that was to become *Noa Noa*, and his contribution to its contents was always to be a source of conflict between himself and Gauguin, and of controversy amongst later generations. Originally part of a publicity build-up for the Durand-Ruel exhibition, it was seen by Gauguin as a co-operative work, a dialogue in which he, with his rough prose and simple feelings, would play The Savage, whilst Morice, with his elegant writing and flowery verse, would be the dichotomous Civilized Man. Gauguin clearly had no doubt in his mind which would be the more highly regarded, and he was not wrong.

Gauguin's first draft, partly based on notes which he brought back from Tahiti and wrote up in Paris, is a mixture of fully developed themes or anecdotes, and notes of ideas to be expanded later. Much of the material about Tahitian beliefs and customs was culled from a two-volume book, *Voyage aux Îles du Grand Océan*, by a Belgian, J. A. Moerenhout, who had worked in Polynesia in the 1820s and 30s in various consular jobs. Gauguin had been lent a copy of this by Auguste Goupil, one of his friends in the French community at Papeete in 1892, and was immediately enraptured, writing to Sérusier in March of that year, 'What a religion the ancient Oceanic one is! What a marvel! My brain is reeling with it and all that it

RIGHT: HER NAME IS VAIRAOUMATI (VAIRAOUMATI TEI OA), 1892 *This woman was, in Tahitian folklore, a beautiful mortal who, chosen by the great god Oro to bear his child, gave birth to the race of Areoi (superior beings to whom free love was permitted). Oro appears behind the girl, who is shown in the pose of maidens in Egyptian friezes.*

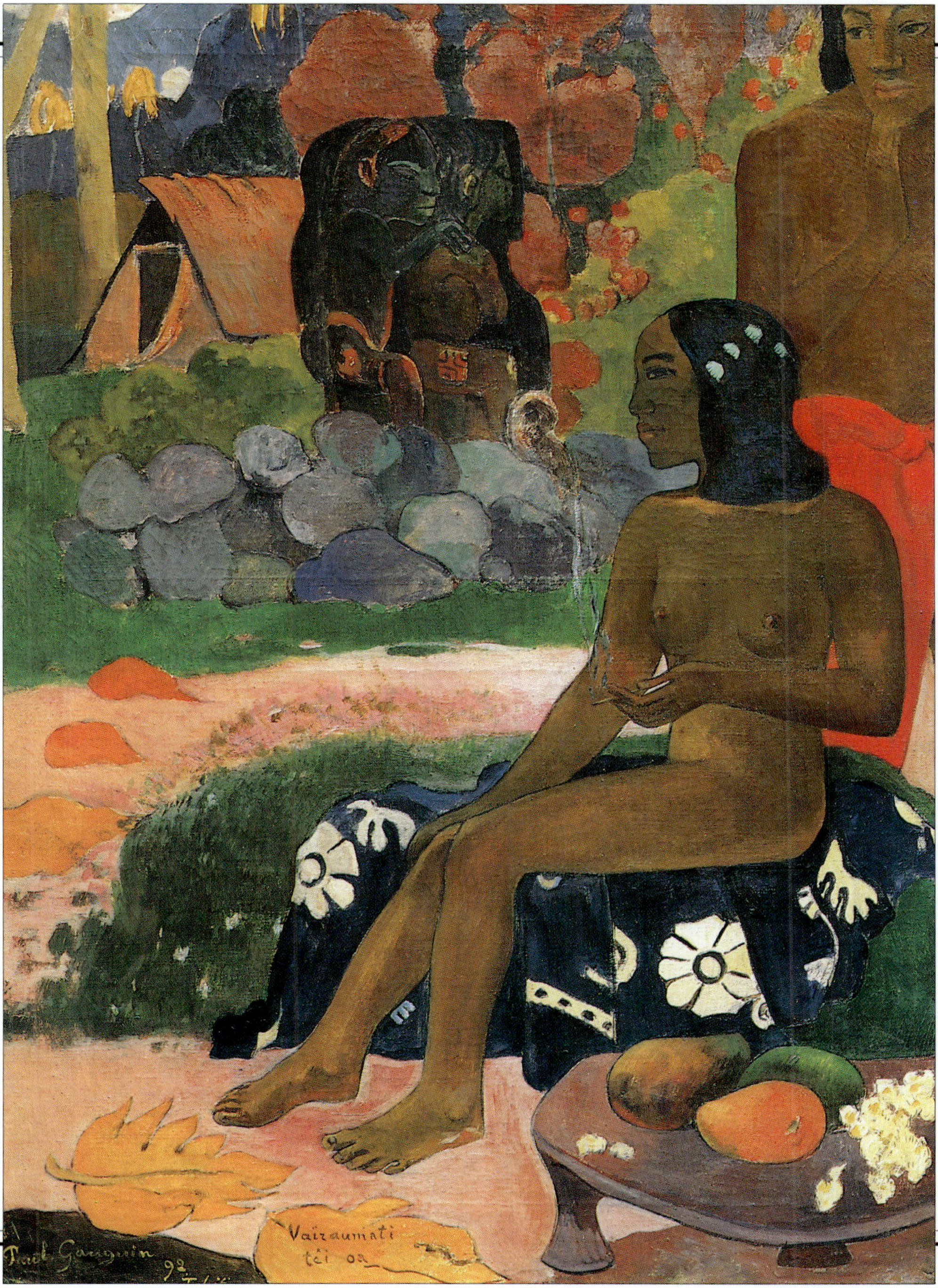

contains is going to frighten people. If people were frightened of putting my old works in their salons, what are they going to make of the new ones?' He saw Tahiti, therefore, not only as a source of iconography for his paintings, but as the source of material for his writings. Amongst his belongings found after his death was a notebook entitled *Ancien Culte Maorie*, which consisted of transcripts and notes on Moerenhout's book, illustrated with delightful watercolour sketches by himself.

It was typical, however, of Gauguin's presentation of himself to the outside world that he should have disguised his borrowings from the book as statements made by various Tahitian girls and presented himself as a sympathetic and knowledgeable interpreter of the island's people and culture. His qualifications for such a role were not profound. Jénot, the naval lieutenant who taught him the local language, commented critically on his 'distressing capacity for forgetting, for mixing syllables, or for turning them upside down'. He could not even get the name of his 'fiancée' right. The correct spelling would be Teha'amana, but Gauguin called her Tehemana, or Tehura, or Téhura. Quite apart, therefore, from the fact that he was almost certainly not in a position to interpret a native girl's account of her religion and its myths, there is also the evidence of the manuscript itself, where he notes 'taken from Moerenhout'. Even the title given to the work, which in 1895 he explained to a journalist from the *Echo de Paris* as meaning 'fragrant', was intended to be 'Noa Noa Fenua'—The Very Fragrant Island.

But, for all the deceptions it incorporates, it must be realized that these were part of Gauguin's reality. He said that the purpose of *Noa Noa* was 'to facilitate understanding of my paintings', and this it did by providing them with an iconographical justification. But it fulfilled Gauguin's aim more completely by giving a vivid picture of himself. A tissue of fact and fiction, an apologia, by implication, for the notion of Gauguin the savage, Gauguin the exiled Messiah, Gauguin the man of sentiment and feeling, *Noa Noa* is, for all its brevity, an autobiographical essay of a singularly persuasive kind.

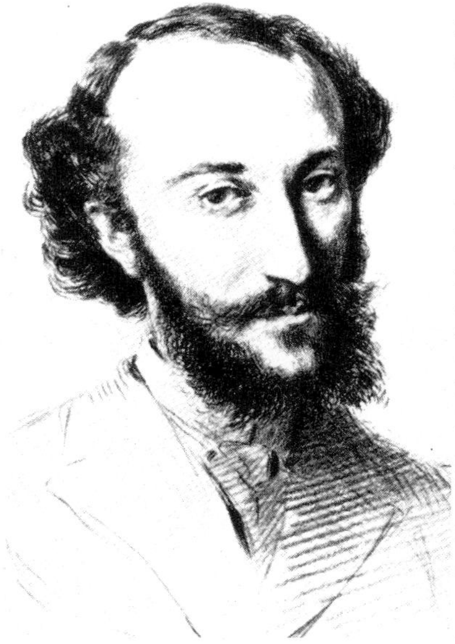

ABOVE: *A drawing of Charles Morice by Baud Bovy, c.1890. Gauguin first met Morice in 1890 and the idea of collaborating on an edition of* Noa Noa *came about during Gauguin's stay in Paris two years later. Morice, a poet and protégé of Mallarmé, has been much reviled for his tampering with Gauguin's vivid prose and savage imagery.*

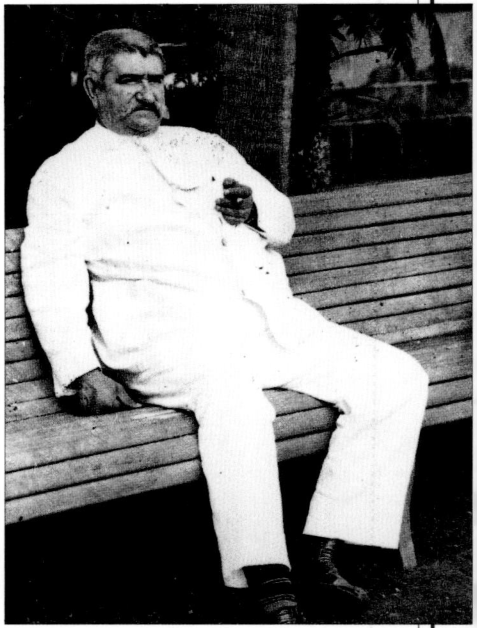

ABOVE: *A lawyer and plantation owner, Auguste Goupil lent Gauguin a copy of J. A. Moerenhout's* Voyage aux Îles du Grand Océan, *an account of the religion, customs and languages of the Polynesians with notes on their political and social systems. From this grew Gauguin's illustrated manuscript* Ancien Culte Maorie.

THE CHARM OF A MAORI SMILE

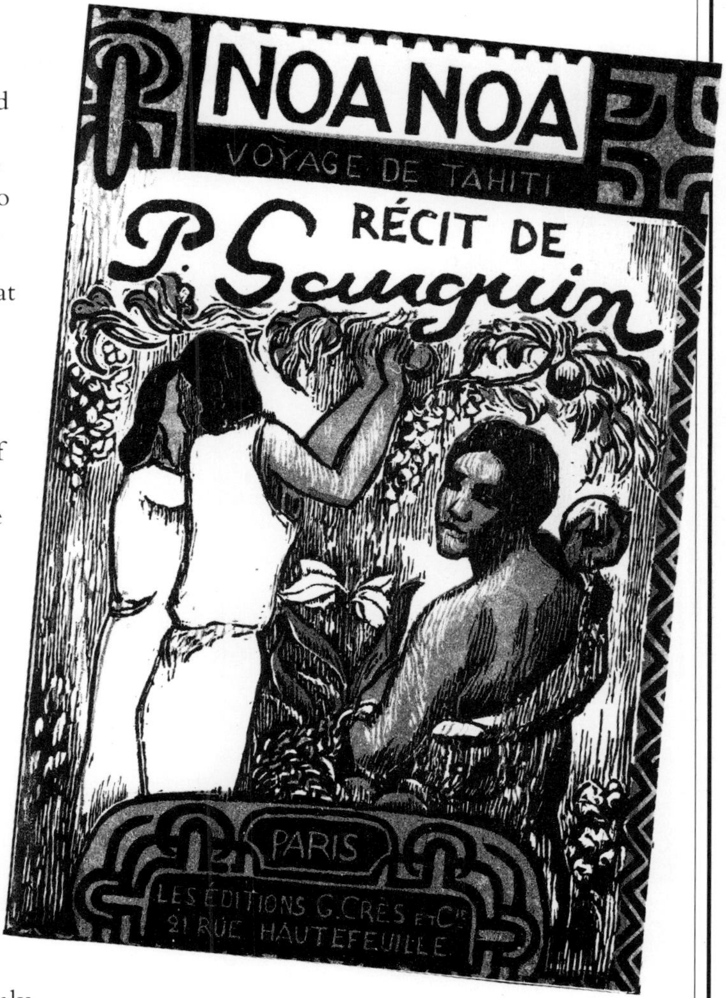

RIGHT: *The cover of the Crès edition of* Noa Noa*, with woodcuts by Daniel de Monfreid. The cover uses one of Gauguin's favourite images: the picking of fruit. In Western art this symbolizes a loss of innocence, but in Gauguin's Tahiti it embodies the harmony of mankind with nature. The text of* Noa Noa *bears out this version of an unfallen humanity in an earthly paradise.*

I began to work: notes, sketches of all kinds. Everything in the landscape blinded and dazzled me. Coming from Europe, I was always uncertain of a colour, making difficulties where there were none; and yet it was so simple just to put naturally on my canvas a red and a blue. In the streams the golden shapes enchanted me. Why did I hesitate to pour on my canvas all that gold and all that joyous sunshine? It was probably because of old habits picked up in Europe—all this fear of expressing oneself which belongs to our degenerate races.

To initiate myself properly into the nature of the Tahitian face and the charm of a Maori smile, I had been anxious for some considerable time to do a portrait of a woman who lived near me and was of real Tahitian descent. I asked her one day if she would pluck up courage to come and look at some images in my hut, photographs of paintings.

She looked with special interest at a photograph of Manet's 'Olympia'.* With the help of the few words I had already picked up in that language—I hadn't spoken a word of French for two months—I asked her some questions. She told me that she thought Olympia was very beautiful. I smiled at this reflection and was very moved. She had a real feeling for beauty—the École des Beaux-Arts found the painting horrible! Suddenly breaking the silence which accompanies a thought, she added:

'Is that your wife?'
'Yes,' I lied. Me, the *tane* (husband) of Olympia! . . .
I asked if I might paint her portrait.

'*Aita* (no),' she said in an almost angry voice, and went away.

Her refusal really depressed me. An hour later she came back, wearing a lovely dress. Was this some internal struggle which had taken place inside her, or a mere whim, a typical Maori trait, or yet again, conceivably, the gesture of a coquette who does not want to give in until she has made some show of resistance?

Caprice, the desire for forbidden fruit. She smelled good, she was ready. I was aware that in my painter's scrutiny of her there was an implicit demand for her to give herself to me, to surrender completely without hope of withdrawal, a penetrating exploration of all that was within. By European standards she was not beautiful, but she was handsome, nonetheless. All her features had a Raphaelesque harmony at the point where their curves met, her mouth modelled by a sculptor for speaking and kissing the languages of joy and suffering; this melancholy of bitterness mingled with that pleasure of surrender which is contained within domination. An entire fear of the unknown.

I worked feverishly; I was uncertain whether this willingness on her part would last. Portrait of a woman: 'Vahine no te tiarare'. I worked quickly—with passion. It was a portrait which was true to what *my eyes veiled by my heart* truly perceived. I believe that above all else it revealed what went on inside her; the strong flame of a restrained force. She had a flower in her ear which absorbed her own perfume. Her face, in its majesty and with its raised cheekbones, reminded me of a phrase from Poe: 'No beauty is perfect without a certain singularity in its proportion.'

Noa Noa

LEFT: WOMAN WITH A FLOWER (VAHINE NO TE TIARE), 1891
This was one of the first portraits made by Gauguin of a native woman; in Noa Noa *he describes how she rushes off to put on her Western style dress before she will be painted (see page 73–4).*

* In February 1891 Gauguin had started copying Manet's 'Olympia', which had at last been hung in the Louvre. He did not complete the work in front of the picture, but finished it off from a photograph. It was a painting which kept echoing in his own works. He had with him in Tahiti a wide range of prints, reproductions and photographs of Greek, Egyptian and oriental art as well as of Renaissance and Baroque paintings and works by contemporary French artists such as Odilon Redon, Degas and others.

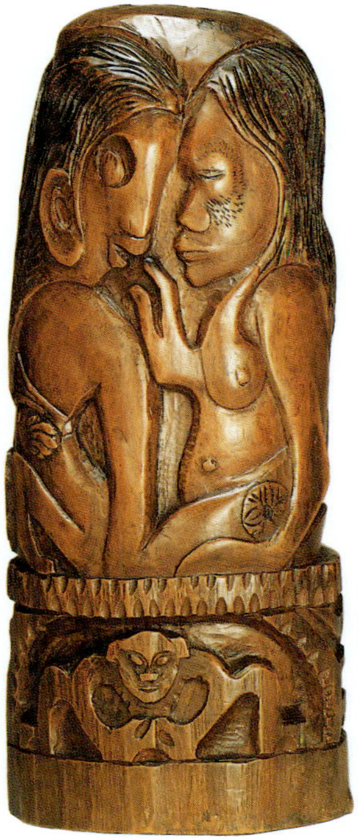

ABOVE: *This sculpture depicts Hina, goddess of the Air (and Moon), with Fatu, the animating spirit of the Earth formed from her union with the supreme god, Taaroa.*

A WEDDING FEAST

I was invited to a wedding, a real legal one of the kind that missionaries have tried to impress on their newly converted Christian faithful.

On the day itself. Underneath an improvised roof rapidly put up by all and sundry, elegantly bedecked with leaves and flowers, a large table. Relatives and friends were all there, and the food for the occasion was magnificent. Young pigs, roasted whole on hot stones, great quantities of fish, bread-fruits, wild bananas, taro, etc.

The local schoolmistress, who was almost white, was marrying an authentic Maori, the son of the chieftain of Punaauia. The Protestant bishop, who was the godfather of the girl who had been brought up in the missionary schools of Papeete, had insisted on the marriage taking place, and that somewhat urgently, between the girl and the young chief. In these parts the will of a missionary is the will of God.

When, after an hour, everybody had eaten and drunk their fill, numerous discourses followed, well-ordered and methodical, eloquent and spontaneous. To know which of the two families present would give a new name to the bride was a matter of great importance, and often indeed the discussion can become almost a fight. But on this occasion there was nothing of that sort; everything was peaceful, everybody happy and joyous and not unpleasantly

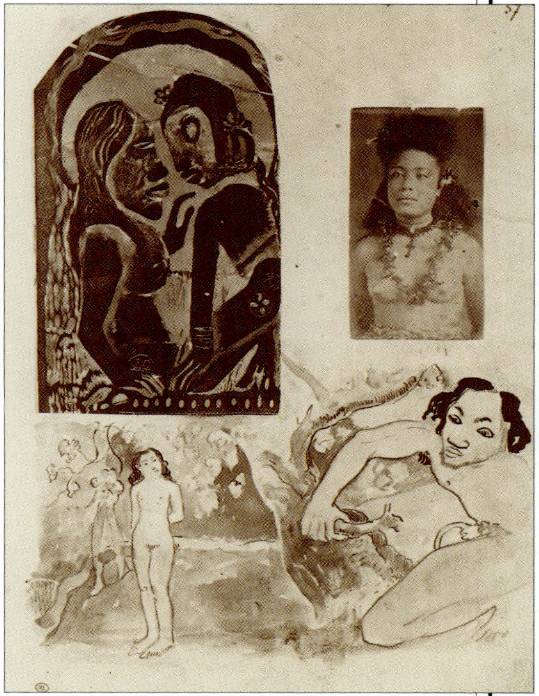

ABOVE: *This page is typical of the way in which Gauguin used his* Noa Noa *notebook to combine different images of Tahitian life in different media.*

drunk. My own poor *vahine*, led astray by somebody—I did not keep her under surveillance all the time—came away dead drunk, and it was not easy for me to get her home. She is very good, but very heavy.

In the centre of the table sat the chieftain's wife, admirably dignified, dressed in a robe of orange velvet—pretentious, bizarre, the sort you buy at a street market. But despite this, the innate grace of this people, the consciousness of her rank, made all that showy dress look dignified. Surrounded by flowers and Tahitian cooking her fragrance was one of the most beautiful of all the *noa noa*.

Near to her sat a centenarian grandmother, now little more than a death mask, made all the more frightening by her perfectly preserved row of cannibalistic teeth. Tattooed on her cheek was an indistinct dark shape, like a letter. I had often seen tattoo marks but never one like that, which was obviously European in origin. (I later discovered that, in the past, the missionaries had reacted very severely to any kind of self-indulgence, and had branded some of their parishioners on the cheek as a foretaste of hell, which covered them with shame, not the shame of a sin committed, but of the ridicule caused by such a distinctive mark.) I then understood why the Maoris of today distrust Europeans so much. Years have passed between the old woman being marked by the priest and the young girl being married by the priest. But the mark is still there.

Noa Noa

A DESIRE FOR THE UNKNOWN

I have a good friend, who comes to visit me every day, though not for any specific purpose. My coloured pictures and my works in wood have surprised him, and my replies to his questions have enlightened him. There is not a day when I am working when he does not come to watch me. One day, when giving him my tools, I asked him to try his hand at producing a piece of sculpture. He looked at me in astonishment, and said in complete innocence and

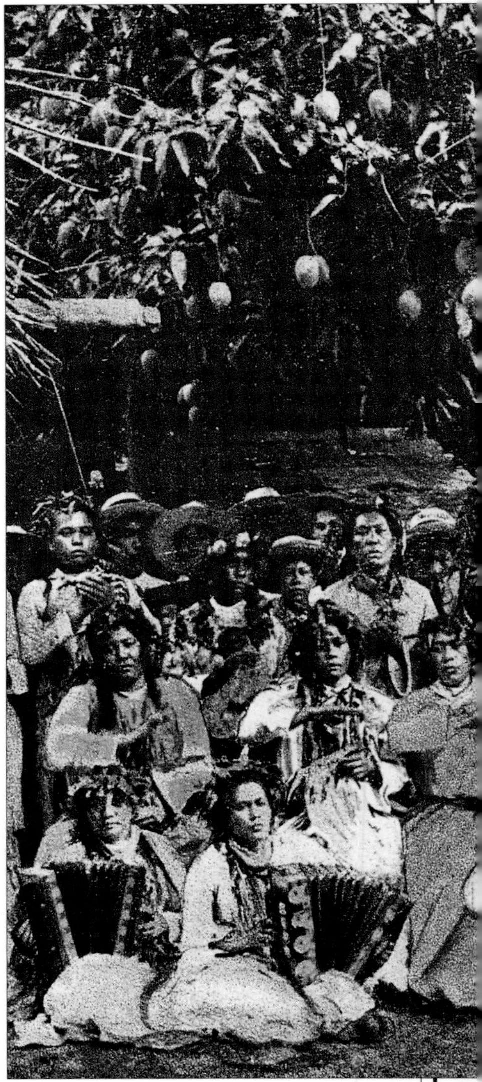

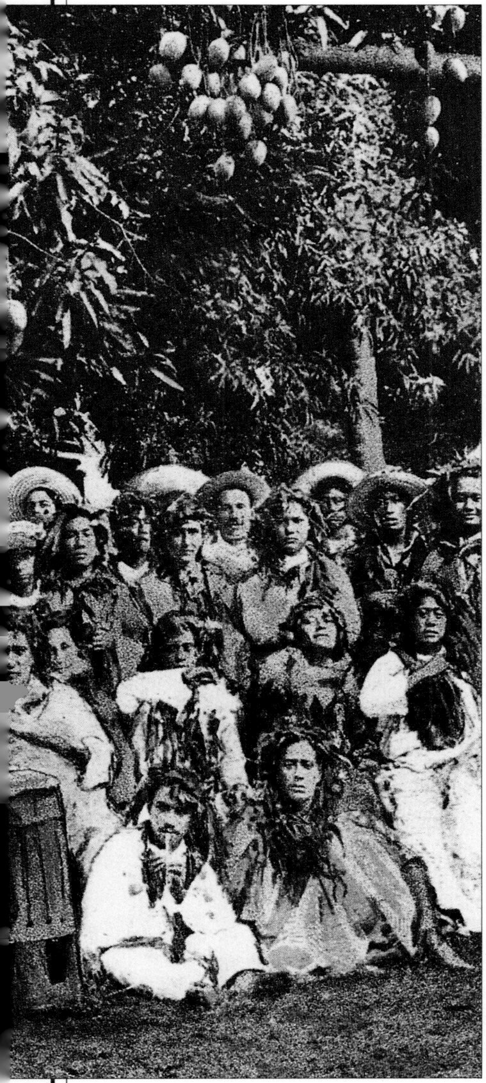

sincerity that I was not like other men, and the first perhaps in the community to be of use to others. What a child! He had to be, to believe that an artist had any use in society.

He was a faultlessly handsome youth, and we were great friends. Sometimes in the evenings, when I was relaxing after my work, he put to me the questions which one would expect from a young savage who was anxious to know more about the nature of how Europeans made love—questions which I often found embarrassing.

One day, I needed a piece of rose-wood for a sculpture I wanted to do; it had to be quite considerable in size, and not hollow.

'To get something like that,' he told me, 'you will have to go up into the hills, to a certain place where I know there are several fine trees of just the kind you need. If you like, I shall take you there and the two of us can carry the wood back.'

We set off early in the morning. In Tahiti, the Indian tracks are very difficult for a European. Between two unscaleable mountains there is a cleft where a stream gushes out across the boulders, pauses for a while and then takes on the life of a torrent, sweeping the loose boulders away as it moves down to the sea. On either side of this cascading stream there is a kind of pathway, trees everywhere, giant ferns, all kinds of vegetation growing wild and getting more impenetrable the closer one gets to the centre of the island.

We were both naked, save for a loin-cloth, and with axes in our hands we crossed and re-crossed the stream to follow, for a short distance, the footpath which my companion seemed to detect by its smell, so obscured and heavily shaded was it. There was complete silence save for the sound of the water babbling on the stones, a noise as monotonous as the silence. We were two people, two friends, he completely young, I almost an old man, in body and soul, in the vices of civilization, and in lost illusions. He, with his body as lithe as that of an animal, walked in front of me, completely sexless.

With all his youth, with all his perfect accord with surrounding nature, he exhaled a beauty, a fragrance (*noa noa*) which bewitched my artist's soul. From this friendship, so closely linked by a mutual

LEFT: *A wedding in Moorea in the last years of the nineteenth century is celebrated with music and singing, as described by Gauguin in a letter to Mette (see page 61–2). The celebrants play a mixture of native and European instruments and wear Western clothes with native headdresses made from flowers and leaves.*

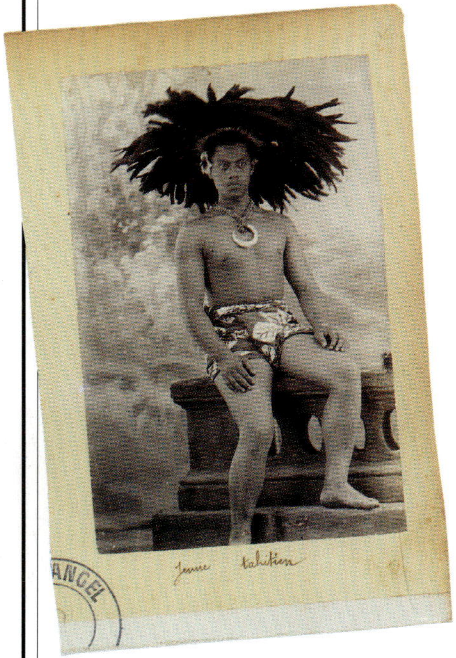

ABOVE: *Gauguin described the heavy-set but handsome young men in an early letter to Mette (see page 65).*

attraction which varied between the simple and the contrived, I found love starting to blossom within me . . .

And the two of us were completely alone.

I had, as it were, a presentiment of sin, a thirst for the unknown, a reawakening of evil. Then, too, I was exhausted by the male role of always having to be strong and protective, of having to have broad shoulders to support everything. Just for once to be the weak one, who loves and obeys!

I drew near to him, without fear of the law, my temples throbbing.

The footpath had come to an end; we had to cross the stream again. My companion turned round to face me at this moment.

The androgyne had vanished; it was a young man after all. His innocent eyes possessed all the limpidity of a stream. Calm suddenly flooded my soul. Plunging into the stream with delight, I savoured its coolness.

'*Toe toe* (it's cold),' he said.

'Oh no,' I replied, and this negation, a response to my earlier desire, penetrated the cliffs stridently, like an echo in a mountain.

Fiercely, I plunged into the thicket which had become increasingly wild. The boy pressed on, his eyes still limpid. He had apprehended nothing. I alone bore the weight of an evil thought. A whole civilization had both pushed me into evil, and saved me from it.

We were arriving at our goal. At this point, the mountain cliffs opened up on both sides to reveal a kind of plateau behind a curtain of tangled trees.

There, several trees (rose-wood) lay fallen with their immense branches stretched out. Savages, both of us, we attacked a magnificent tree with axes, which had to be broken up to get a branch of the size I desired. I struck furiously, and, my hands

BELOW: *Photograph of a native drinking at a waterfall taken in the 1880s by Charles Spitz, who organized the Tahitian exhibit at the Paris World's Fair in 1889.*

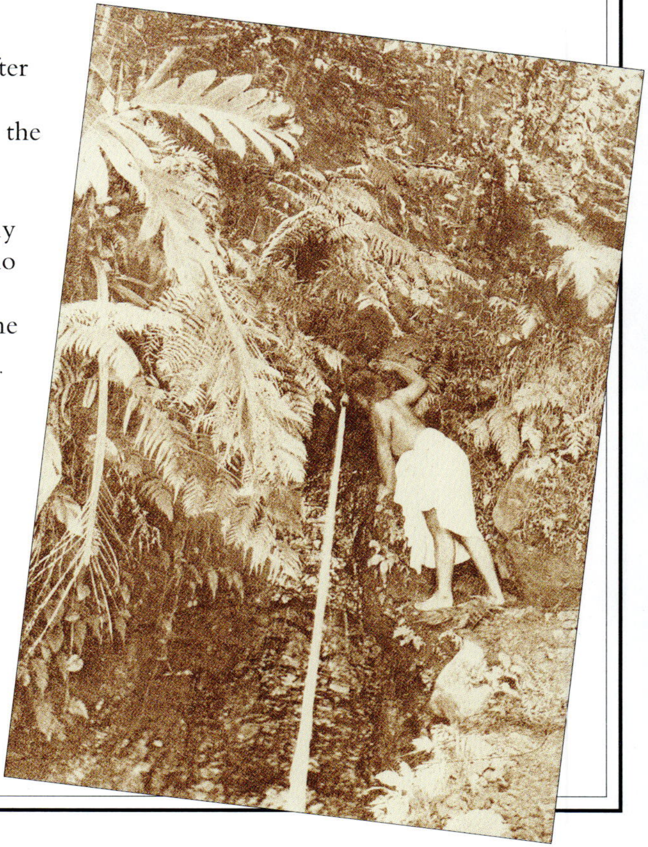

RIGHT: MYSTERIOUS WATER (PAPA MOE), 1893 *This painting follows the description of an event during Gauguin's expeditions into the interior of the island (see page 77), which may, however, be imaginary. Though so closely based on the photograph opposite, the painting evokes a more mythical world of legends and spirits.*

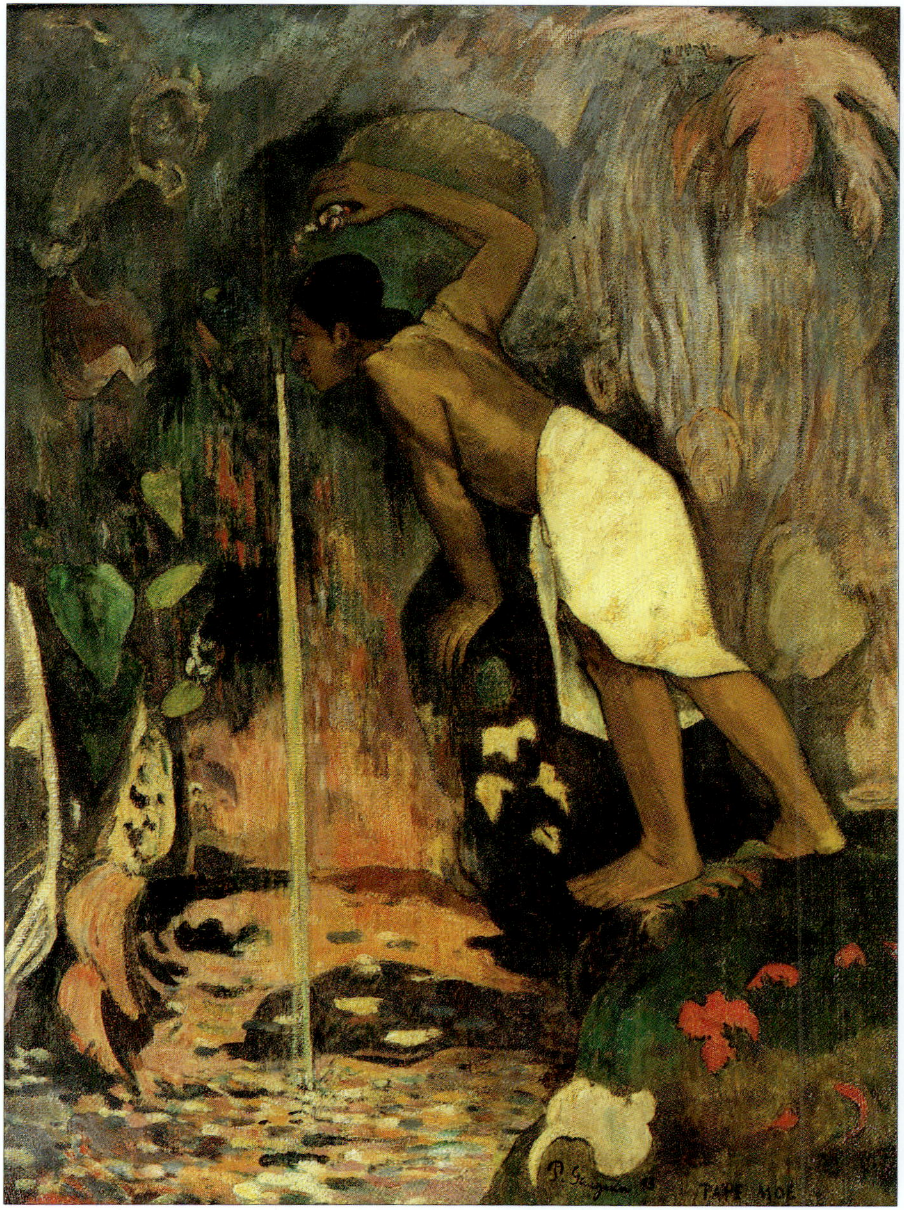

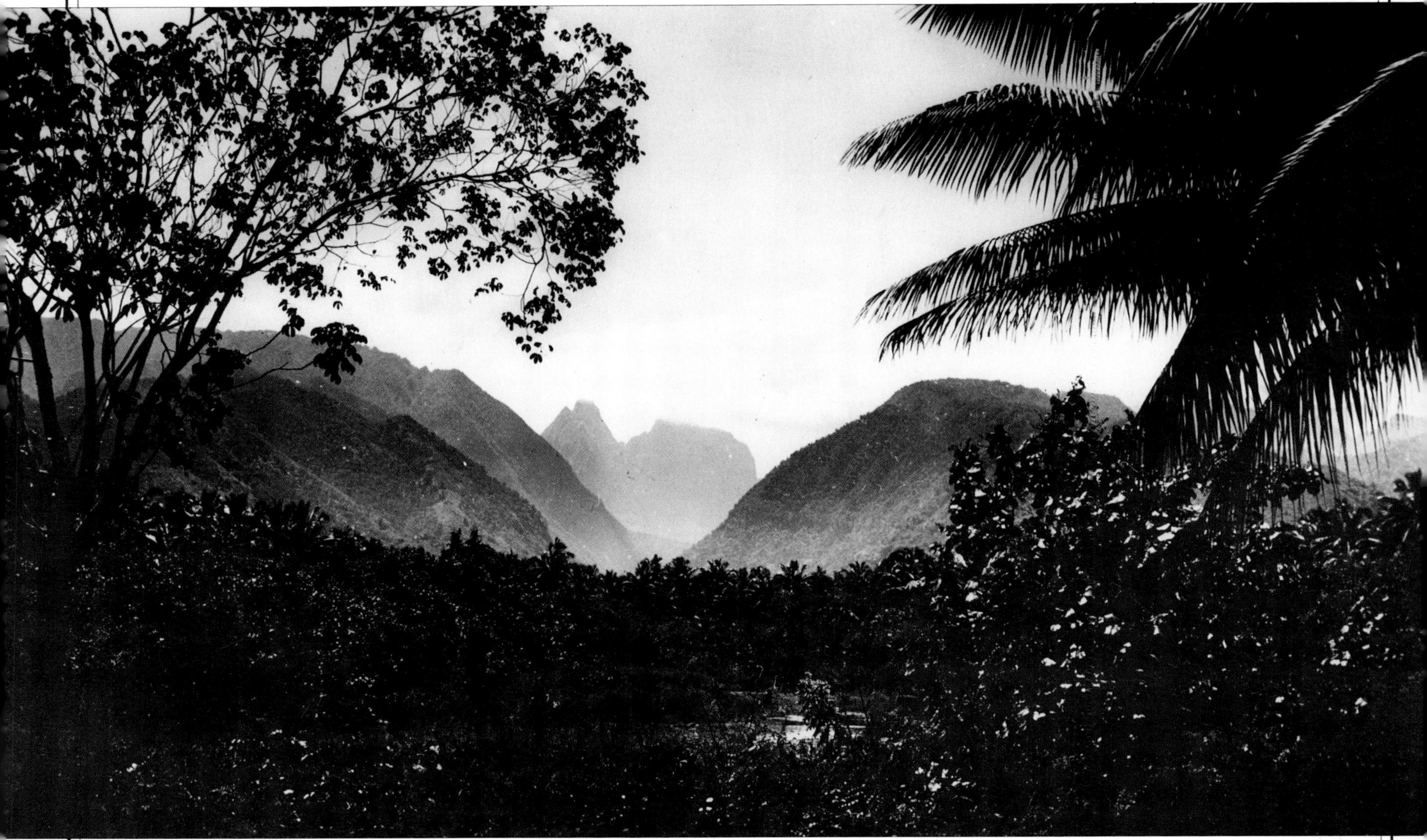

covered in blood, hacked away, rejoicing in assuaging my brutality by destroying something, no matter what it was.

To the sound of the cadence of the axe, I sang:

Trample down the entire forest (of desires),
Hack away in thyself all self-love,
As a man in autumn would cut down with his hand,
The Lotus.

Completely destroyed in me were all the old remnants of civilized man. I came back in peace, already feeling myself a new man, a Maori. The two of us carried our heavy load cheerfully, and I could admire in front of me the gracious figure of my young friend, as robust as the tree we were carrying, and could do so in tranquillity. The tree smelt of roses—*noa noa.*

On our return journey in the afternoon we were tired.

'You are satisfied?' he asked me.

'Yes,' I replied, and repeated it to myself. Yes, I was already at peace.

Never have I been able to give a single blow of the chisel to this piece of wood without having memories of a sweet peacefulness, of a fragrance, of a victory and a rejuvenation.

Noa Noa

LEFT: *A typical enclosed valley in the mountainous interior of Tahiti, graphically described by Gauguin in* Noa Noa.

THE WOODCUTTER

The nearly naked man was wielding a heavy axe with both hands that left, at the top of its stroke, a blue flash against the silvery sky, and, as it came down, its incision on the dead tree, which would soon live again in a moment of fire, time-honoured heat which would be built up each day. On the purple ground there were long serpentine leaves of a metallic yellow, a whole oriental vocabulary, the letters, or so it seemed to me, of an unknown mysterious alphabet. I seemed to see that word of Oceanic origin: *Atua*, 'God' . . . A woman was stowing away some nets in a canoe, and the

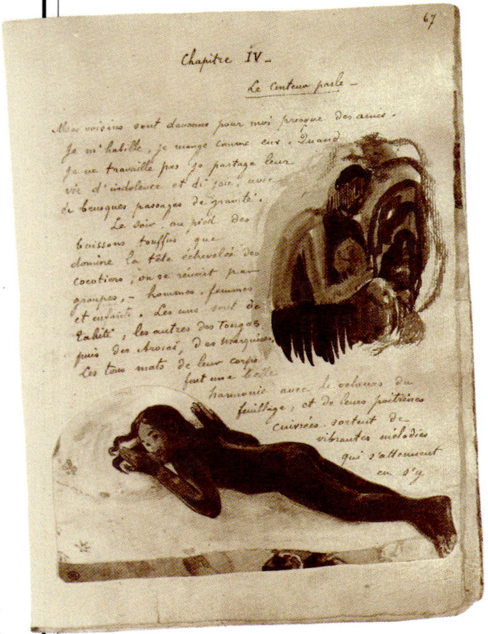

ABOVE: *Gauguin's* vahine, *Tehemana, and a mysterious man, sketched in* Noa Noa.

horizon of the blue sea was often broken by the green crests of the waves as they broke on the coral reefs.

Noa Noa

TUNNY FISHING

For about a week the flies, which till then had been scarce, started appearing in great numbers and became insufferable; but the Maoris rejoiced for it meant that the bonitos and the tunny-fish would come in from the open sea towards the coast. They started checking the condition of their lines and fish-hooks.

Women and children all gave a hand at dragging nets, or rather long palisades of coconut leaves, along the beach and over the coral rocks that form the seabed between the land and the reefs. In this way they caught the small fish to which the tunny are partial.

The day came when two large pirogues were launched into the sea, coupled together and bearing at the prow a very long fishing rod which could be raised quickly by two ropes that stretched as far as the stern. With this device, as soon as the fish has bitten, it is hauled in and brought aboard.

We make our way out past the reefs, and move out into the open sea. A turtle stares at us as we pass by.

We reach a place where the sea is very deep, and which they call the Tunny Hole, for it is there that the fish sleep at nights and very soundly too, out of the reach of sharks.

A cloud of sea birds watches the tunny. When they rise to the surface the birds swoop down from the sky and then soar up again with a lump of flesh in their beaks. There is carnage everywhere.

When I asked why they did not lower a fishing line into the Tunny Hole they replied it was a sacred place, the abode of the God of the Sea—*Rouahatou*—a kind of Neptune who sleeps in the depths of the sea at this spot . . .

One of the crew was told by the skipper to cast the hook clear of the boat. Time passed without any hint of a fish biting. Another was

RIGHT: THE SPIRIT OF THE DEAD WATCHING (MANAU TUPAPAU), 1892 *This canvas, a Tahitian version of Manet's 'Olympia' and one on which Gauguin placed great importance, is based on an incident when Gauguin found Tehemana lying rigid with fear in the darkness, prey to the Tahitian sense of powerful spirit presences embodying the malignant power of the dead. To these Gauguin gave a simple form which he explained as being within the power of the girl's childlike imagination (see letter page 69).*

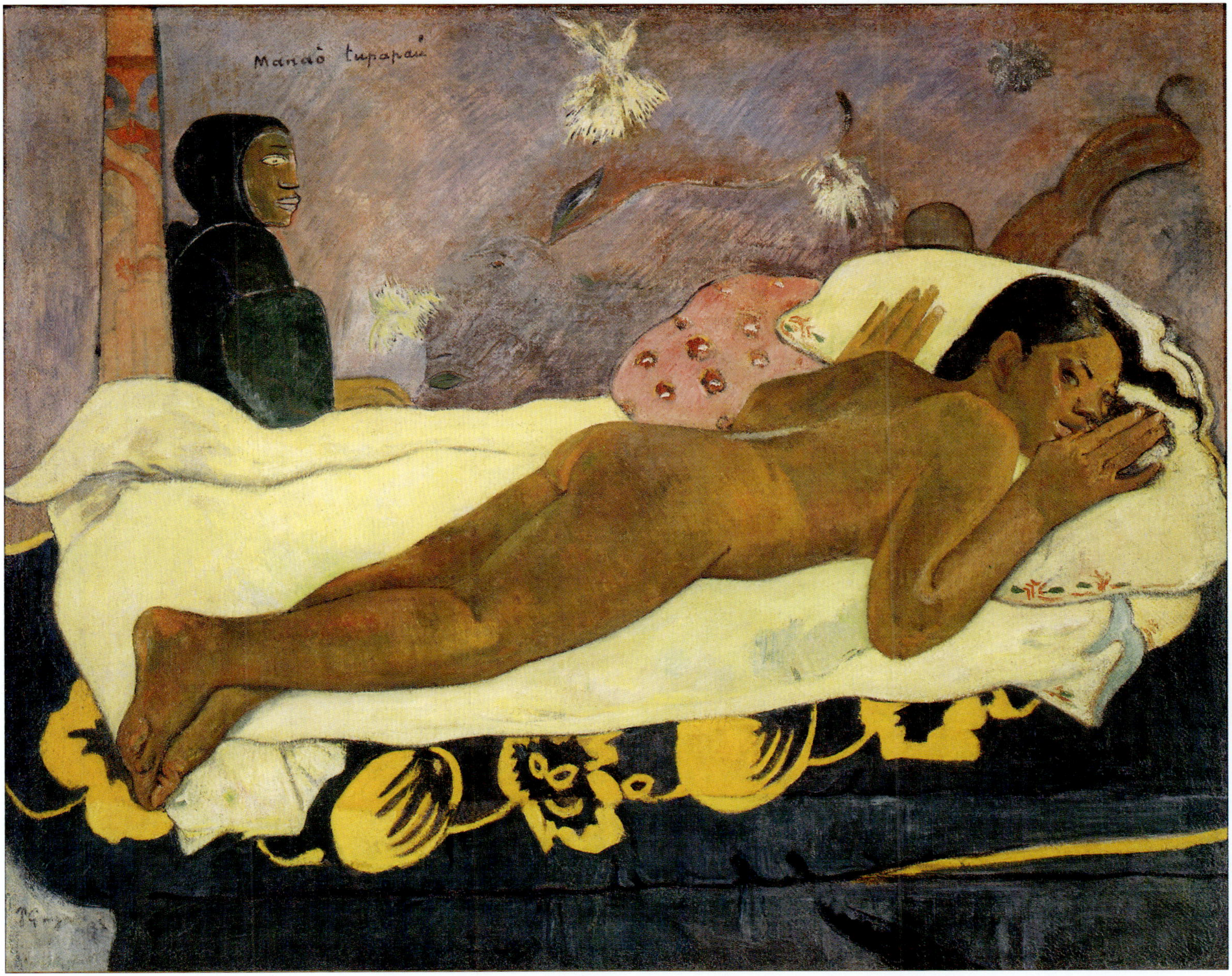
Manaò tupapaù

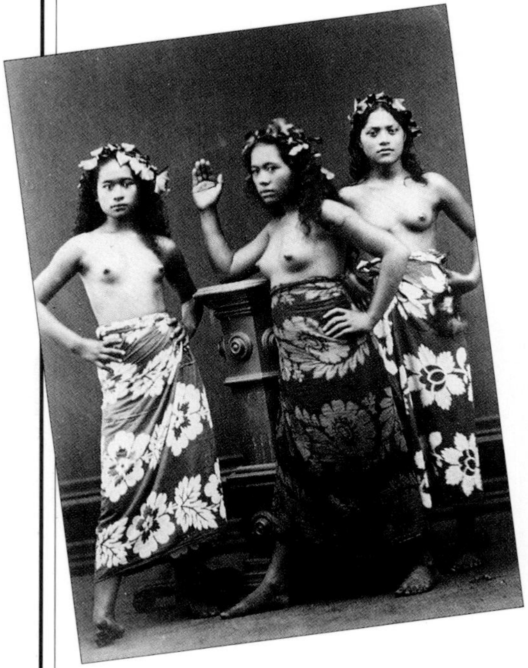

ABOVE: *A photograph of three young Tahitian women taken c.1890. Their ritual poses are powerfully reminiscent of some of the statuesque stances in Gauguin's paintings.*

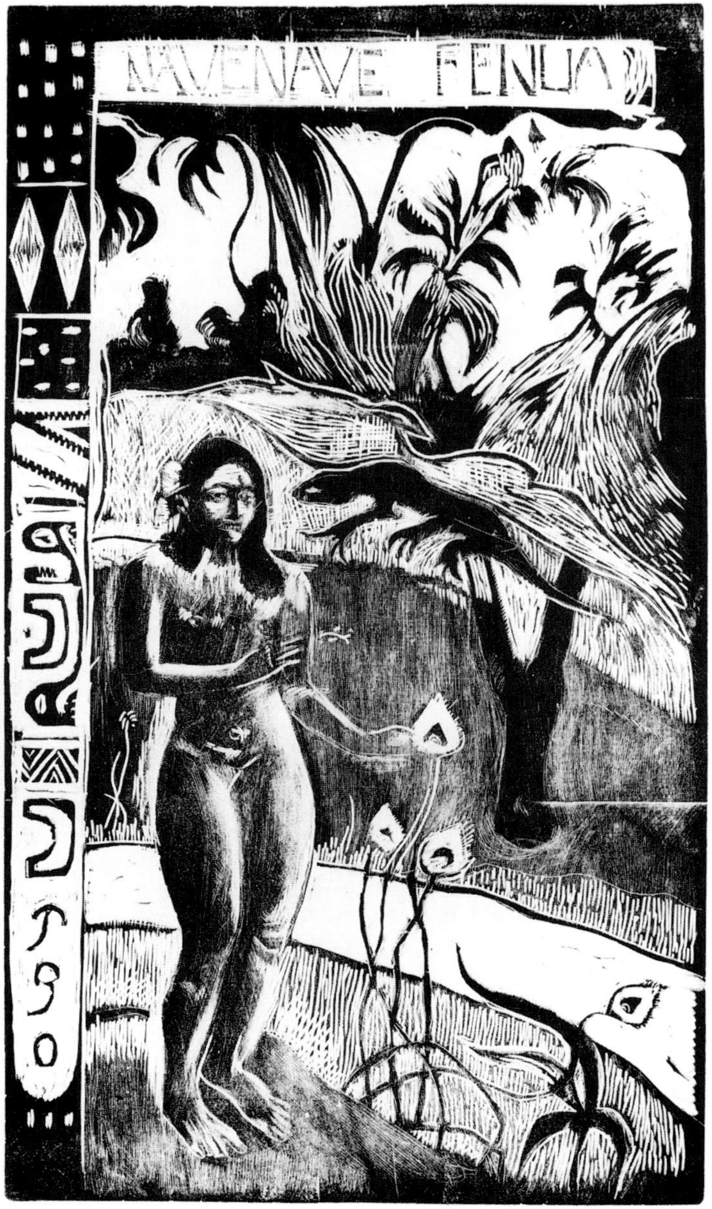

LEFT: DELICIOUS LAND (NAVE NAVE FENUA), 1893–4 *One of Gauguin's series of woodcuts, this image, reworked in watercolour, sculpture, and charcoal and reproduced in monotype and woodcuts, confronted Gauguin's Western audience with a new conception of Eve.*

RIGHT: *Gauguin is known to have taken several photographs with him to Tahiti of the reliefs from the friezes decorating the temple of Borobudur in Java. The Bhuddist legends carved in stone provided many of the artist's most reworked images and poses.*

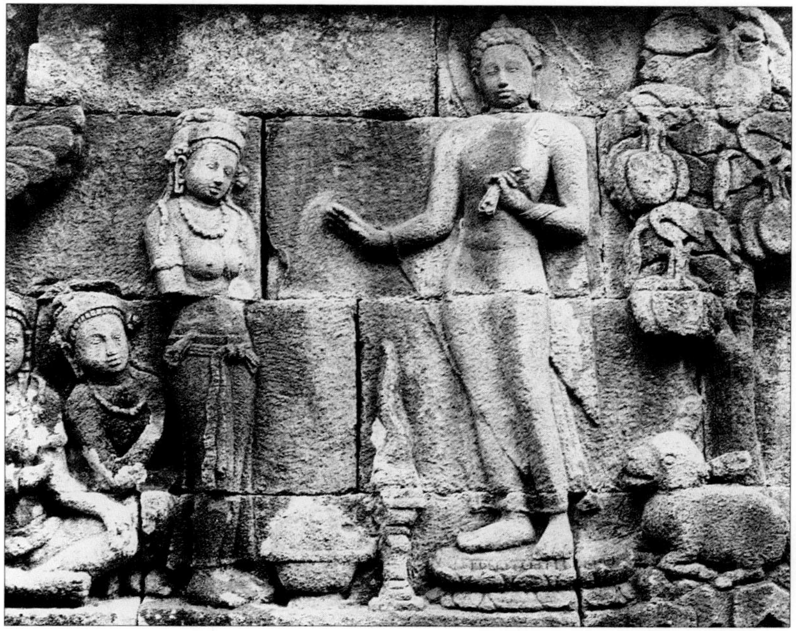

called to throw. This time a superb fish was caught, so heavy that it made the rod bend.

Four sturdy arms lifted up the rod, and with the tugging of the rope from the stern, the tunny was gradually pulled to the surface. Then a shark pounced; a few slashes of its teeth and all that we pulled on board was the head. It was a bad start.

My turn came and I was chosen. After a few moments we landed a huge tunny; a few blows on its head with a stick and it was in its death-throes, its body twisting and transformed into a silvered mirror, flashing with a thousand glittering lights.

A second time we were successful; the Frenchman had certainly brought good luck. All proclaimed that I was a marvellous fellow, and, full of pride, I didn't gainsay them. We went on fishing till nightfall . . .

RIGHT: *In this illustration to the woodcutting expedition in* Noa Noa *the two naked figures, absorbed in the water and one another, turn their backs on us and civilization.*

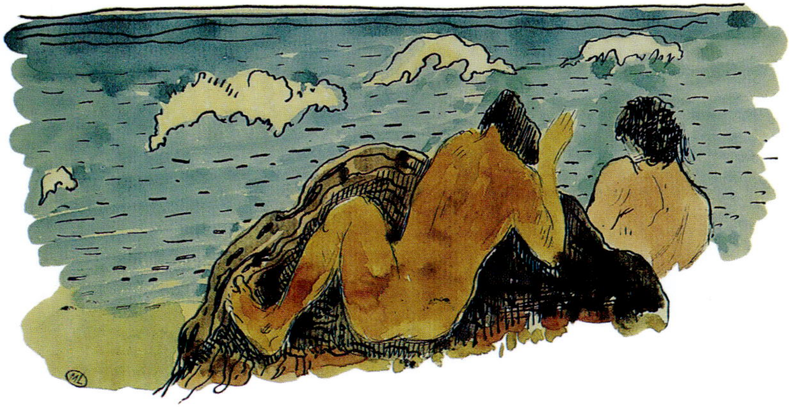

BELOW: *Gauguin illustrated his manuscript* Ancien Culte Maorie *with many pen and watercolour sketches. On this page he writes, in the native language, of the legend of the 'Birth of the Stars'.*

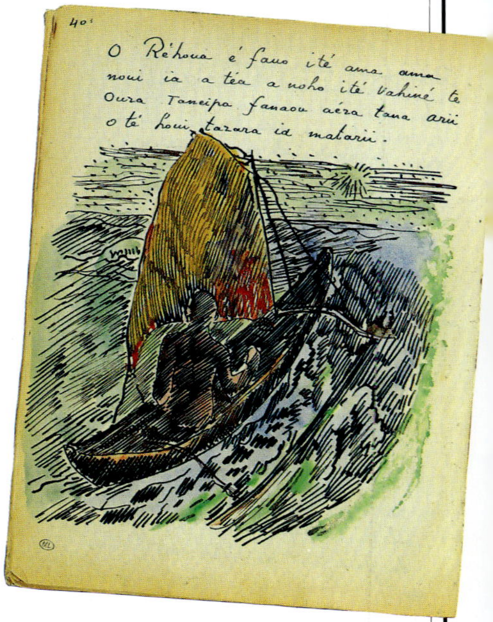

As everything was being put away, I asked a young boy what was the reason for all the giggling and whispering when my two fish were being hauled aboard. He refused to explain to me, but I insisted, knowing what little resistance a Maori has, especially when he is being pressed. He succumbed and told me that when a fish is caught by its lower jaw it means that your *vahine* has been unfaithful to you whilst you have been away fishing. I smiled incredulously, and we returned . . .

All our catch was laid out on the sand, and the captain cut as many pieces, equally divided, as there were people engaged in the fishing, women and children included, irrespective of whether they were fishing for the tunny or the smaller fish. Thirty-seven shares.

Immediately afterwards, my *vahine* took the axe, chopped wood and lit a fire, while I cleaned myself up and put on some clothes because of the cool night air. I had my share of the fish cooked; she ate hers raw.

Thousands of questions. All that had happened on the trip. Bedtime came. One question was gnawing at me, but it seemed futile. At last it came out:

'Have you behaved yourself?'

'*E* (Ha).'

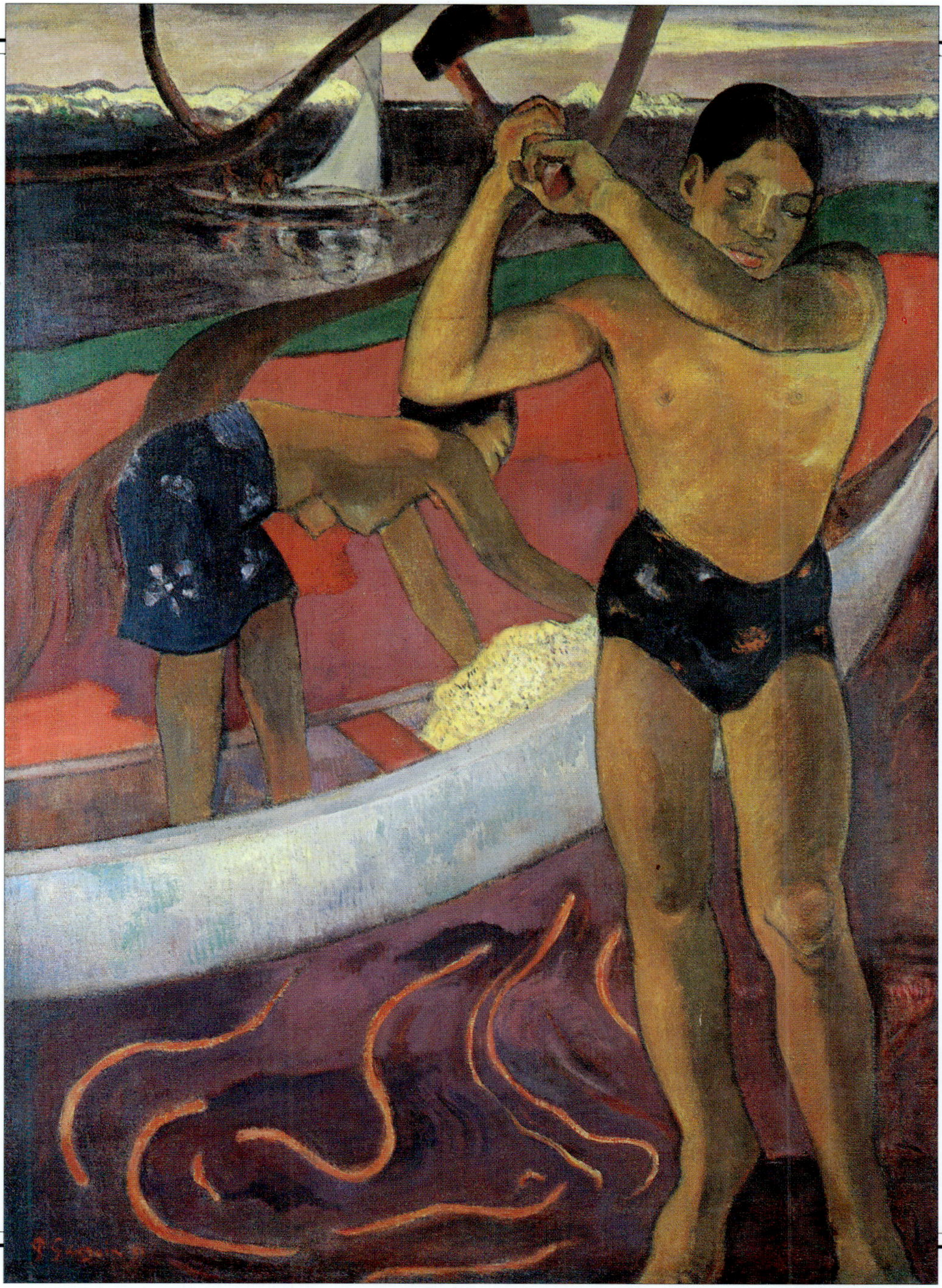

RIGHT: MAN WITH AN AXE, 1891 *This monumental figure – a rare instance of Gauguin painting a man as his central image – is the artist's idea of the 'noble savage'. He describes the scene in* Noa Noa *almost as vividly as the painting depicts it (see page 81–2).*

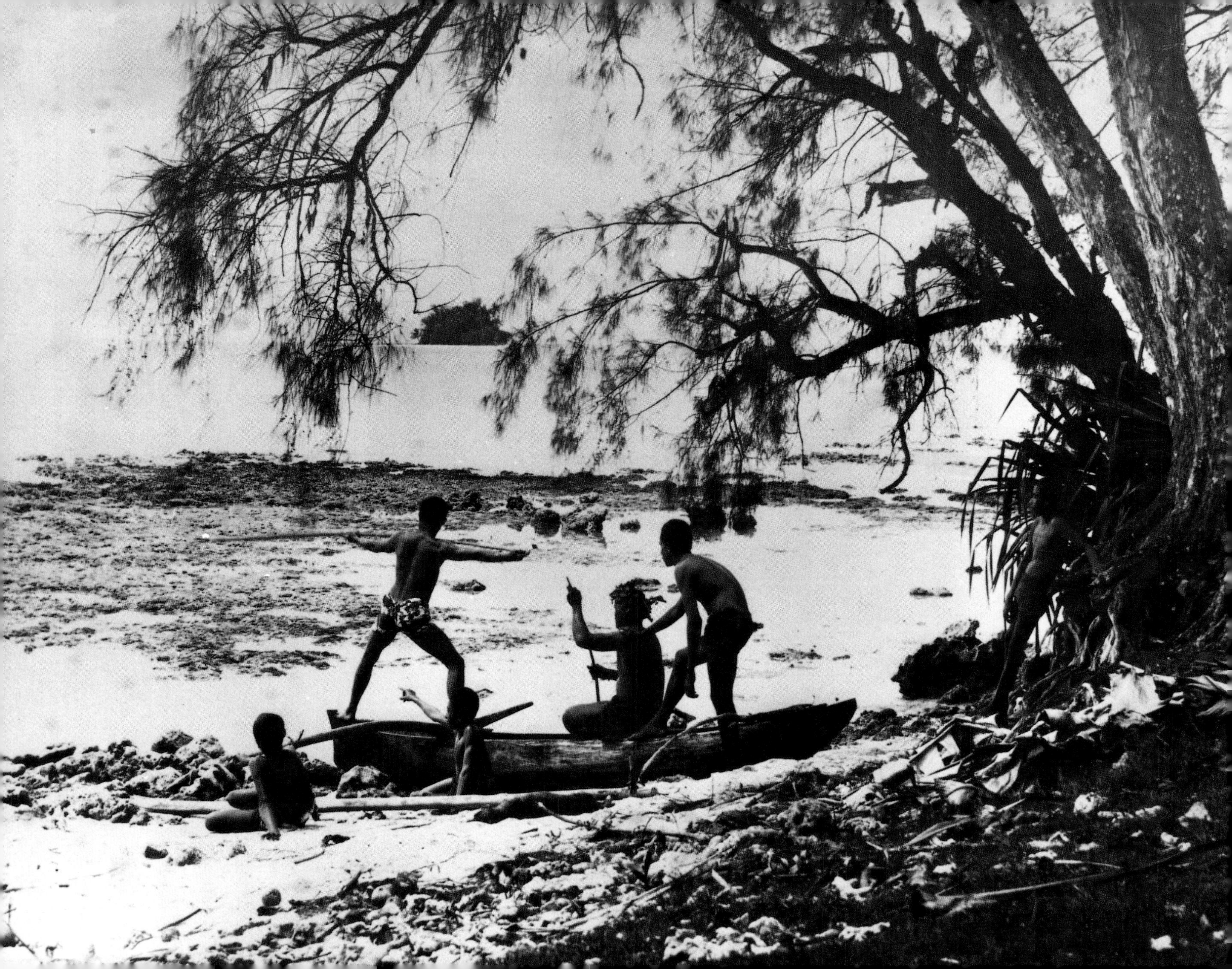

LEFT: *Fishermen testing their harpoons on the beach at Afuahiti, c.1890.*

'And was the lover you had today any good?'

'*Aita*—I haven't had a lover.'

'You're lying. The fish has spoken.'

Her face took on an appearance I had never seen before; her brow seemed furrowed in prayer. Despite myself, I followed her in her faith. There are moments when warnings from above are useful.

An awareness of the difference between the superstitious faith inborn in a race, and the scepticism of our civilization.

Gently she closed the door and prayed in a loud voice, '. . . Keep me free from the bewitchments of sin . . .' That evening I prayed, almost.

She, having finished her prayer, came close to me with a look of resignation on her face, and said to me, with tears in her eyes:

'You must beat me—strike me hard.'

And in front of that resigned face, that marvellous body, I was put in mind of some superb ancient idol. Might my hands be for ever accursed if they ever scourged one of creation's masterpieces. Naked in this way, she yet seemed to be clothed in an orange-yellow garb of purity—the saffron mantle of *Bhixu* (Buddha). A beautiful gilded flower, whose Tahitian *noa noa* impregnated everywhere with its fragrance, and which I adored as an artist, and as a man.

'Beat me, I tell you, otherwise you'll be resentful for a long time, and that will make you ill.'

I kissed her and my eyes spoke these words of Buddha: 'It is by gentleness that one must overcome anger, by goodness that one must overcome evil, and by truth that one must overcome falsehood.'

It was a tropical night. The morning came with radiance.

Noa Noa

CHAPTER 4

Interlude

1893–1895

GAUGUIN ENDED *NOA NOA* WITH THE STATEMENT, 'I had to return to France; pressing family obligations recalled me. Farewell hospitable soil. I was leaving after two years, feeling twenty years younger, more barbaric too, and yet better informed.' But family obligations had never really influenced his behaviour, and he had never really regarded his stay in Tahiti as permanent; at one point he even toyed with the idea of getting a job in France as a school inspector of art. But above all else, he was anxious to 'stir up Paris' by exhibiting 'the savage fruits' of his Tahitian experiences. He arrived in Marseille on 30 August 1893 with four francs in his pocket and was only able to get to Paris after Sérusier had telegraphed him 400 francs.

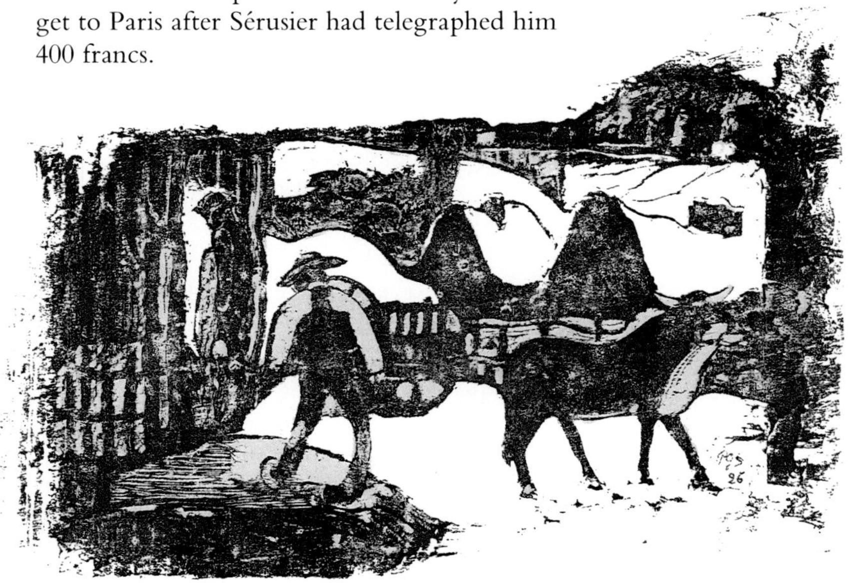

RIGHT: THE OX CART, 1898–9
This work formed part of the suite of woodcuts which Gauguin sent to Vollard in 1900. There were over 500 sheets of fine Japanese tissue paper in the packet, all printed from native hardwood blocks. Most of the images were Tahitian in theme; this is one of two recalling Gauguin's period in Brittany.

RIGHT: CHRISTMAS NIGHT: THE BLESSING OF THE OXEN, *c.*1896
This version of the Christmas story (painted before the accompanying woodcut) was probably painted in Tahiti. The canopied 'shrine' housing the Holy Family has a primitive simplicity, but also recalls Breton wayside shrines and calvaries. Working from memory – it was many years since Gauguin had seen it – the artist uses snow to great decorative effect, as a backdrop to highlight the important features.

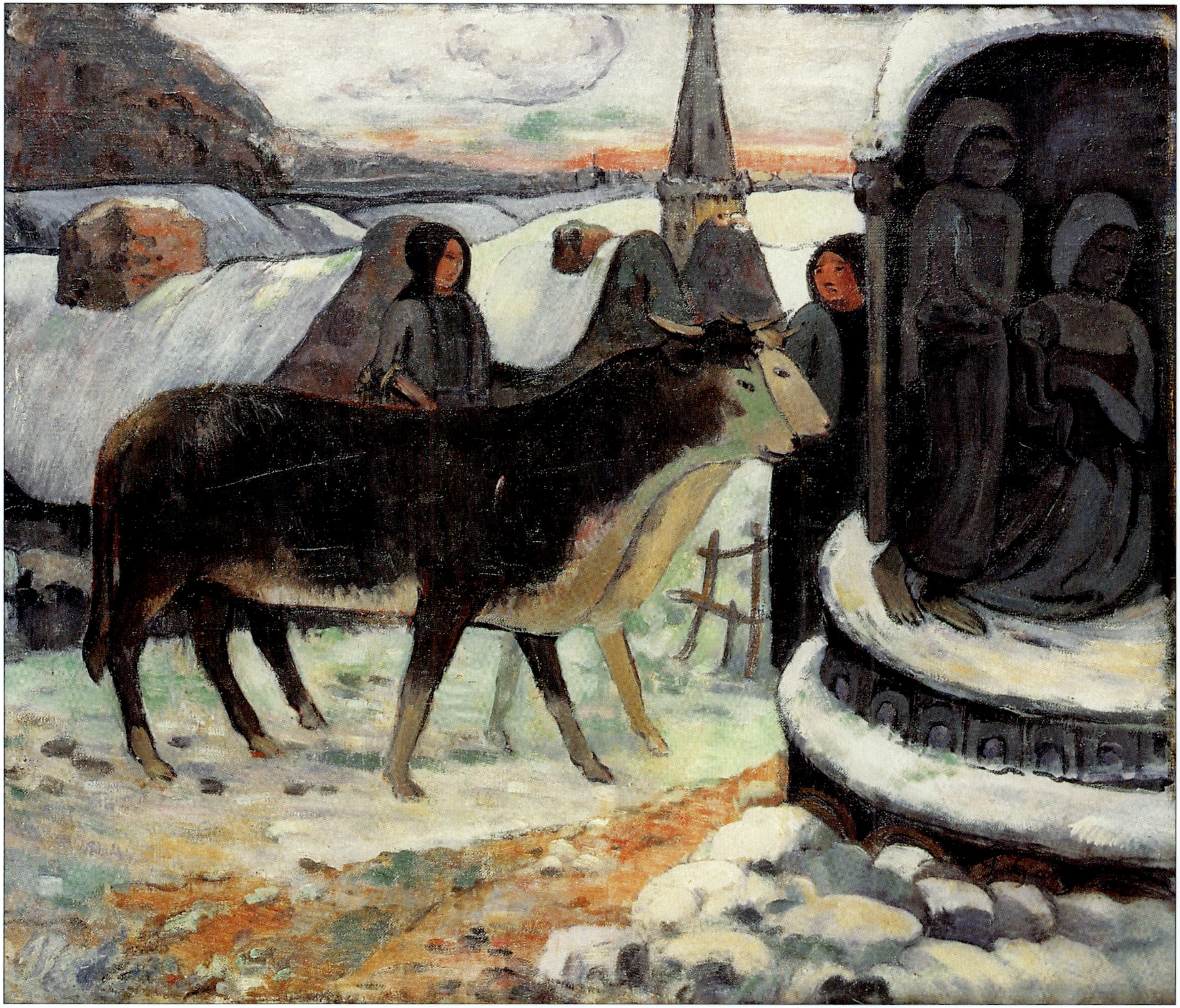

Renting a room over a dairy shop, and using a studio lent by Alphonse Mucha, he set about making an impact again, having fortuitously inherited nearly 10,000 francs from an uncle, only 1,500 francs of which he sent to his wife. He exhibited at various mixed exhibitions, and in November had a one-man show at Durand-Ruel's, pricing his works between 1,000 and 4,000 francs; eleven were sold. His efforts to put himself forward as the returned savage, who had brought back from an uncontaminated paradise impulses that would rejuvenate effete French art, were vigorous. He held Thursday receptions, in the style of Mallarmé; he established contact with the avant-garde group of *La Libre Ésthetique* in Brussels, and exhibited there in February 1894. In April of that year he renewed his Breton experience, visiting Pont-Aven and Le Pouldu, where he failed to collect the paintings and sculpture he had left with Marie Henry, the inn-keeper, when he had left for Tahiti.

In May, when visiting the nearby fishing port of Concarneau with a group of friends and his newly acquired mistress and model, the diminutive Annah, who was half Indian, half Malaysian and passed as Javanese, he was involved in a fight with some sailors and was incapacitated for two months. Unsuccessfully involved in lawsuits against both the sailors and Marie Henry, he returned to Paris at the end of the year, only to find his apartment ransacked and the faithless Annah disappeared. She had taken many of his belongings, but left his work untouched.

He announced his intention of returning to Tahiti and, in an attempt to finance this, in February 1895 he arranged an auction of his works at the Hôtel Drouot, selling only nine out of forty-seven. Undeterred, Gauguin pressed ahead with his plans to leave. Not only could he not now back down from his elaborately constructed persona as rebel, outsider and primitive, but he was increasingly disillusioned with the Paris art scene, especially after the *Mercure de France* of June 1895 ran a swingeing attack on his integrity by Émile Bernard. For once, Gauguin left the arguing to others, and quit the scene. He left Paris on 28 June, this time for good.

INTERLUDE

Paris To Daniel de Monfreid *12 September 1893*

Ever since I arrived here I have been running about all over the place. But all my excursions have been useless; there is nobody in Paris. I did, however, manage to see Durand-Ruel, who received me favourably, and who has started dealing in the Impressionists again, something he abandoned some time ago. It seems that Pissarro and Guillaumin are selling very well. He has promised to come and see my works when they are ready, and to hold an exhibition at his gallery* . . .

I have come a cropper at Boussod's; Joyant† has left the establishment, disgusted with the gentlemen who run it; nothing at all remains of mine in the gallery. Let us hope that I shall have a breakthrough with Durand-Ruel.

* On the persuasion of Degas, Durand-Ruel, who was not partial to Gauguin's work, gave him an exhibition in November, which included thirty-eight canvases from Tahiti, six from Brittany and two sculptures. Although the exhibition was not a financial success, it did help to make Gauguin's work better known.

† Maurice Joyant had taken over the running of Boussod and Valadon's gallery in Montmartre from Théodore van Gogh in 1890, and, like him, he had helped Gauguin by stocking some of his works.

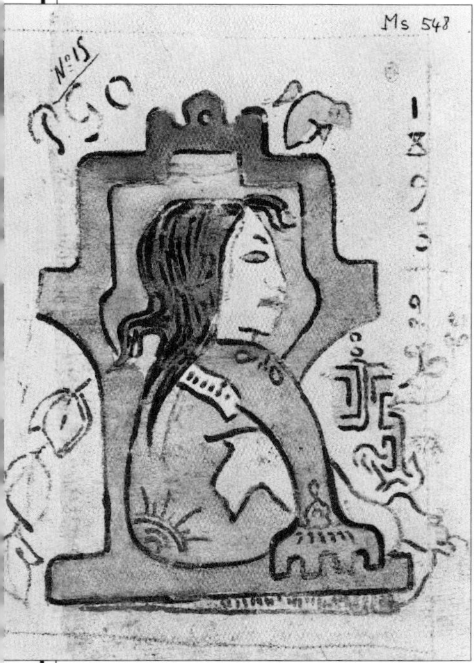

ABOVE: *The cover of* Cahier pour Aline*, a notebook Gauguin began for his much-loved daughter in December 1892. He had not seen her since March 1891 and was never to see her again; she died in 1897 without seeing the* Cahier.

Paris To Aline Gauguin* *end December 1893*

Very dear Aline. Here you are grown up already—sixteen years old. I even thought it was seventeen—weren't you born on 25/12/1876?† . . .

Mademoiselle is off to the ball. Can you dance well? I hope the answer is a graceful YES, and the young gentlemen talk to you at length about your father. It is a way of indirect courtship. Do you remember three years ago when you said you would be my wife? I sometimes smile at the recollection of your simplicity.

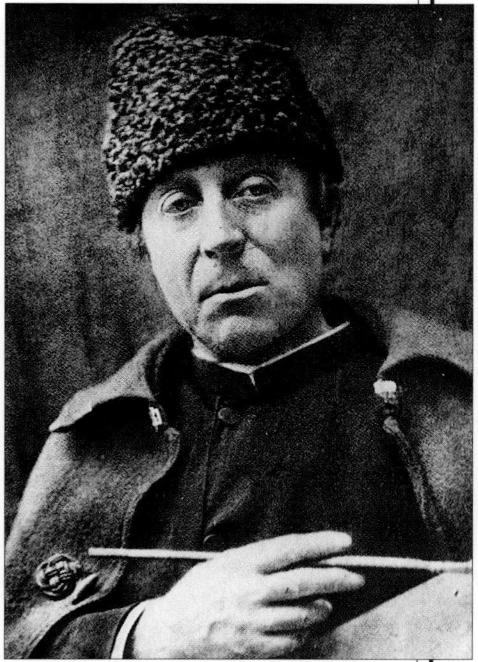

ABOVE: *Gauguin painted a self-portrait based on this photograph. The artist's flamboyant dress was a constant source of comment; according to Séguin, he 'looked to the Parisians like a sumptuous, gigantic Magyar, or like Rembrandt in 1635'.*

You ask me if I have sold many pictures; unfortunately, no, otherwise I should take great delight in sending you some pretty things for your Christmas tree.

You see, my poor children, you must not be too cross with your father if money is not plentiful in the house. A day will come when, perhaps, you will find that he is the best father in the world.

Kiss all the children and your mother, dear Aline, for your papa.

* Enclosed as a postscript to a letter to his wife.
† Gauguin was wrong. Aline was born in 1877.

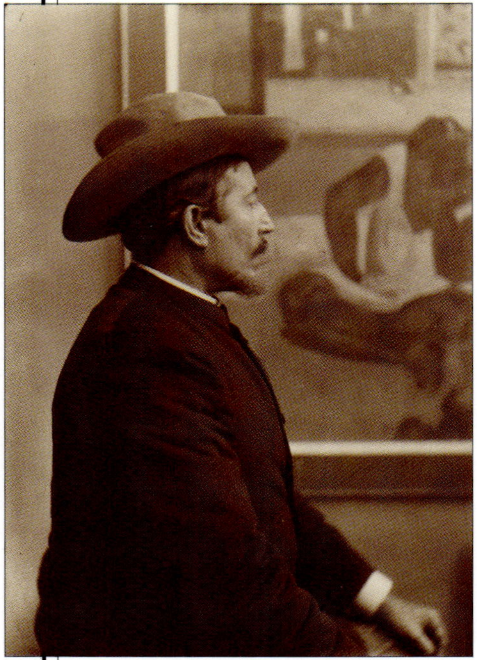

ABOVE: *Gauguin in his Paris studio. Taken in 1893 for publicity purposes, this photograph demonstrates the importance of the painting 'The Brooding Woman' to the artist.*

Pont-Aven To William Molard ***May 1894***

. . . I feel too seedy to write much. My leg is broken close to the ankle. They started throwing stones at Concarneau, when I was walking with Annah. I knocked down a sailor who attacked me. He then rallied the crew of his boat and fifteen men fell on me. I took them all on, and kept the upper hand, until my foot caught in a hole and in falling I broke my leg. I was kicked mercilessly and had to be carried to Pont-Aven, where I am nursing my wounds.

Pont-Aven To William Molard ***September 1894***

Your letter surprised me in utter idleness: in front of me a heap of unanswered letters growing higher each day.

I have had to take morphine every night for two months and I am now very weak. To ward off insomnia, I must take alcohol every day, which gives me four hours sleep a night. But this weakens and disgusts me. Yes, I can manage to limp with a stick, but it is most disappointing not to be able to get far enough to paint a landscape. However, during the last eight days, I have begun to handle the brushes again. All these misfortunes, the difficulty of earning a *regular* income in spite of my reputation, reinforced by my taste for the exotic, have led me to make an irrevocable decision.

RIGHT: THE BROODING WOMAN (TE FAATURUMA), 1891 *This image is taken directly from Degas's studies of exhausted dancers; to Gauguin's great pride, Degas himself bought the canvas. The model, presumed to be Tehemana, typifies the way in which Gauguin observed the Tahitian ability to remain silently seated for hours on end.*

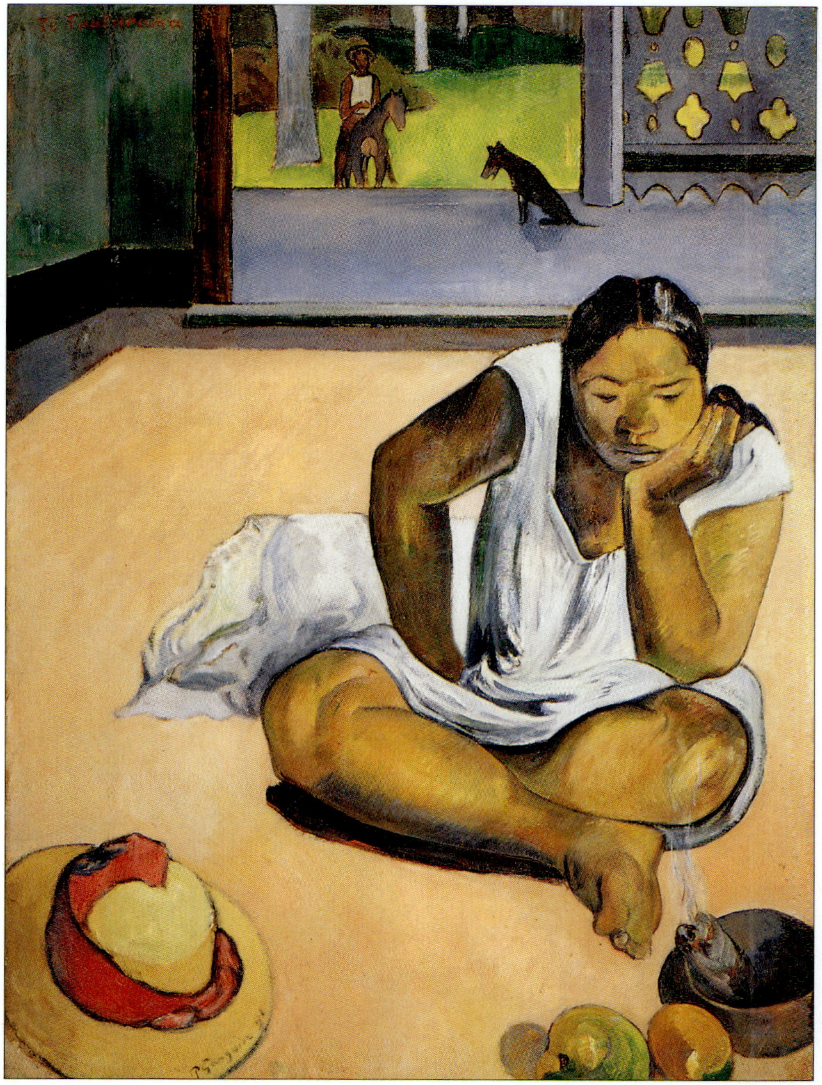

In December I will return to Paris and aim to sell everything I have. With the proceeds, I will set out again for the South Seas . . . Nothing will stop me, and it will be for good. How foolish European life is! . . .

Paris **To August Strindberg** ***5 February 1895***

I have just received your letter today, a letter which is in itself a preface to the catalogue.* I had the idea of asking you for this preface when I saw you the other day in my studio, playing the guitar and singing, your Nordic blue eyes looking attentively at the pictures hung on the walls . . . In front of the Eve of my choice, which I have painted in the forms and harmonies of another world, your chosen memories evoked perhaps a melancholy past. The Eve of your civilized conception makes you and us all misogynists.
To make you understand my thinking properly, I shall not

RIGHT: *Gauguin with a group of friends in his studio at 6 rue Vercingétorix, Paris, 1894. Gauguin painted the walls chrome yellow and hung them with his own and his friends' paintings. The group includes (standing) Sérusier, Annah the Javanese, and Georges Lacombe, and (seated) the musicians Fritz Schnedklud and Larrival. Gauguin (seated, centre) owned several instruments and enjoyed playing music in company.*

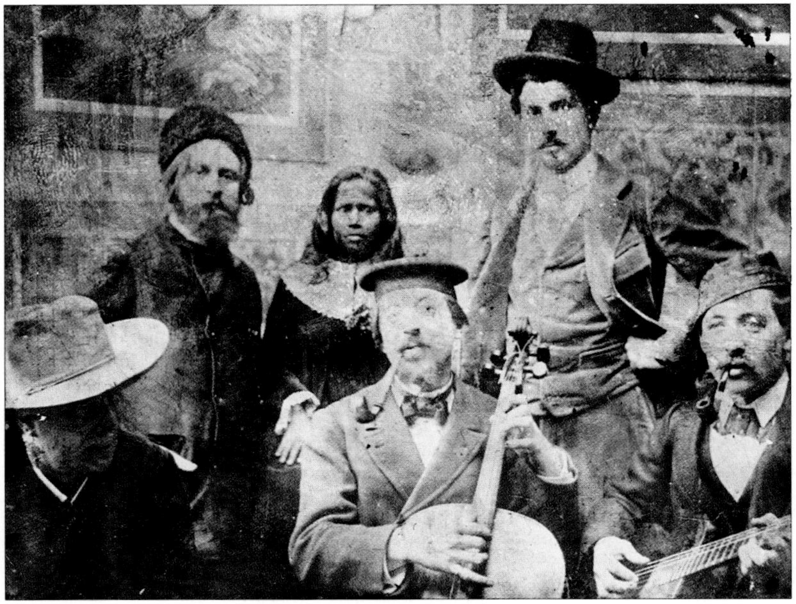

RIGHT: ANNAH THE JAVANESE, 1893–4 *Gauguin's new mistress, Annah, was a thirteen year old from Ceylon introduced to him by Vollard. She lived with him from December 1893 to the autumn of 1894, when she fled his studio, looting it of everything except his canvases.*

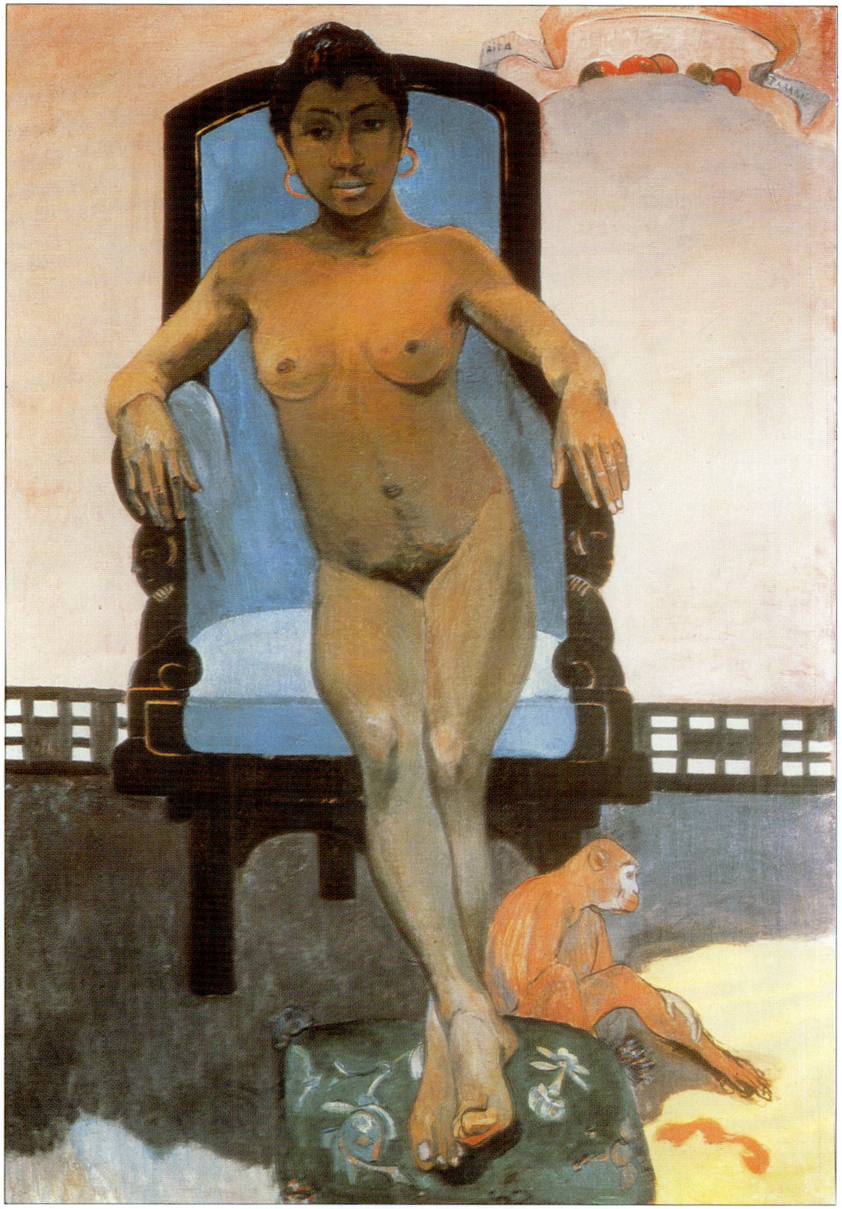

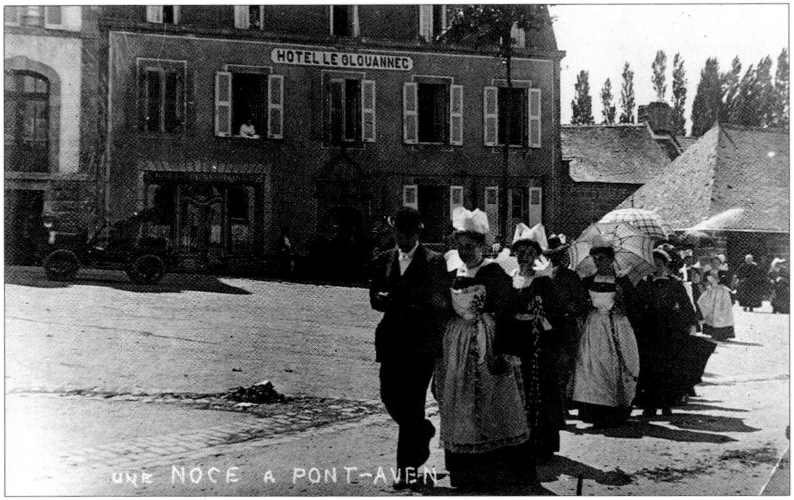

LEFT: *A wedding party passing the new Hotel Gloanec, which looks just as it did when Gauguin and Annah stayed there during the summer of 1894. The Gloanecs had been obliged by the increase in numbers of tourists and artists visiting Pont-Aven to move out of their original inn to larger premises.*

compare these two women directly, but the Maori or South Sea language, which my Eve speaks, with the language your chosen woman speaks, the inflected European language. In the languages of the South Seas, with the essential elements preserved in their simplicity, isolated or linked without any care for refinement, all is naked and primordial. On the other hand, in those languages that have flections, the roots, by which, as in all languages, they have their origin, have disappeared in the course of daily usage, which uses their shapes and their contours. It is a finely wrought mosaic, in which one no longer sees the lines that divide the stones, which seem more or less melded together: a fine painting in stone. Only an expert eye can catch the process of the construction.

Excuse this long philosophical digression; I thought I ought to explain the savage drawing with which I have felt it necessary to adorn a South Sea country and population.

* Gauguin had asked Strindberg to write an introduction to his sale catalogue, but Strindberg courteously refused. This is Gauguin's reply.

INTERLUDE

IN MAY 1895, Gauguin gave an interview to the well-known journalist Eugène Tardieu, which was published in the *Écho de Paris*.

ORANGE RIVERS AND RED DOGS

He is the most anti-social of innovators, the most intransigent of the 'misunderstood'. Many of those who have met him have backed away; for most people, he is pure humbug. Yet he goes serenely on, painting his orange rivers and red dogs, every day exaggerating his own personal style.

Herculean in build, his greying hair hanging in ringlets, his face radiating energy, his eyes clear, he has his own special smile, gentle, modest, and a little mocking.

Copy nature, what does that mean? Follow the masters? But why follow them? They themselves are only masters because they followed nobody. Bouguerau* talks about women awash with rainbows. He denies blue shadows, but one can equally well deny his brown shadows . . .

So what about your red dogs and rose-coloured skies?

They are absolutely intentional! They are necessary; everything in my work is calculated, and thought about for a long time. It is a sort of music, if you like. I create, by arrangement of lines and colours, using as a pretext some subject drawn from nature or life, symphonies, harmonies, which do not represent anything real in the ordinary sense of the word, not directly expressing any idea, but which make you think as music makes you think, without the help of ideas or images, simply by the mysterious affinities which exist between our minds and such arrangements of colours and lines . . .

Why did you go to Tahiti?

I had been seduced at one point by this virgin land and by its simple and primitive people. I returned, and I am going back again. To create something new, it is necessary to go back to the sources, to the infancy of humanity . . .

* A famous academic painter.

CHAPTER 5

'Where Have We Come From? What Are We? Where Are We Going?'

1896–1900

'ALL THAT I HAVE LEFT TO DO,' Gauguin said to Morice, on his departure for Tahiti, 'is to carve my tomb out there, in the silence, and amongst the flowers.' He was right, and yet he was entering what was to be artistically the most fruitful period of his life, one in which he was to be obsessed

RIGHT: DELICIOUS WATER (NAVE NAVE MOE), 1894 *In a letter of 1 March 1899 Gauguin refers to 'violent terrors in the harmonies of nature which intoxicate me', as his palette grew less and less naturalistic.*

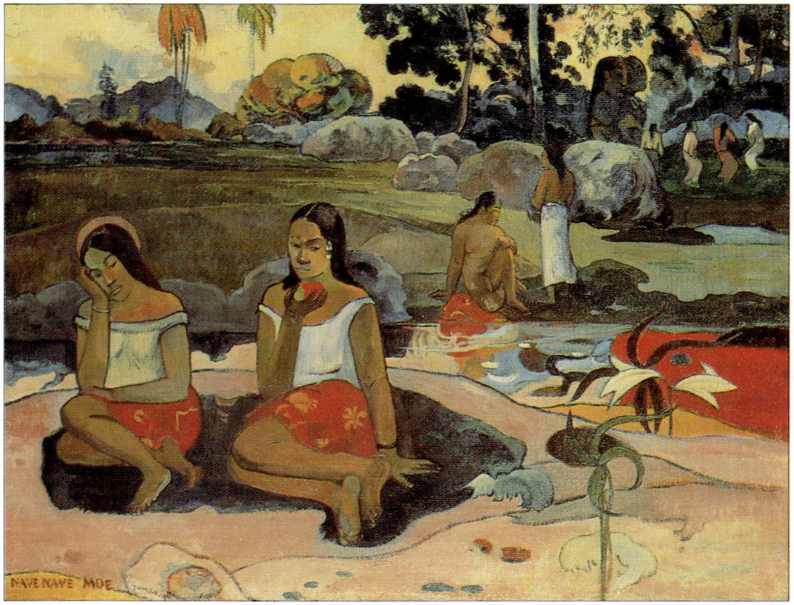

RIGHT: DELIGHTFUL DAY (NAVE NAVE MAHANA), 1896 *The frieze-like composition and the classical, almost archaic poses of the women in this painting hint at Gauguin's debt to Puvis de Chavannes's Arcadian compositions. The tiny figure of the child, separate and dark and somehow reminiscent of the 'tupapau' spirits (see page 83), may be a memorial to Gauguin's child by his mistress Pahura, who died at this time.*

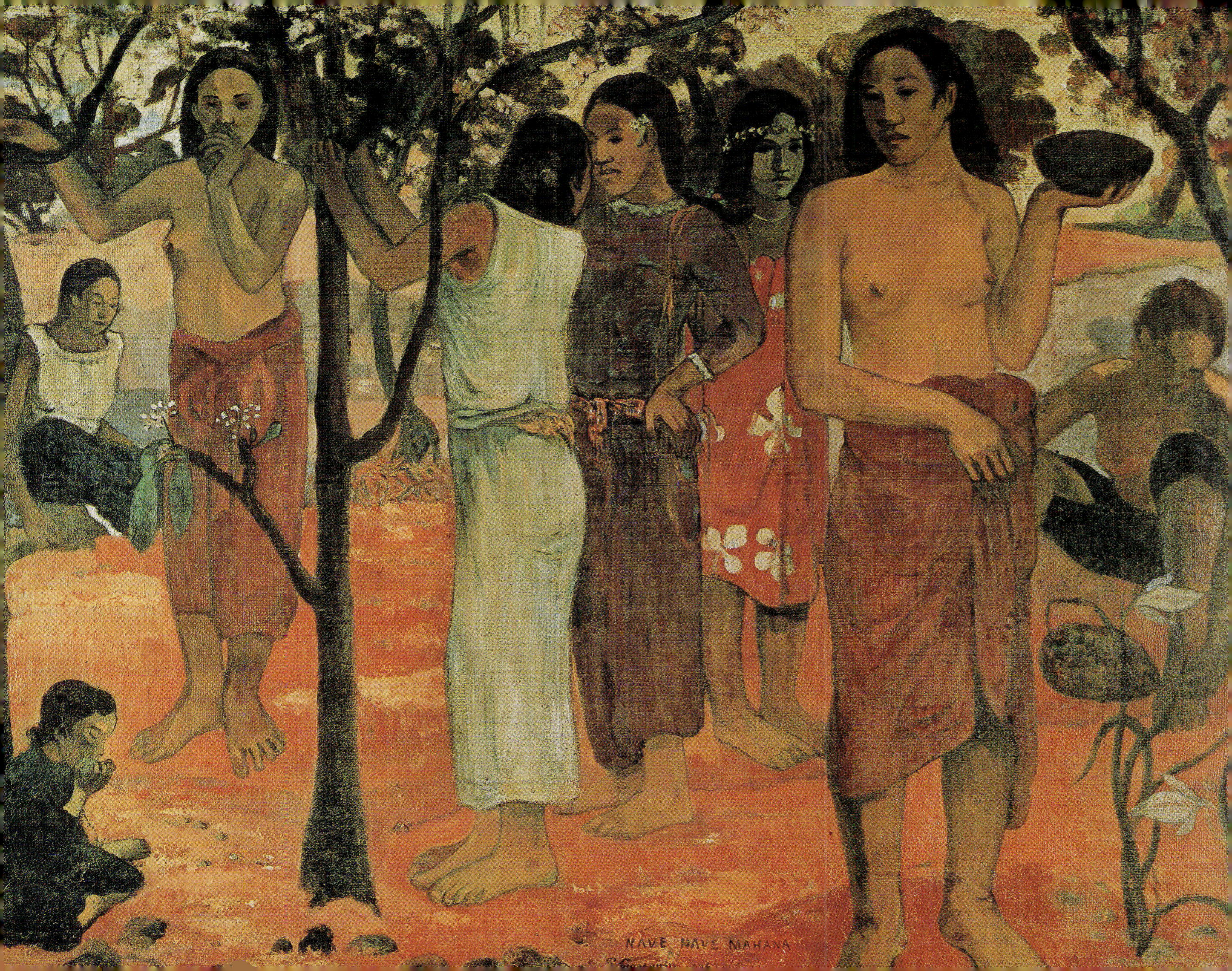
NAVE NAVE MAHANA

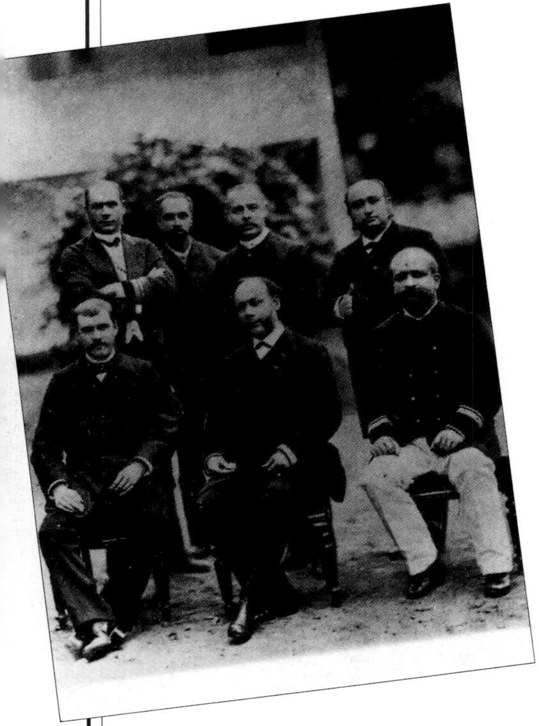

ABOVE: *Governor Lacascade and members of the élite 'Military Circle'. Gauguin's support for the natives was to cause antagonism.*

about the nature of life, of morality, of sexuality and religion, but also one in which he was to be wracked with illnesses of different kinds, ranging from syphilis to heart attacks, and tormented by poverty. The nigh on 100 paintings he produced during this period, notably including what posterity has concurred with him in believing his masterpiece, 'Where have we come from? What are we? Where are we going?', the 400 woodcuts and twenty sculptures and wood carvings, must be seen as representing the apex of his career.

Immediately on arriving back in Papeete, Gauguin was disillusioned by the real or imaginary changes that seemed to have taken place during his absence, though he had always fought against what he saw as the encroaching westernization of the islands. Gauguin's Tahiti, if it ever were a paradise, was always a contaminated one, dominated as it was by a reasonably benevolent but unimaginative colonial administration. An army detachment and a group of gendarmes controlled the lives of a handful of French settlers—a few of whom were merchants or professionals, the rest being ex-soldiers or sailors who had married local women—and the indigenous inhabitants. Catholic missionaries, ably helped by an earlier king, Pomaré IV, who massacred those of his subjects who did not convert to Christianity, had dominated the educational system and enforced their own, alien codes of behaviour. Throughout his time in Tahiti and subsequently in the Marquesas Islands, Gauguin quarrelled with representatives of all the governing classes. Partly from instinct, partly because in doing so he found a useful outlet for his ingrained hatred of authority, he supported the natives, even encouraging them not to pay their taxes. Now, from 1899 to 1900, he went so far as to produce his own four-page, stencilled satirical broadsheet, *Le Sourire* (The Smile), in which he ridiculed the local authorities.

He took rooms in an unfurnished bungalow, announcing his intention of going to live in the Marquesas Islands. But after a tour around some of the smaller neighbouring islands with a group of

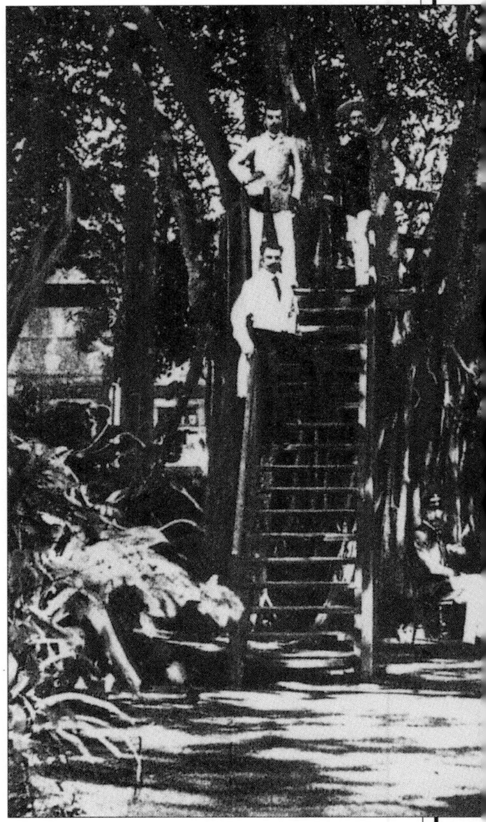

ABOVE: *The garden of the Military Circle, where Gauguin lunched from time to time.*

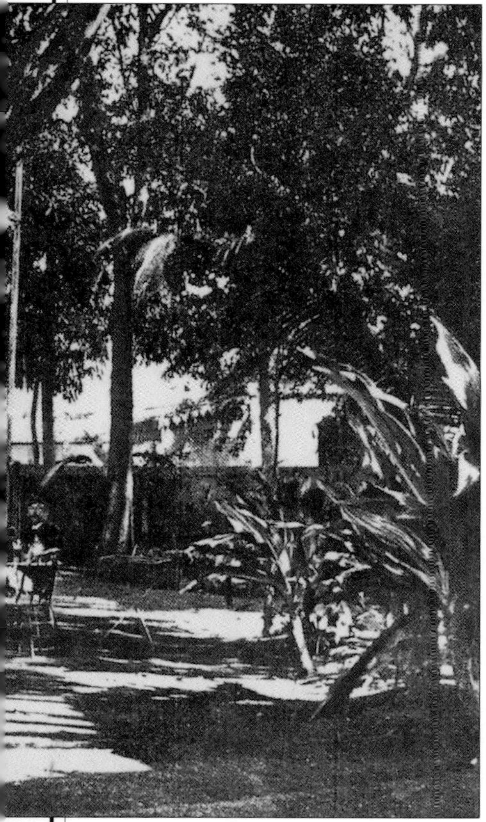

government officials, he abandoned this idea and, renting a plot of land at Punaauia on the west coast of the island, three miles from Papeete, built a hut there in the local style with help from the natives. He tried to re-establish contact with his old mistress, Tehemana, who had got married during his absence, but she was so taken aback by the sores that had appeared on his leg, and which may have been of syphilitic origin, that she left him.

By now his mental and physical condition was getting serious. He had got into the habit of taking morphine to alleviate the pain in his leg, and confessed to Morice that he was on the verge of suicide. In July 1896 he went into hospital, where he was described on the admissions register as 'indigent', but left after a week, without paying the bill of 140 francs. His health and finances gradually improved, and he was obtaining wider recognition; but then, in May of the following year, misfortune struck again. He received what he saw as a short and brutal letter from Mette informing him of the death of their nineteen year old daughter Aline from pneumonia on 19 January. His reply, written in August, was vitriolic, terminating all contact between them.

Meanwhile, his French landlord had died, and the new owner of the land forced him to pull down his hut and move. His health began to deteriorate again. He developed an eye infection, his leg sores and other symptoms of his various diseases began to torment him, he had fainting fits and, during the closing months of the year, several heart attacks.

At the same time, however, he was working feverishly on what he saw as his great contribution not only to art, but to human understanding of the nature of life itself. It was finished early in 1898 as the culmination of a series of six large works, which were shown with it at Vollard's gallery in November and December of that year. 'Where have we come from? What are we? Where are we going?' and its attendant works seem like the icons of some new cult intermingling elements from the primitive and the sophisticated, from the religious traditions of the East and the West. Nearly 4.5

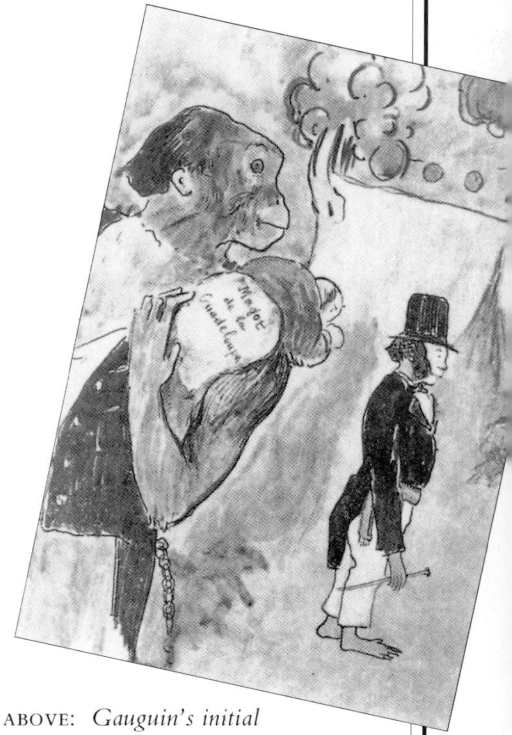

ABOVE: *Gauguin's initial friendship with Governor Lacascade, who vetoed Gauguin's free passage back to France in 1893, did not last; here he is pilloried as a 'monkey' for his negro appearance.*

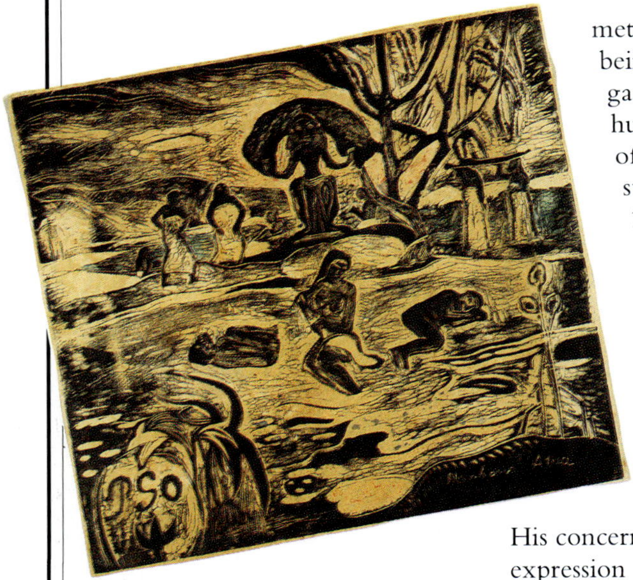

ABOVE: *Woodcut of 'The Day of the God', 1894.*

metres long and over 1.5 metres high, it blended human beings and landscape in a way that was quite alien to avant garde painting of the time. Representing each stage of a human life, it mocks the futility of mere words as a means of coming to terms with reality, and is laden with gnomic symbols, explained in a letter to Charles Morice dated July 1901 (see page 137).

The canvas took only a month to complete. Then all the despair Gauguin had suppressed during this time resurfaced; he went up into the mountains, took an overdose of arsenic and waited to die. But his body rejected the poison and he survived. Curiosity about the future of the picture he described as 'a philosophical work on a theme comparable to that of the Gospel' helped to dispel his depression, and his feelings of morbid hopelessness gradually subsided. His concern with religion at the time was insistent and found expression in the summer of 1897 in a long tract, *L'Église Catholique et les Temps Modernes*, which expressed his very complex and mostly critical ideas about the role the Church and religion generally should play in the affairs of man. Despite his strictures on the 'futility' of words, he seemed to be turning to them with increasing frequency, encouraged perhaps by the fact that *Noa Noa* had been published in October and November 1897 in the pages of the influential magazine of the literary avant garde, *La Révue Blanche*.

At the end of March, he unsuccessfully applied for a job at the Caisse Agricole in Papeete, and was forced to take one as a draughtsman in the Public Works department at the derisory salary of 6 francs a day. To be nearer to his workplace, and a hospital, he moved to Paofai, a western suburb of Papeete, where he rented a small house and gave up painting for five months. His foot began to trouble him again, and in September he spent twenty-three days in hospital. By the end of the year, he confessed to De Monfreid that he had 'lost all moral reasons for living'. Early in the following year, he

RIGHT: THE DAY OF THE GOD (MAHANA ATUA), 1894
This painting, unlike any other in Gauguin's canon, combines a 'realistic' with a totally abstract landscape, in which figures from his previous works are gathered together round a central deity. Gauguin invented all his idols from the descriptions of the Easter Island statues in Moerenhout's book; none existed in Tahiti.

BELOW: *Fragment dedicated to 'The Unknown Amateur' with a sketch for 'The Day of the God'.*

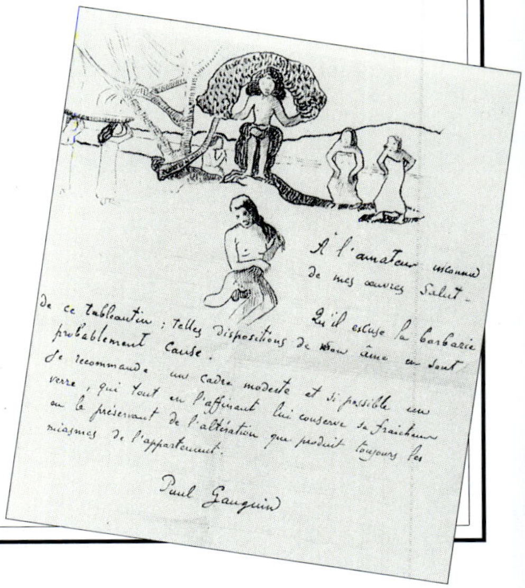

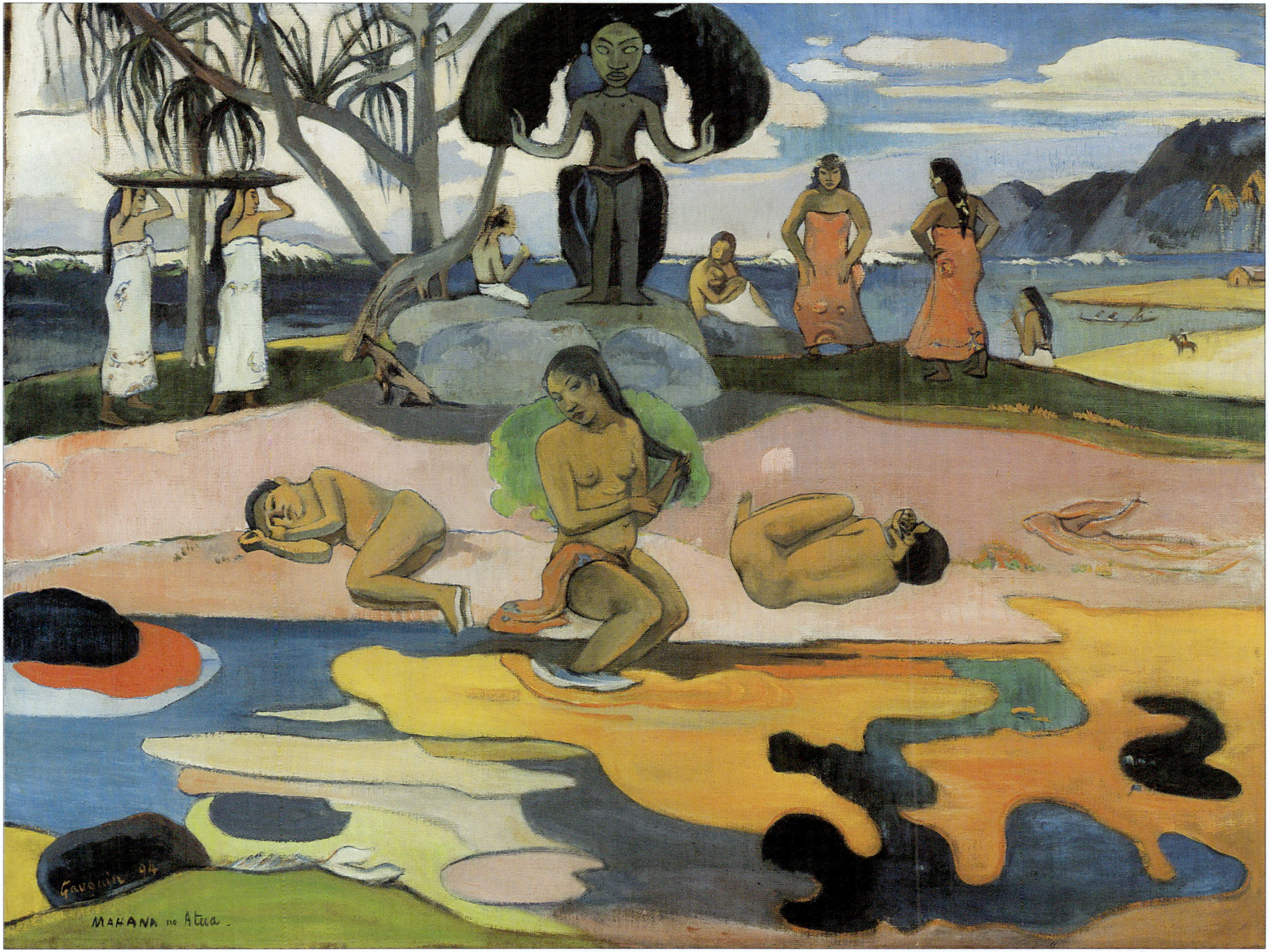
Gauguin 94
MAHANA no Atua

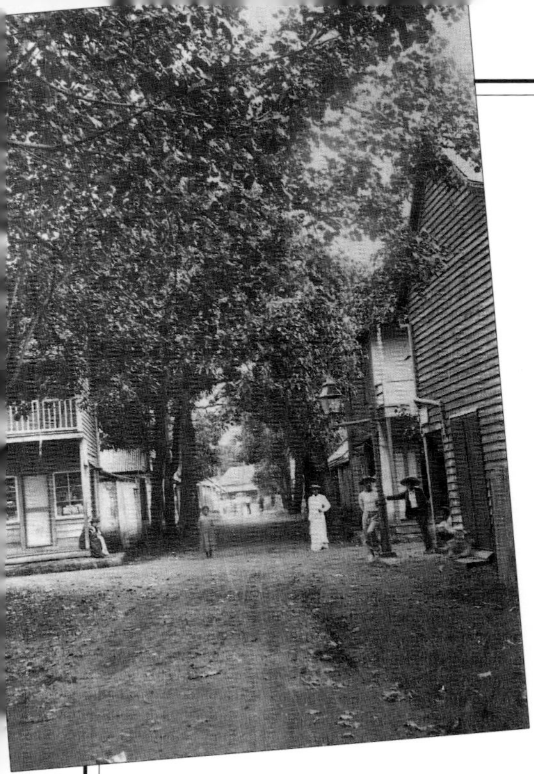

ABOVE: *The rue de la Petite Pologne, Papeete, c.1900. It is now the rue Gauguin.*

gave up his job and returned to Punaauia, where he found Pahura pregnant, the roof of his house destroyed by rats, and several of his works eaten by cockroaches.

The new century opened with more disappointment. The paintings that he had sent to Paris for the Exposition Universelle did not arrive in time, and he was represented only by a Breton landscape. On the other hand, in March, he signed a contract with Vollard, naming De Monfreid as his representative, whereby he would send him twenty-four paintings a year in return for a monthly salary of 300 francs. The final phase of his career was opening with greater financial security than he had known for a long time.

Tahiti — **To William Molard** — ***July 1895***

Here I am, safely arrived, and tomorrow the post goes, so I hasten to let you have reassuring news of my situation. I arrived in good health. What changes have taken place here since I left! Papeete, the capital of this Eden Tahiti, is now lit by electricity. The great lawn in front of the old Royal garden is now ruined by merry-go-rounds, which cost 25 centimes a ride; and there is a gramophone, etc.

My ears tell me all the gossip about the political situation, which is very complicated. Chené, the Commissaire-Général is here on a special government mission to pacify the insurgents on the neighbouring islands, and on the diplomatic front. After all the blunders that have been made, nothing is happening, so troops and gunfire will be necessary if we are not to give in to the natives, who are being stirred up by the English. But after all, this kind of thing doesn't really interest me. In fact, what is a disaster for commerce and the colony is a blessing for me because of the exchange rate. Just think: I used to get 125 Chilean francs for 100 French francs; now I get 200, and my little fortune is considerably increased* . . .

Next month I shall be at Dominique,† a small island in the Marquesas which is absolutely enchanting, where living costs nothing, and I shall be free of Europeans.

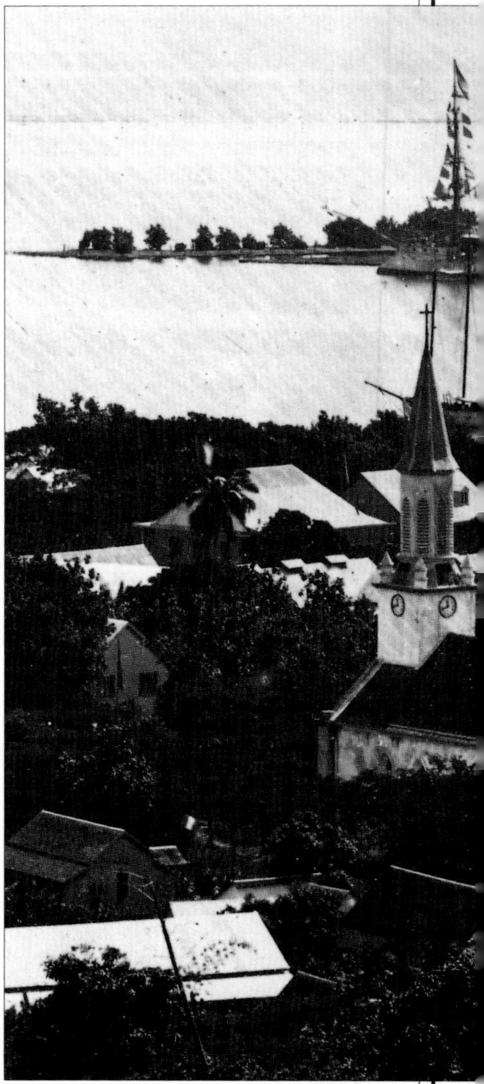

RIGHT: *The port area of Papeete. The church, in Gauguin's opinion source of much spiritual and physical pollution, is clearly visible.*

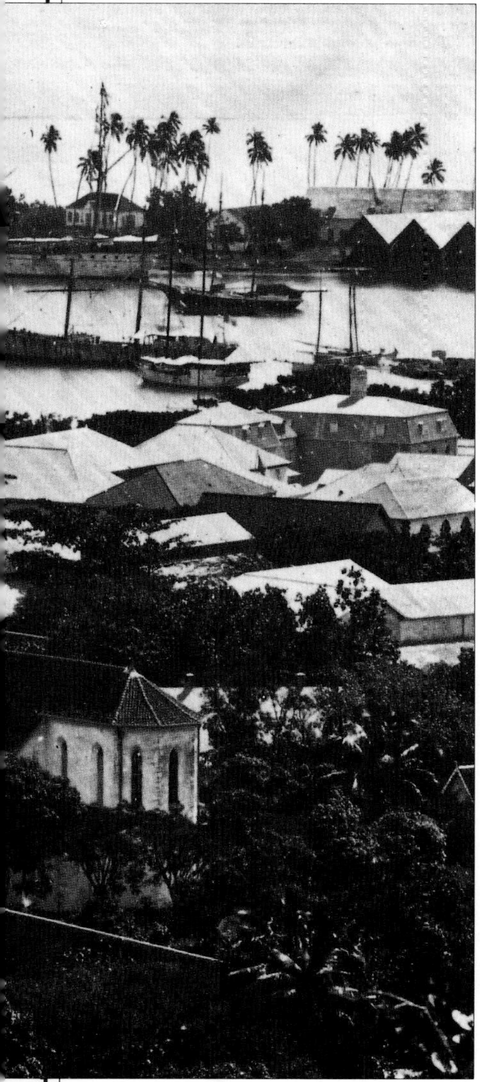

I shall live like a lord with my small fortune and my nicely arranged studio . . .

* Gauguin must have had a fair amount of money left from his uncle's legacy and the final auction of his pictures when he arrived in Tahiti. It has been estimated that a single man could live very comfortably in Tahiti on 250 francs a month, but he very rapidly ran through the money he had brought.
† In fact, he settled at Punaauia, near Papeete, and did not go to Dominique until September 1901.

Tahiti **To Daniel de Monfreid** ***November 1895***

At the time I received your delightful letter I hadn't touched a brush, except to do a window in my studio. I had to pitch a temporary camp at Papeete, until I eventually made the decision that I would build a large Tahitian hut somewhere in the countryside. Its situation is marvellous—a shady spot by the roadside, and at the back a breath-taking view of the mountain. Imagine a huge birdcage made of bamboo and divided in two by my old studio curtains, the roof thatched with coconut leaves. One half is the bedroom, with very little light, to keep it cool. The other half, with a very large window, acts as my studio. On the floor are rush mats and my old Persian carpet. The whole place is decorated with curios, drawings and fabrics.

You can see that for the moment I don't have much to complain about. Every night, wild young girls invade my bed—last night I needed three of them to function properly. But I am going to put an end to this life of wild promiscuity; I intend to set up a serious

BELOW: *The penal settlement of Noumea, New Caledonia, in about 1890. The French colonial administration created quite a large town to contain recalcitrant natives, with barracks, factories, shops, and compulsory barbering and exercise.*

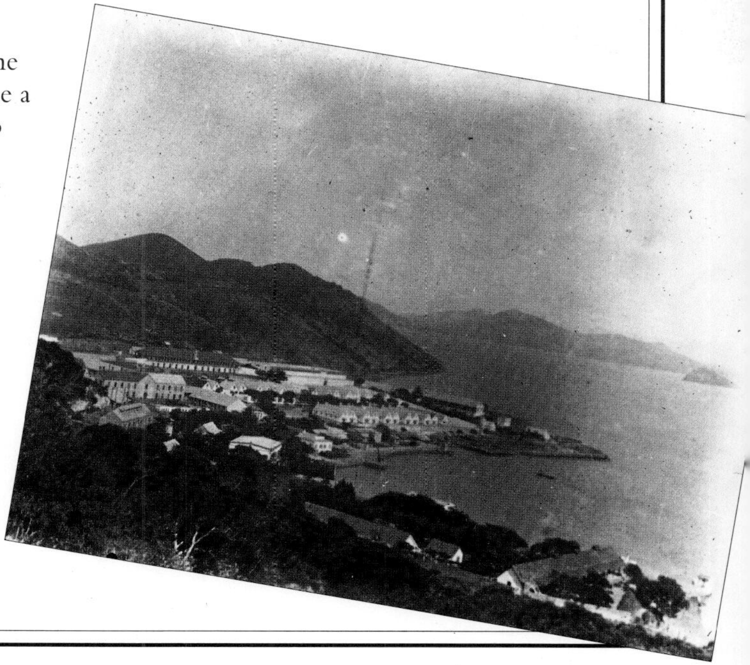

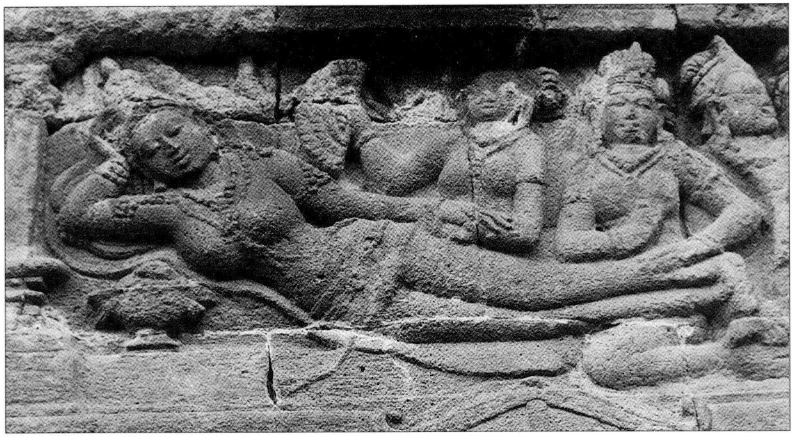

LEFT: *Another image from the Bhuddist friezes at Borobudur, depicting the mother of the Buddha. Gauguin borrowed the figure – even down to the fan – for his painting 'The Queen'.*

BELOW: *A letter to Daniel de Monfreid of April 1896, in which Gauguin describes his painting and affirms that until now he has never created one of such 'great and sombre sonority'.*

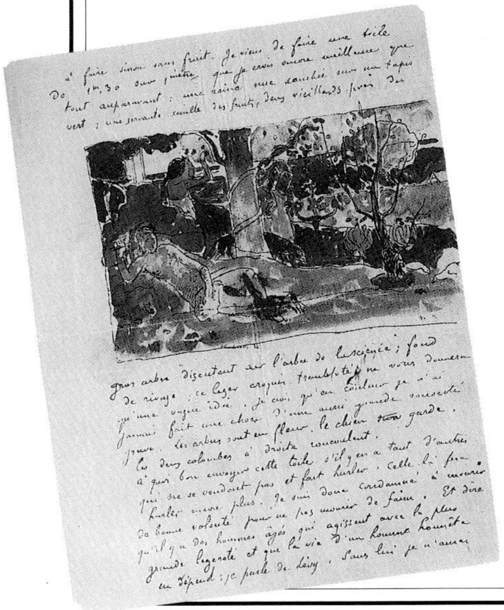

à faire sinon sans fruit. Je viens de faire une toile
de 1m,30 sur 1 mètre que je crois encore meilleure que
tout auparavant : une reine nue couchée sur un tapis
vert ; une servante cueille des fruits, deux vieillards près du
gros arbre discutant sur l'arbre de la science ; fond
de rivage ; ce léger croquis tremblotté ne vous donnera
qu'une vague idée. Je crois qu'en couleur je n'ai
jamais fait une chose d'une aussi grande sonorité
grave. Les arbres sont en fleur. le chien [illegible] garde.
les deux colombes à droite roucoulent.
à quoi bon envoyer cette toile s'il y en a tant d'autres
qui ne se vendent pas et font hurler. Celle-ci fera
hurler encore plus. Je suis donc condamné à mourir
de bonne volonté pour ne pas mourir de faim. Et dire
qu'il y a des hommes âgés qui agissent avec la plus
grande légèreté et que la vie d'un homme honnête
en dépend ; je parle de Lévy. Sans lui je n'aurais

woman in my home,* and start working hard. I believe that I am now going to produce better works than ever before . . .

Look what I have done with my family life; I ran away without any warning, letting my family solve its problems by itself, for I am the only person who could help it in any way. But I really am going to finish my life here, and, as far as I'm concerned, in complete tranquillity. Of course, this means that I am an utter scoundrel. But what does it matter? Michelangelo was too, and I'm not Michelangelo . . .

* Gauguin installed, in January 1896, a girl of nearly fifteen (he claimed she was thirteen) whom he called Pahura, his own rendition of her real name, Pau'Ura. In December she bore him a child which died. Three years later she produced a son, whom Gauguin named Émile, the same name as that of his first child by Mette. When, however, he left Tahiti in 1901 for the Marquesas, she did not accompany him.

RIGHT: THE QUEEN, OR THE NOBLE WOMAN (TE ARII VAHINE), 1896
The woman's pose recalls Manet's 'Olympia' (of which Gauguin made and exhibited a copy) as well as the mother of the Buddha; her face may be that of Queen Marau, widow of King Pomaré V.

Tahiti — To Charles Morice — ***May 1896***

I have just received a letter from Séguin which makes me think that for some considerable time I have owed you a letter in reply to the

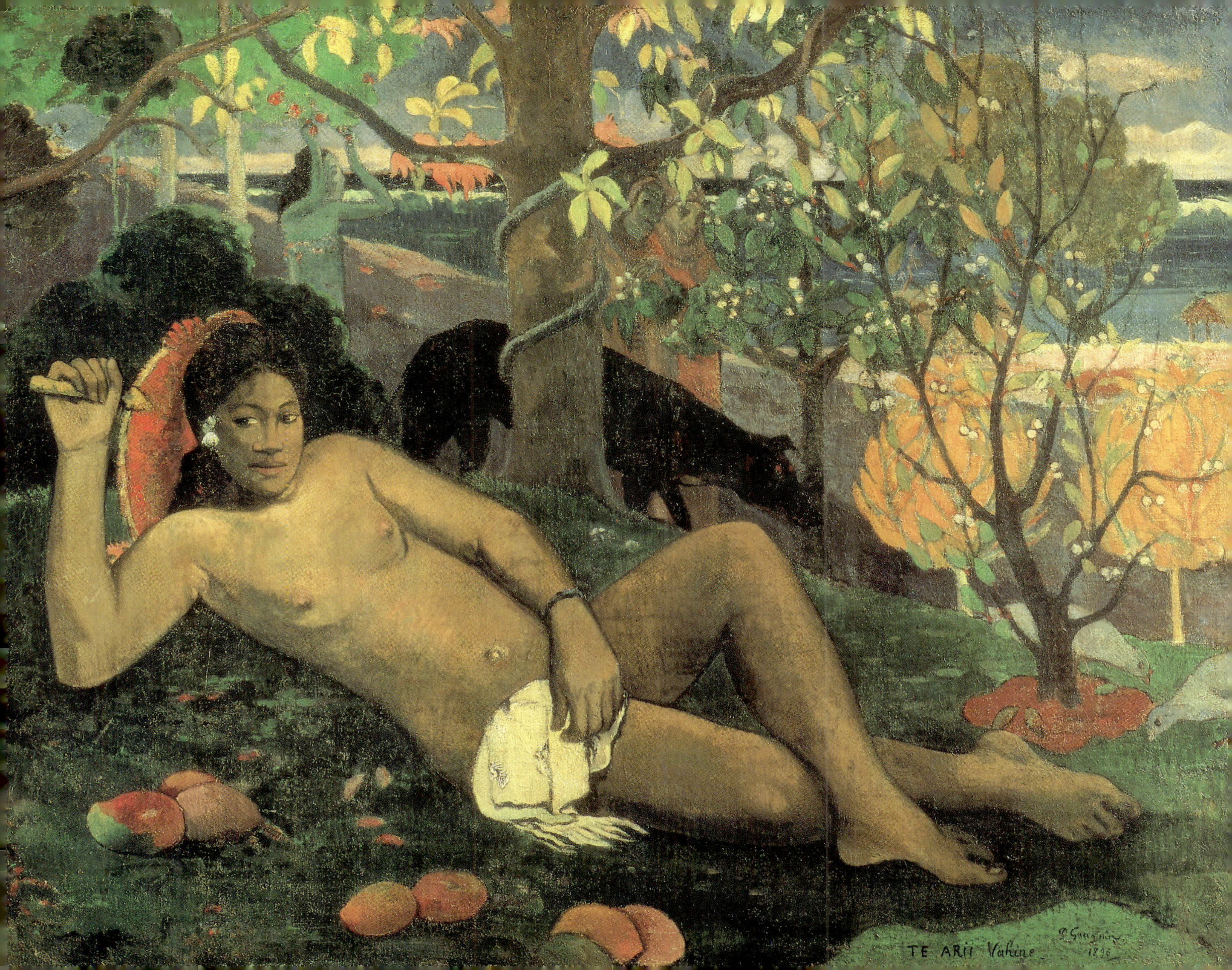
TE ARii Vahine
P. Gauguin
1896

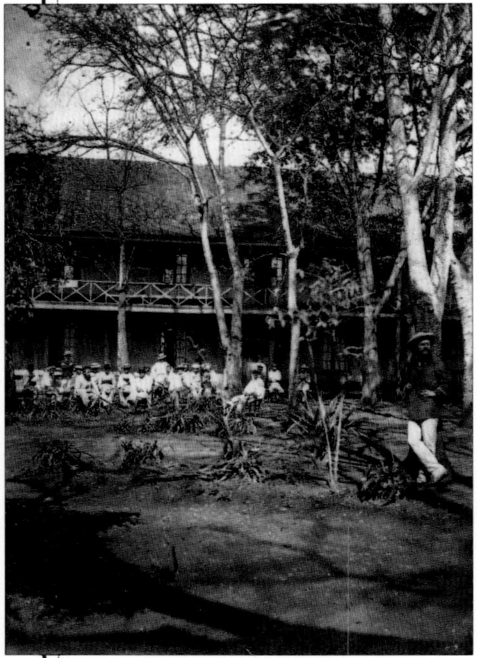

ABOVE: *The courtyard of the military hospital, where Gauguin went for treatment in July 1896 after his eczema reacted in the tropical heat to produce running sores which refused to heal.*

only one I received from you when we arrived in Tahiti. But I am in bed with a broken foot, which is giving me terrible pain. Large sores have appeared, and I do not seem to be able to heal them, which saps all my energy, even though, at the same time, I have greater need of it than ever before to solve my problems, such problems as harass a man of fifty who today, thanks to his friends, is entirely without resources . . . You say that I do not believe enough in your friendship, and that you will prove it to me some day. If only I could believe it—but I also know how impossible it is for you; I know what your life is like and that you do not have a minute to concern yourself with anybody else, despite all your good intentions. Séguin tells me that he heard from *you* that the *Noa Noa* book *was on sale in Brussels* and it didn't occur to you that this news coming from somebody other than yourself could have profoundly upset me, for you know the penury in which I live, abandoned by Lévy, indeed by *everybody*. If the book is selling, who is getting the money? You know, by the way, that I gave Molard the job of representing me in anything connected with publishing. And if this is the situation (I cannot bring myself to believe it), how, despite all appearances, can one judge an act of this kind? Is this a thing that a friend would do? You must get it into your head that I am on the verge of suicide (a ridiculous thing to do, it's true, but probably inevitable)—in a matter of months; it depends on the replies I get, replies containing money. I believe that your friend Talboum is due to pay me 800 francs, in June I think, which is next month. I doubt whether he will though, and will gaily go off to the café to have his apéritif without any thought for what is happening to his creditor. What does the death of an artist matter? Think about all this Morice, and reply with actions; there are cruel moments when words have no charm at all.

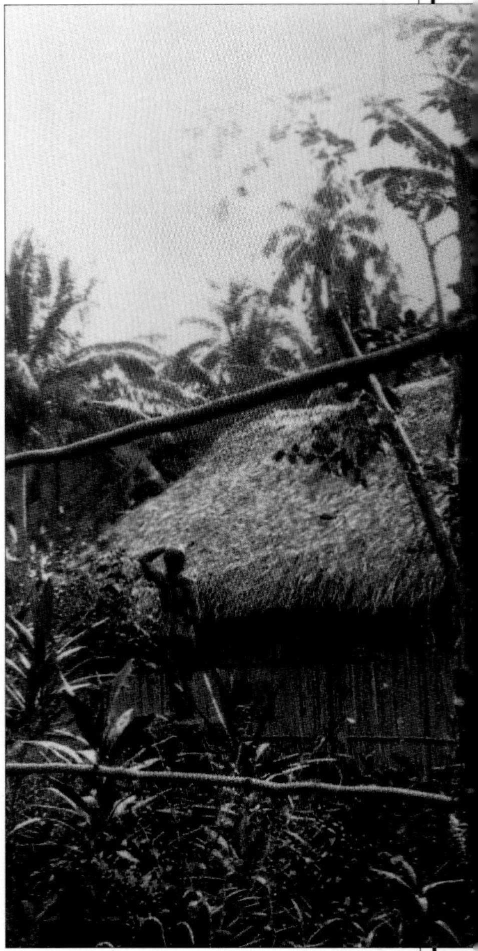

Tahiti — **To Alfred Vallette** — **July 1896**

I am in a colonial hospital having treatment for my foot, which has deteriorated badly. It is from this hospital that I am writing to thank

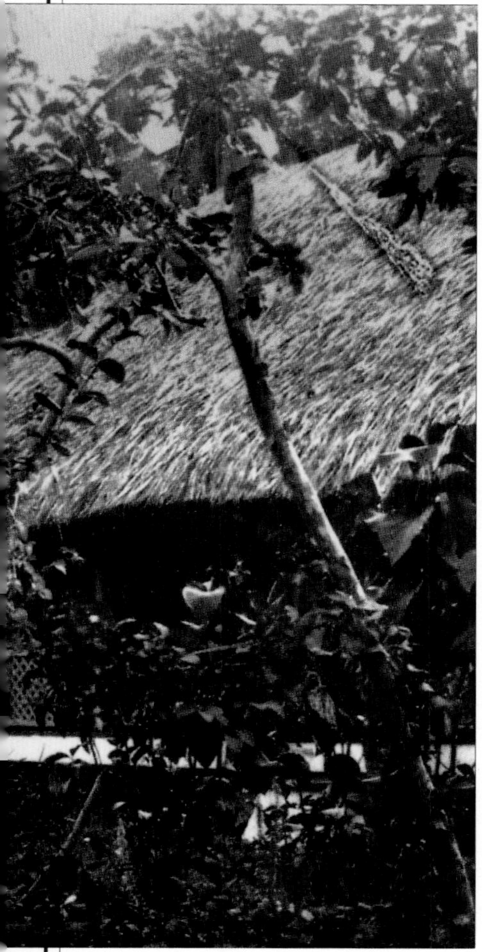

you first of all for sending me the *Mercure*. Reading your review every month makes me feel that I am not alone; and if I do not follow all the political and social tittle-tattle, for which I have no use, I am able, to my great pleasure, to keep abreast of all the main currents of activity in the intellectual world . . .

But may I touch on something more intimate? What do you think of work which on the one hand is admired by people such as Degas, Carrière, Stéphane Mallarmé, Jean Dolent, Albert Aurier, Rémy de Gourmont, and on the other has as an antagonist Camille Mauclair and various other mechanical scribblers?

This is to explain to you that between the subtle, literary and scholarly criticism of Viélé-Griffin, De Gourmont and others and the art criticism of Camille there is such a gulf that I cannot think the *Mercure* can be enlightened in all things. Subscribers to the *Mercure* consist of painters as much as of writers. Let Mauclair do his criticism in the *Revue des Deux Mondes* or in the *Journal de la Mode*; that I could understand; but in the *Mercure*!

I am not saying this because in each issue, in every exhibition review, he denigrates me (on the contrary, as I have told you above, the esteem in which Degas and others hold me is enough for me) but rather because, like a bull in a china shop, and lacking all the knowledge necessary to judge paintings, he condemns anything that has the audacity to express an idea of anything that is not official or suitable for the Salon . . . To listen to him, any writer who has not been to an École Normale is a bumptious ignoramus. But beware, Mauclair, who is the warden of artistic security, is there: 'Who are you citizen, you whom the young so wrongly praise? Show me your passport. Were you at the École des Beaux-Arts? Get back you conceited ass, you who are not prepared to do as others do.' I assure you, my dear Editor (and it is as a shareholder that I speak to you), Mauclair isn't right for the *Mercure*.

It only remains for me to tell you that Tahiti is as charming as ever, that my new spouse is called Pahura, that she is fourteen and that she is very debauched (though that is not immediately apparent

LEFT: *Gauguin's house with its tagged-on studio, in Punaauia. This was the building which he began in May 1897, when his landlord forced him to move from the house he had just finished; this time he owned the land. He added the statue in mockery of the 'classical' sculptures in Goupil's garden; the lawyer had sacked him as teacher of his daughters the previous year. The building is now the Gauguin Museum.*

RIGHT: THE NIGHT (TE PO), 1893–4 *Seemingly intended as an illustration for* Noa Noa, *this one of a series of woodcuts creates a dark and vaguely threatening world peopled with idols, spirits, and isolated figures, barely discernible as human.*

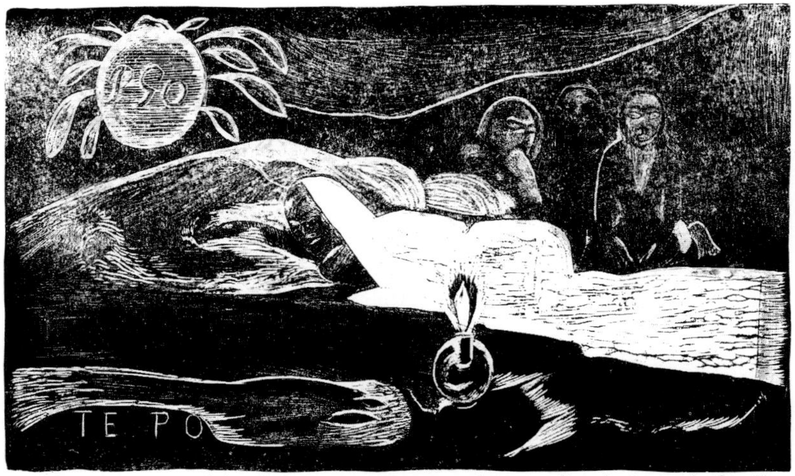

RIGHT: THE BIRTH OF CHRIST, OF THE CHILD OF GOD (TE TAMARI NO ATUA), 1895–6 *Christmas had a special significance for Gauguin, resonant with symbolic and important moments of his life. This is the last painting he made at this season, and it combines Christian and Polynesian themes. Death as well as birth is present; the girl (probably Gauguin's new wife, Pahura) seems lifeless and the child is held by an old woman resembling Gauguin's earlier representations of the Spirit of the Dead* *(see page 83)*.

as there is no model of virtue to assess such a quality by), and, finally, that I continue to paint pictures that are grossly repellent . . .

Tahiti **To Daniel de Monfreid** **_August 1896_**

I have received a letter from you and from Shuff, and that's all. You both seem to believe that I have had some money from Maufra—not a penny. And so, for the year that I have been here, despite my having described my appalling situation, I have not received a centime from those who owe me money. You must agree that it is enough to make the strongest of characters despair, especially when, as in my case, he has been racked by a cruel illness. When I came out of hospital you can imagine what went through my head when I had to confess that I couldn't pay the 140 franc bill until later. Thank God I don't feel any more pain, even though I am only half cured; but I do feel very weak, and to get my strength back I have only water to drink and a little cooked rice in water for nourishment.

Shuff has written me a mad and totally unjust letter, and I don't know how to reply, for he has a sick mind. His exhibition was a

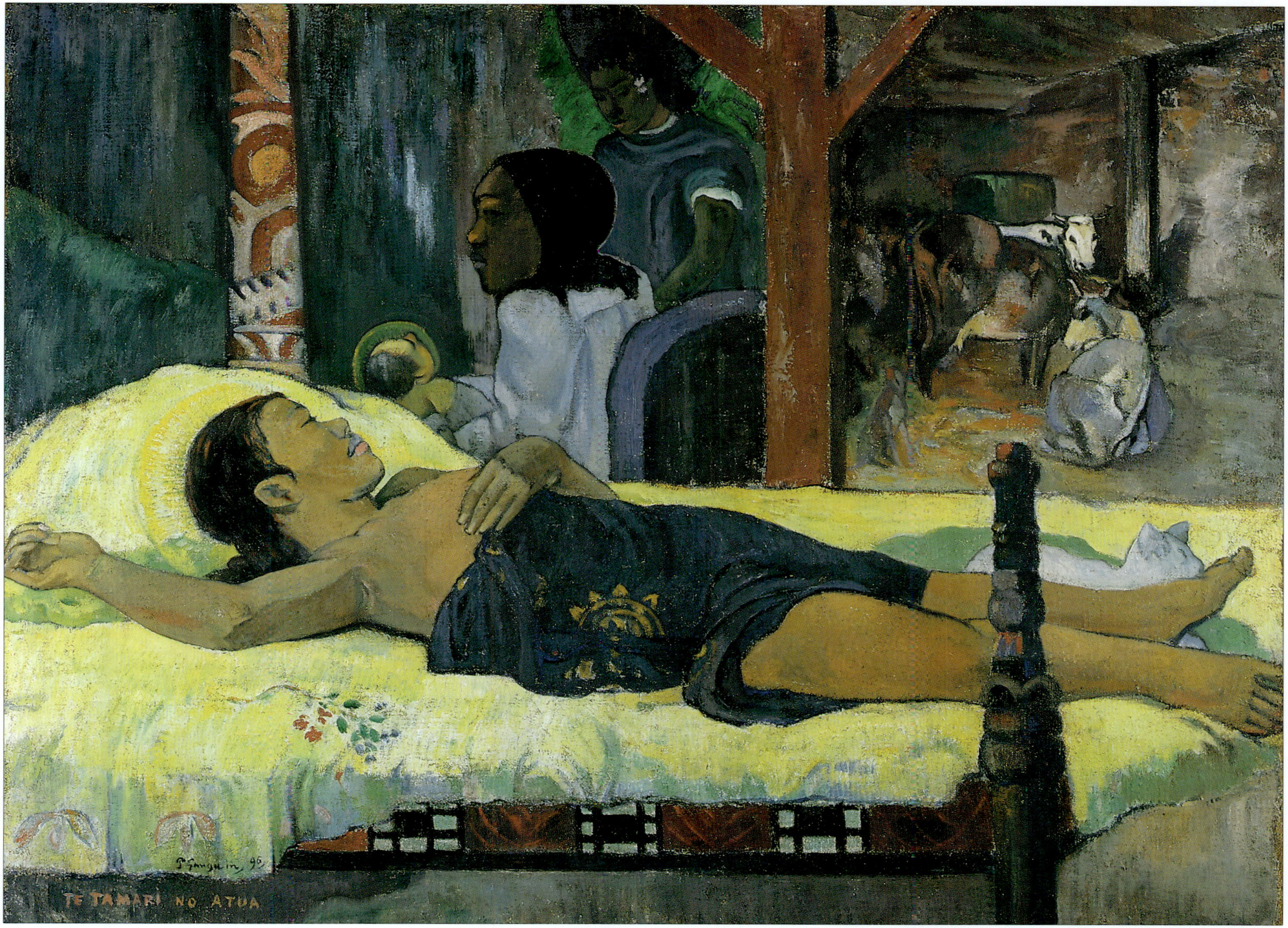
P Gauguin, 96
TE TAMARI NO ATUA

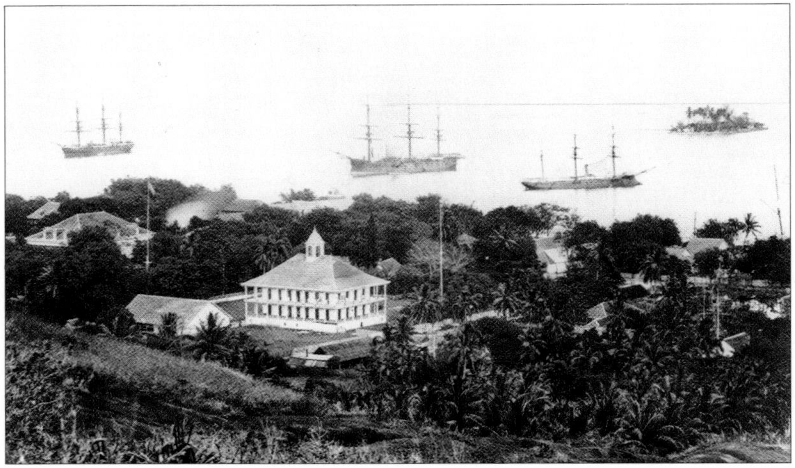

LEFT: *The coastal area and administrative district of Papeete in the early 1890s. The large building in the centre, then the seat of colonial power, was formerly the royal palace.*

complete flop and he claims, therefore, to be more unlucky than I, who have fame, strength and good health. That's a likely story! I am, he says, endowed with qualities that make others jealous, and he adds, 'If you had been prudent and far-sighted you would now be in a comfortable position, and, with a little more thought for the future, a little more goodwill to people, and a more sociable spirit towards your contemporaries, you would have had a very happy life.'

So I examine my conscience—I find nothing. I have never done anything evil, even to an enemy; on the contrary, in the most difficult periods of my life I have shared everything with the unfortunate, and the only thanks I have had is in being completely let down. I saved Laval from suicide and gave away more than half I possessed. I helped Bernard, and Morice and Leclercq with contacts and money. You know the result . . . I have been attacked for the faults of others; my leg has been broken. During my last stay in France I was as munificent as possible to the Molards, with an ever-open purse. From them, not a single letter.* I commissioned Molard to recover a debt of 800 francs for me in May—not a word, not a penny. In this context *will you do something about it?* And all this is

You see, my dear Morice, how well it would look, and all in a very simple style such as the natives speak.

If you are successful in placing the article in a magazine, send me some copies. I shall be glad to let some skunks here know that I still have teeth. It must be understood, of course, that my name appears on it, to give it some importance. To work!

* Morice published this 'interview' along with extracts from *Noa Noa* in *La Révue Blanche* of 1 November 1897.

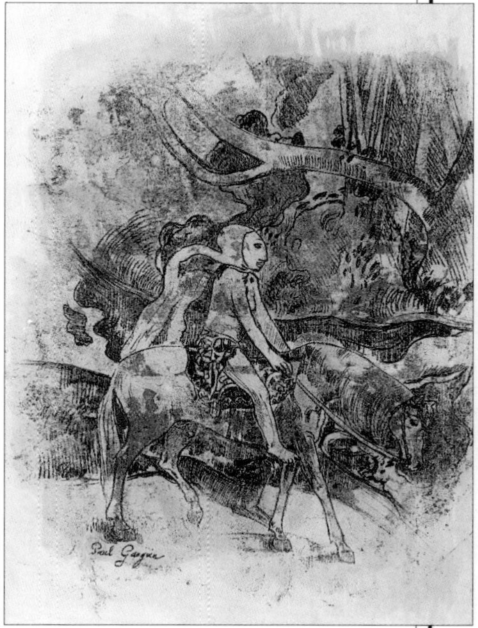

RIGHT: RIDER, 1901–2 *Dürer's medieval visions of Death on a white horse seem to be the inspiration for this hooded figure in a spirit-haunted landscape.*

Tahiti To Daniel de Monfreid *14 February 1897*

. . . You will soon be receiving some paintings from me. With my physical and mental suffering, I am not in a position even to judge them; you will be able to see them more sanely than I can: 'Nave nave mahana', Delicious days; Bouquet of Flowers; 'Note aha oe riri', Why are you upset?; Barbaric poems; Still-life; Study after myself. The history of painting*—I offer you this as a very small token of friendship in return for your devotion, and if there is any of the paintings which *pleases* you a lot, take it; I shall be delighted to give it to you.

I am trying to finish a painting† to send with the others but *shall I have time?* I would recommend you to pay good attention to the vertical when you are putting it on the stretcher. I may be wrong, but I do think that this is an important thing. I wanted to portray, by means of a simple nude, a suggestion of a certain barbaric opulence from the past. The whole is drenched in colours that are deliberately sombre and sad. It is not silk, or velvet, or cambric, or gold that creates this opulence, just the hand of the artist. There is nothing ostentatious about it . . . the mind of a man alone has enriched the place with his imagination . . .

Will you also be good enough (yet another commission) to order from my shoemaker (Tholance, 4 rue Vavin), a pair of lace-up boots. I want them to be in Russian leather, as soft as possible, and not

RIGHT: NEVERMORE, O TAHITI, 1897 *'I wished to suggest by means of a simple nude, a certain barbaric luxury,' Gauguin wrote to De Monfreid. He added that the bird represented 'not exactly the raven of Edgar Allen Poe, but the bird of the devil who is keeping watch'. In Poe's poem, the raven prevents the poet from uniting with his ideal woman. Characteristically, Gauguin implies the reverse meaning to that in his source; his young wife Pahura rests at ease and in intimacy with the artist.*

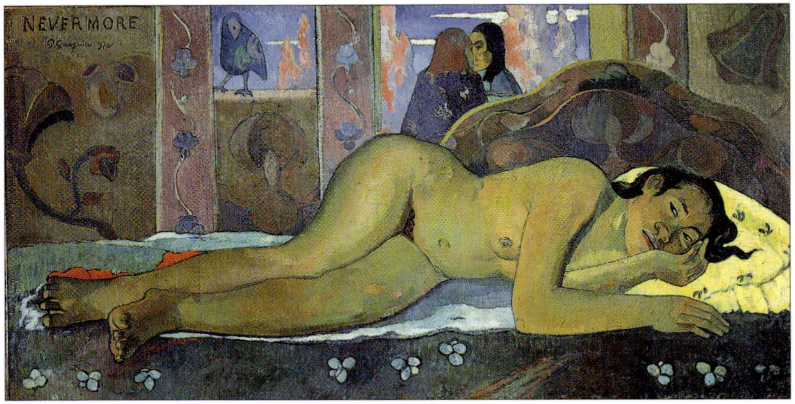

RIGHT: THE DREAM (TE RERIOA), 1897 *Gauguin often described himself as a failed decorative artist, and we see here perhaps the most elaborate of his decorative interiors. Painted in a period of relative calm, this picture shows us the painter's new home, with a frieze of human love and watching gods. His* vahine*, Pahura, watches over their new child.*

lined; boots like a woman's ankle-boot, with laces and eyes, a bit like the boots of an acrobat (by 'eyes' I mean holes pierced in the leather), with the welts of the soles exaggerated, and the toecap squared. My crippled foot demands a well-structured shoe and yet one which can be flexed at will. Also, a large jar of red shoe polish. You know what to do about the cost and its payment.

* Gauguin wrote a number of reflections on the history of art between 1896 and 1897. It is presumably some of these which he sent to De Monfreid.
† The painting was 'Nevermore'.

Tahiti — To William Molard — *August 1897*

. . . I must confess to my shame that on receiving a short letter from my wife informing me of the tragedy* my eyes were dry. I did not reply, and my feelings were of anger and rage, like the delirium of a victim who is being tortured, and yet asks for more suffering.

Ever since my infancy, misfortune has flayed me. I've never had a chance, never any ray of joy. Everything has been against me, and I cried: My God, if you exist, I accuse you of injustice and

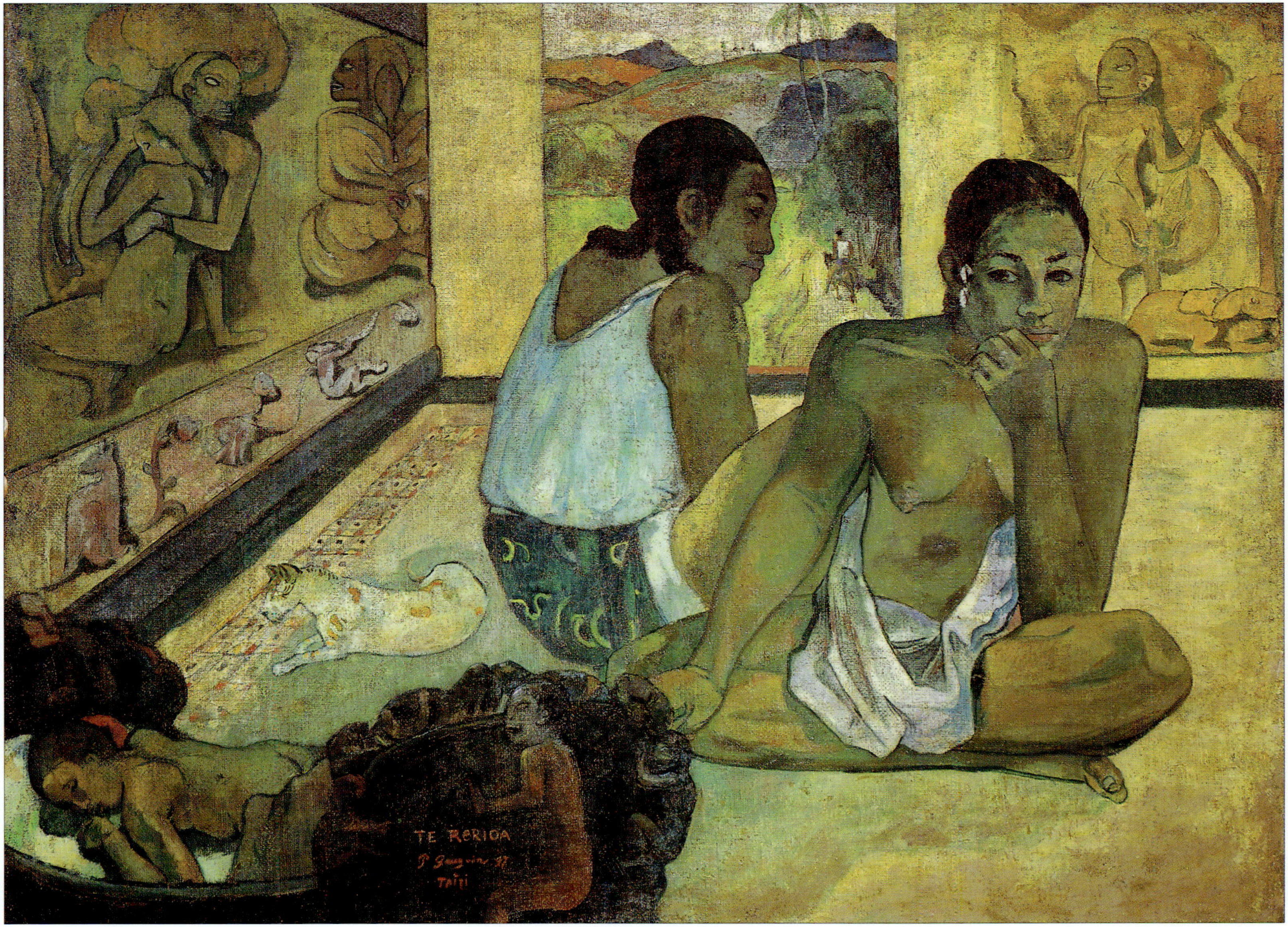
TE RERIOA
P Gauguin 97
TAÏTI

malevolence. Yes, on the death of my poor Aline, I came to doubt everything. I laughed like a madman. What is the good of virtue, work, courage and intelligence? Only crime is logical and right.

Then one's vitality wanes; sheer anger ceases to stimulate, and wearily one thinks. Ah, those long, sleepless nights, how they age you. So that is why today I feel the sorrow of the death of Aline; the numbness has gone, and my illness takes over. Although in essence mental, my sorrows have now started to take over my body, and I shall never get better without some peace. But when?

* The death of his daughter Aline from a bronchial infection at the age of nineteen.

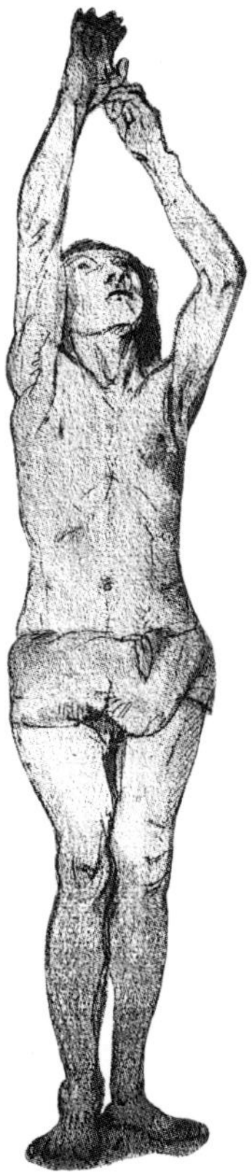

ABOVE: *This study by Rembrandt of 'Christ at the Pillar' seems to have inspired Gauguin's central figure. He probably had a print or etching, hence the reversed pose.*

Tahiti — To Mette Gauguin — *August 1897*

. . . Madame, I asked you that on 7 June, my birthday, the children should write 'Dear Papa' to me with a signature. You replied, 'You have no money, don't count on it.'

I shall not say, 'God guard you', but, more realistically, 'May your conscience sleep to save you waiting for death as a deliverance.'

Tahiti — To Daniel de Monfreid — *February 1898*

. . . I have decided before I die to paint a great picture, which is in my head, and all this month I have worked on it in a kind of unaccustomed frenzy.* It's not a picture made like a Puvis de Chavannes, with drawings from life, a preparatory cartoon and all that sort of thing. It's all done in a spontaneous way, straight from the tip of the brush, on a canvas made of sacking, full of knots and coarse textures, so that the general appearance is incredibly rough.

People will say that it isn't properly finished. It's true that I can't judge it properly myself, but I still believe that in value this picture surpasses anything else I have done, and that I shall never produce a similar or a better one before I die. I have put all my energy into it,

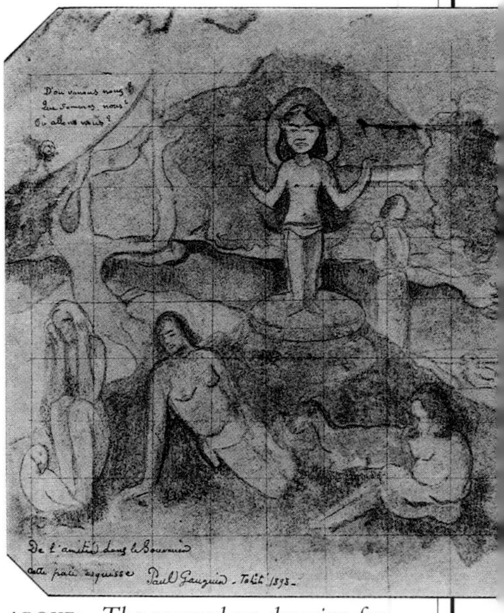

ABOVE: *The squared-up drawing for 'Where have we come from? What are we? Where are we going?'. Gauguin denied making a preparatory study (see letter to De Monfreid, this page), and seems to have preferred the explanation that the canvas was made in the white heat of grief and despair of impending suicide.*

and a sad passion created by terrible circumstances. It is so sharp and uncorrected a vision that all the sins of the speed at which it was painted disappear, and life surges out of it. It smacks not at all of models, technical skill or the so-called rules, from which I have always been free, sometimes, it is true, not without fear.

It is a canvas of four and a half metres wide, by 1m 70 high. The two upper corners are yellow, with an inscription on the left and my signature on the right, so that it looks like a fresco which has been bent down in the corners and affixed on to a gilt wall. On the lower right-hand side there is a baby asleep and three crouching women. Two figures dressed in purple confide their thoughts to each other. A huge squatting figure, deliberately painted without regard to perspective, lifts its arms in the air, astonished by these two people who dare to talk about their own destiny. A figure in the centre is gathering fruit; there are two cats beside a child; a white goat. The idol, its two arms rhythmically and mysteriously raised, appears to indicate the hereafter. A crouching figure is apparently listening to the idol. And, finally, an old woman near to death seems to accept everything, to resign herself to her thoughts, and to end the story. At her feet, a strange white bird, holding in its claws a lizard, represents the vanity of useless words. The whole scene is set beside a stream under the trees; in the background, the sea and then the mountains of the neighbouring island. Despite certain tonal passages, the general aspect of the work from one end to the other is blue and green, like Veronese. All the naked figures stand out in strong orange. If one said to students from the Beaux-Arts: 'The painting you must do will represent Where have we come from? What are we? Where are we going?' what would they do? I have completed a philosophical work on a theme comparable to that of the Gospel; I'm sure it's good. If I have the strength to make a copy, I shall send it to you . . .

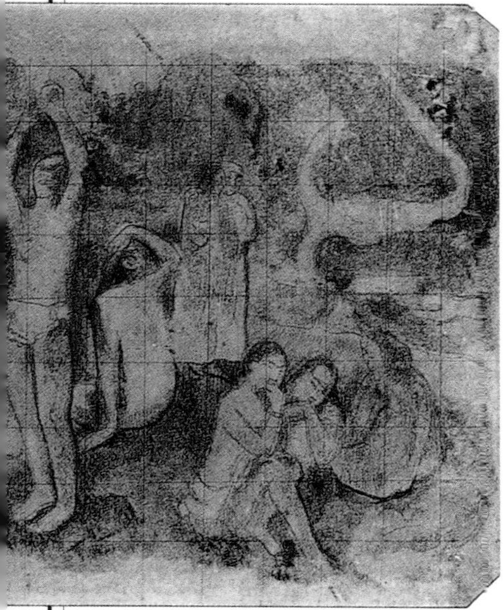

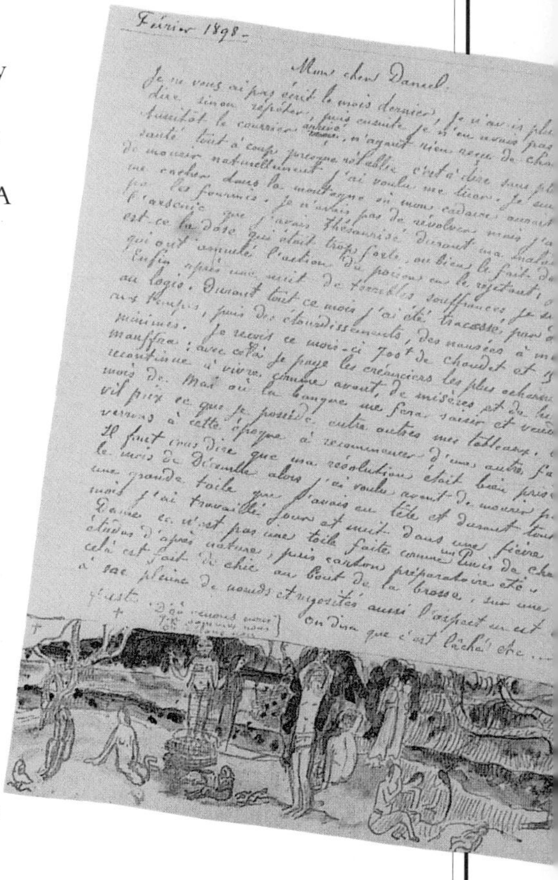

Février 1898 –

Mon cher Daniel.

RIGHT: *Letter to Daniel de Monfreid, February 1898, with a sketch for the painting and an explanation of its production.*

* 'Where have we come from? What are we? Where are we going?', which he sketched at the foot of the letter.

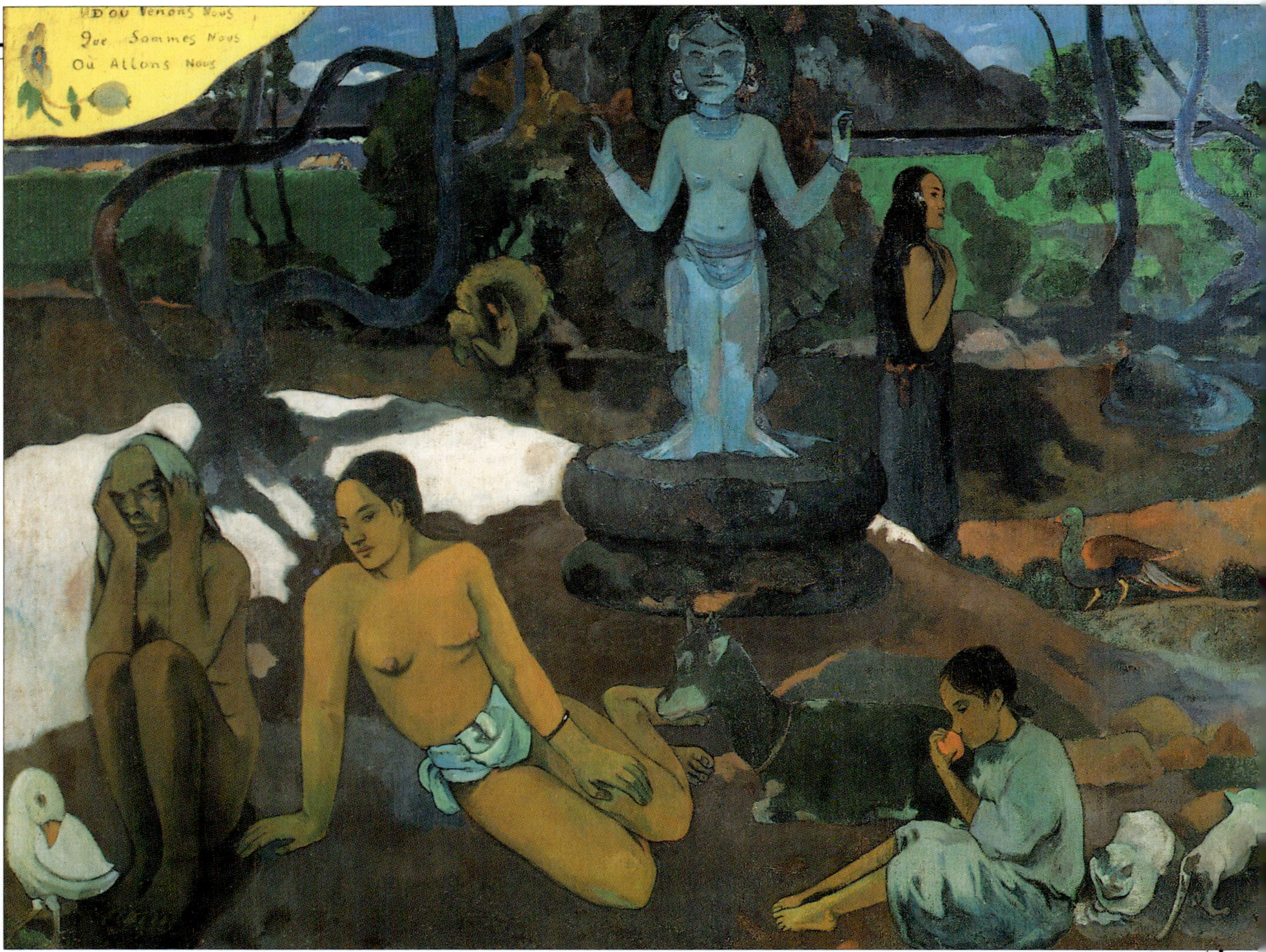

THE PICTURE I WANT TO PAINT

It is six metres long, two metres high. Why these measurements? Because the length is that of my studio, and I cannot paint any higher without extreme fatigue.

The canvas is already stretched, prepared, smoothed with care, not a knot in it, not a crease, not a spot. So think then; it will be a masterpiece.

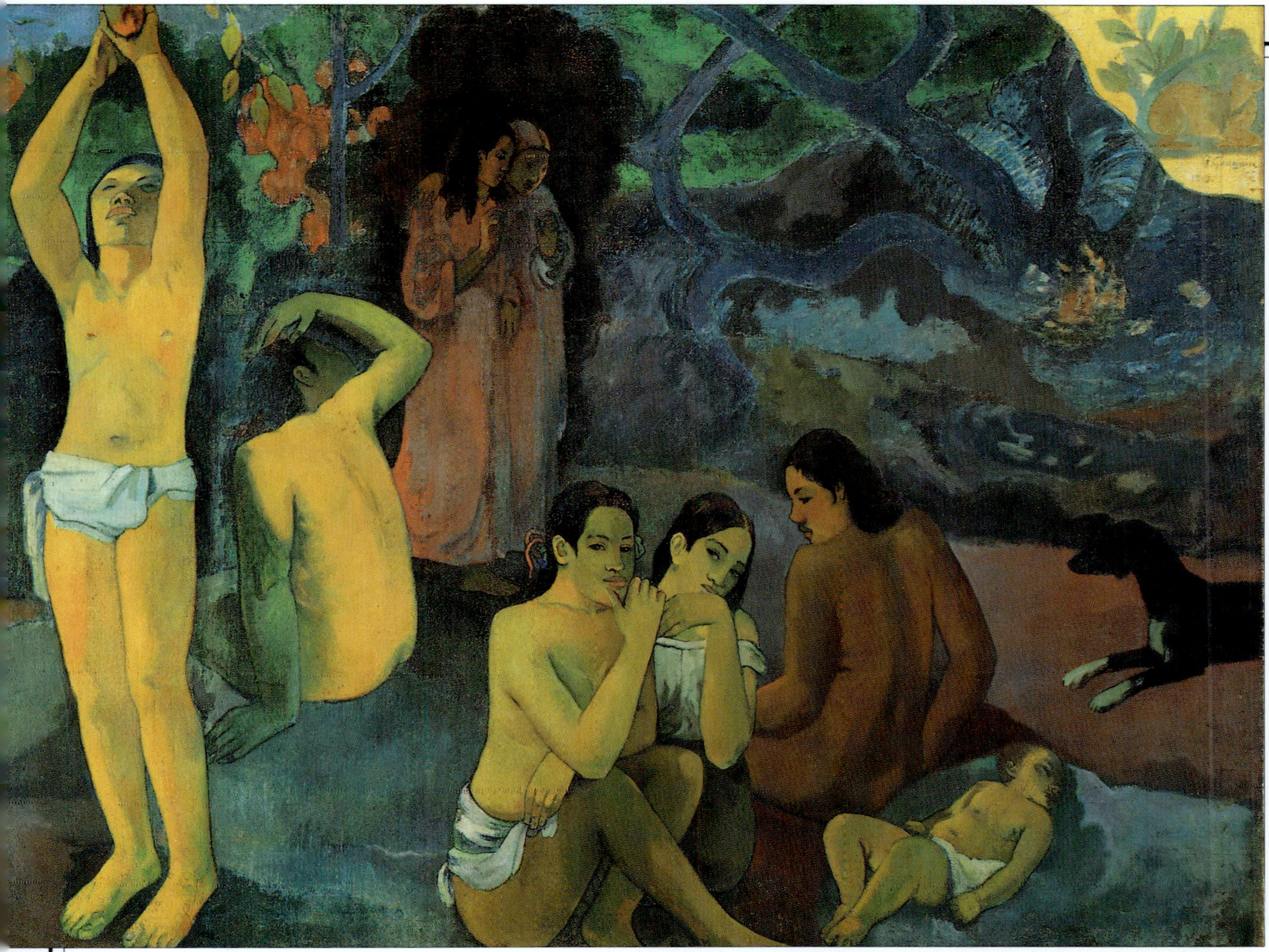

LEFT: WHERE HAVE WE COME FROM? WHAT ARE WE? WHERE ARE WE GOING?, 1897 *Gauguin claimed that he painted this, his largest and he felt greatest, work in 'an unparalelled fever' before attempting to take his own life, driven to despair by worry, ill-health, and the death of his daughter. In this mural-like composition, the goddess Hina presides over a primitive landscape peopled with the recurring icons of Gauguin's idyll.*

From the geometric point of view, the composition of lines will start from the middle, with eliptical lines undulating towards the extremities. The central figure will be a woman transforming herself into a statue, still retaining life, but being transformed into an idol. The figure will stand out against a clump of trees which look as though they are growing not on this earth but in paradise. You see? It is not a statue of Pygmalion becoming alive. Nor is it the daughter of Lot being changed into a pillar of salt. Good God, no!

From all sides, fragrant flowers rise; children frolic in the garden; young girls collect fruit; the fruits pile up in huge baskets; lithe young people in gracious attitudes bring them to the foot of the idol. The general aspect of the picture should be grave, like a religious evocation, melancholic, yet as gay as children. Ah I forgot; I also want some adorable black piglets snuffling up grain, the good things that one will eat, signalling their satisfaction by the laughing gestures of their tails.

The people will be life-size in the foreground, but because of the rules of perspective I shall have to have an elevated horizon. But my canvas is only two metres high, so I shall not be able to give due space to the superb mango trees in my garden.

How difficult painting is. I shall trample on the rules, and shall be stoned for it.

To be serious, the colours must be serious. To be gay, the colours must sing like ears of corn and should be clear. How can one produce painting which is both dark and bright? There is of course the 'midway-between', which satisfies the generality of people but gives me no pleasure.

My God, how difficult painting is when one wants to express one's thoughts with pictorial and not literary means! Decidedly, the picture that I want to do is far from being done; the desire is greater than my power; my weakness is immense (immense and weak, ha!) Let's go to sleep . . .

*Noa Noa**

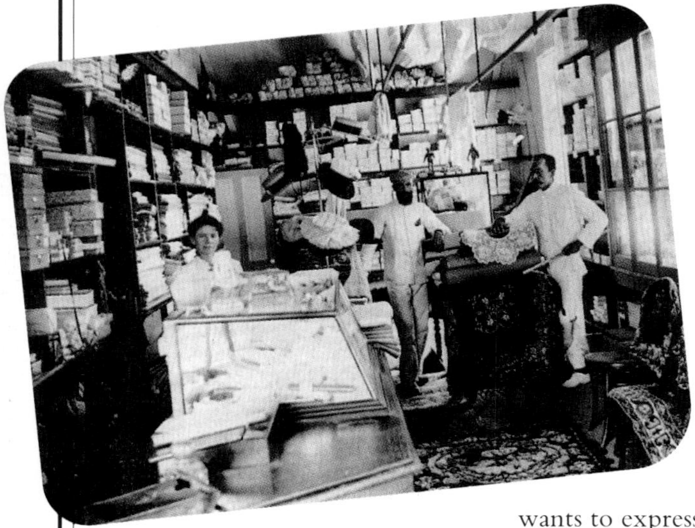

ABOVE: *Interior of a draper and haberdasher's shop in Papeete. On sale is a collection of hats, including the straw boaters worn indiscriminately by men and women islanders, and a selection of cloth and lace for the adornment of colonial wives.*

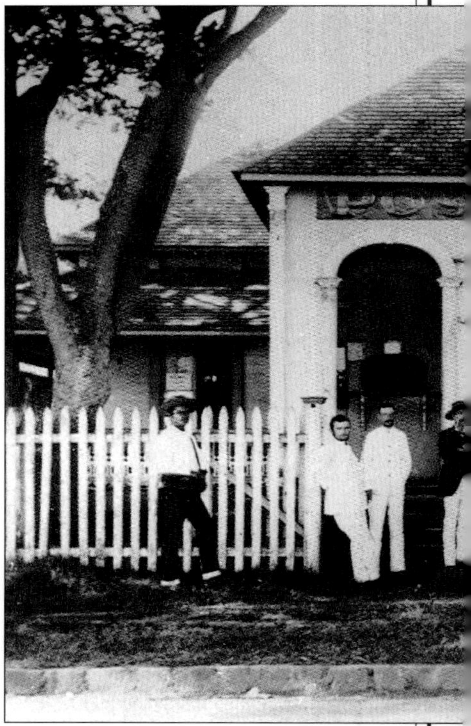

ABOVE: *The post office in Papeete, where Gauguin must have been a frequent visitor. He sent a huge number of letters and was unfailingly irate if his numerous correspondants did not reply quickly.*

* *Noa Noa* was written and drawn in an album, of which it did not occupy all the pages. On the remaining pages Gauguin jotted down various haphazard reflections on art—both on his own works, and on art in general. This account of a picture, which was not realized in this form, contains elements of 'Where have we come from? What are we? Where are we going?' and others.

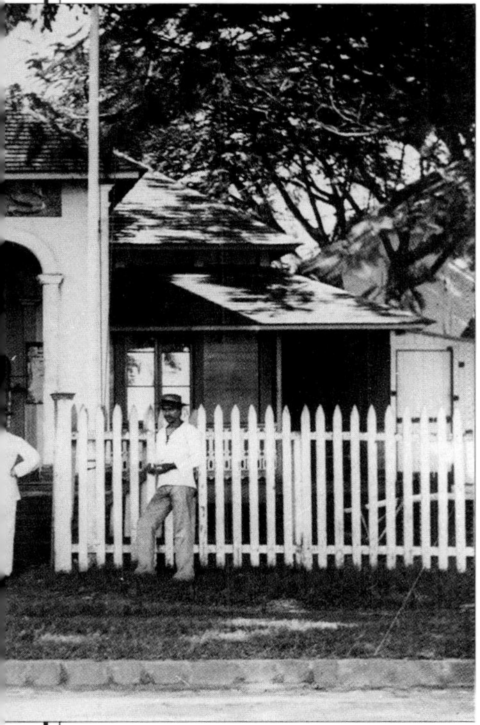

Tahiti * To Dr Gouzer *15 March 1898*

. . . I cannot come back to France as you advise me to, even if I could afford the journey.

Every day—my recent important works are proof of it—I realize that I have not said all I want to about Tahiti; there is much more to be said.

In France, with the disgust I have for it, my brain would perhaps become sterile—the cold freezes me up physically and spiritually, everything seems ugly to me.

It is true that as far as I am concerned at the moment, being adaptable is becoming easy, and I could produce work which is commercially viable, but considerations such as these I cannot view without horror and revulsion. It would be unworthy of me and of my career, which I have continually pursued (nobly, I believe).

Finishing badly when one has started well! But at least I shall live, you will say. But why go on living when one has to lose the considerations which make you live? . . .

And then, too, a martyr is often necessary for a revolution. My work, considered as a current pictorial production, has little importance compared to its definitive and moral result: the *liberation* of painting, already freed from all its fetters, from that infamous tissue knitted together by schools, academics, and above all else by mediocrities.

Look at what people are daring to do today compared with the timidity that held sway ten years ago. Fantasists are profiting from it—much good may it do them. There are others of the same kind and, at the moment, a whole constellation of names. My own may disappear; what does it matter?

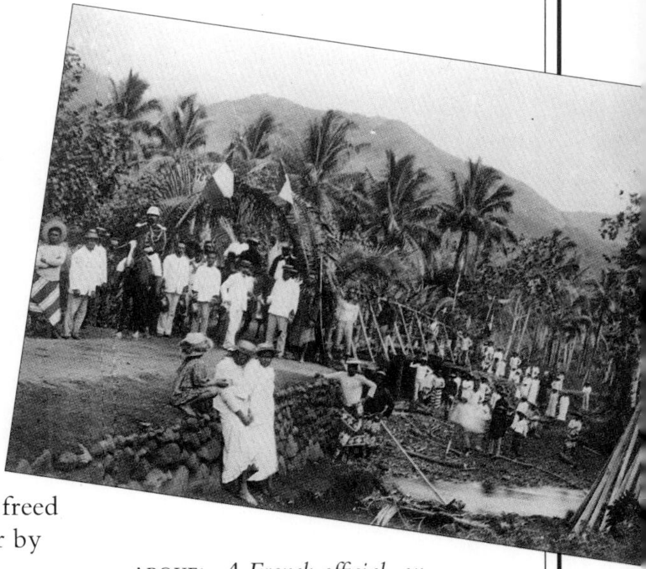

ABOVE: *A French official, on horseback, ceremoniously opens a new bridge built by the administration.*

* Dr Gouzer was the ship's doctor on the French warship, the *Douguay-Trouin*, and had got to know Gauguin when the boat made a prolonged stop at Tahiti in connection with the trouble in the Windward Isles. He

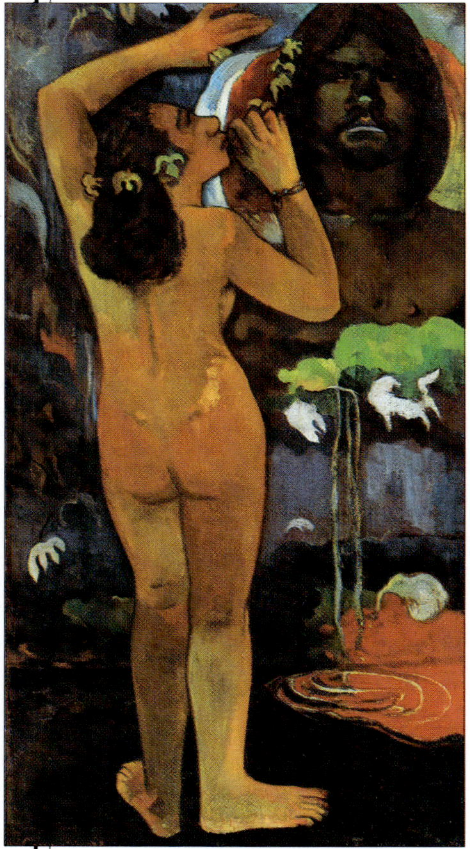

ABOVE: THE MOON AND THE EARTH (HINA TEFATOU), 1893 *An ancient myth: Hina (the Moon) whispers to Fatu (the Earth), who refuses her request that Man have eternal life. She replies that the Moon shall never die but be always reborn.*

bought one of his paintings, and Gaugin made him a present of some drawings.

Tahiti — To Daniel de Monfreid — *15 May 1898*

. . . The 575 francs that you and Annette sent me were entirely unexpected, while Chaudet and Maufra don't send me what I have been expecting; no news at all from them.

The small sum you sent will be of use to me, if not to live, at least to keep out the bailiffs, who will be sent by the bank in regard to a debt of 1,200 francs that I owe them. After a lengthy struggle, I persuaded them not to take action for five months on condition that I made a payment of 400 francs, plus 60 francs interest due for the last six months. What a monstrous comedy, to borrow with difficulty at a rate of ten per cent, simply to make up the deficit created by Bauchy* and company, who themselves have no thought of paying any interest!

The rest of the money has gone in paying some pressing debts to the chemist† and for bread from the Chinese. This, then, is my present situation. Happily, the small job I have with the Office of Works and Surveys saves me from accumulating any further debts, but I shall leave it when I have in front of me a thousand franc note, after my debt is paid. It is necessary, therefore, that we continue to go on selling. In your letter, you give the impression of fearing that I shall be upset about the low prices you are charging for my pictures. Not at all; I have already told you that what you have done has been well done. I would also like to know, each time you sell anything, *what pictures you have sold, with the price*. Certainly, Lerolle, who is *very rich* and an artist, pays very little; but what can one do about it? A painting in his house is very well placed, in the sense that everybody goes there and that the best proof that my painting has a certain value is that an artist, *an official one* or not, buys it. Ah, if only I were able to sell all my paintings for 200 francs each as quickly as I produced them, I would be very happy and could afford to live very

BELOW: *The young man posing here for his portrait is shown with the bananas, mangoes and pineapples he has brought for sale to market.*

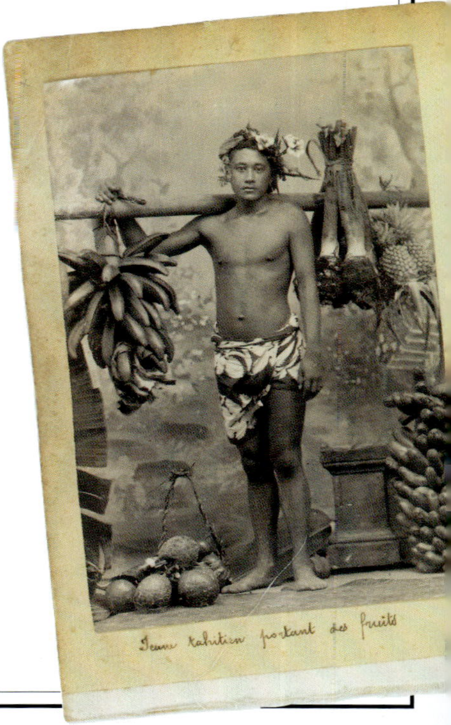

agreeably in Tahiti. Sell, therefore, at any price. There will be time enough to increase the prices when there is a crowd of people clamouring for them . . .

* Bauchy was a Parisian café owner who sold some of Gauguin's works.
† François Cardella, who was Mayor of Tahiti, and a good friend to Gauguin.

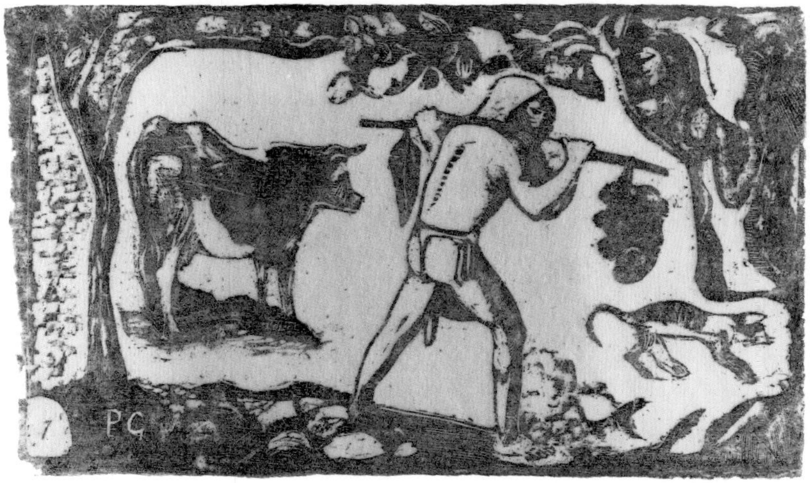

RIGHT: THE BANANA CARRIER, 1898–9 *Woodcut printed in black on Japan paper. In this late suite of prints Gauguin found a stylized and decorative means to show the daily lives of the Tahitians: 'I have tried, within a symbolic background, to translate my dream.'*

Tahiti To Daniel de Monfreid *15 August 1898*

. . . I am very glad that you have met Degas, and that through your desire to be of service to me you have secured some good connections for yourself. Yes, indeed, Degas does pass as being biting and satirical, but *so do I*, according to Schuffenecker.

But this does not apply to those whom Degas *judges* as being worth his attention and esteem. He follows his heart and his intelligence. I am not at all astonished that he commented on your

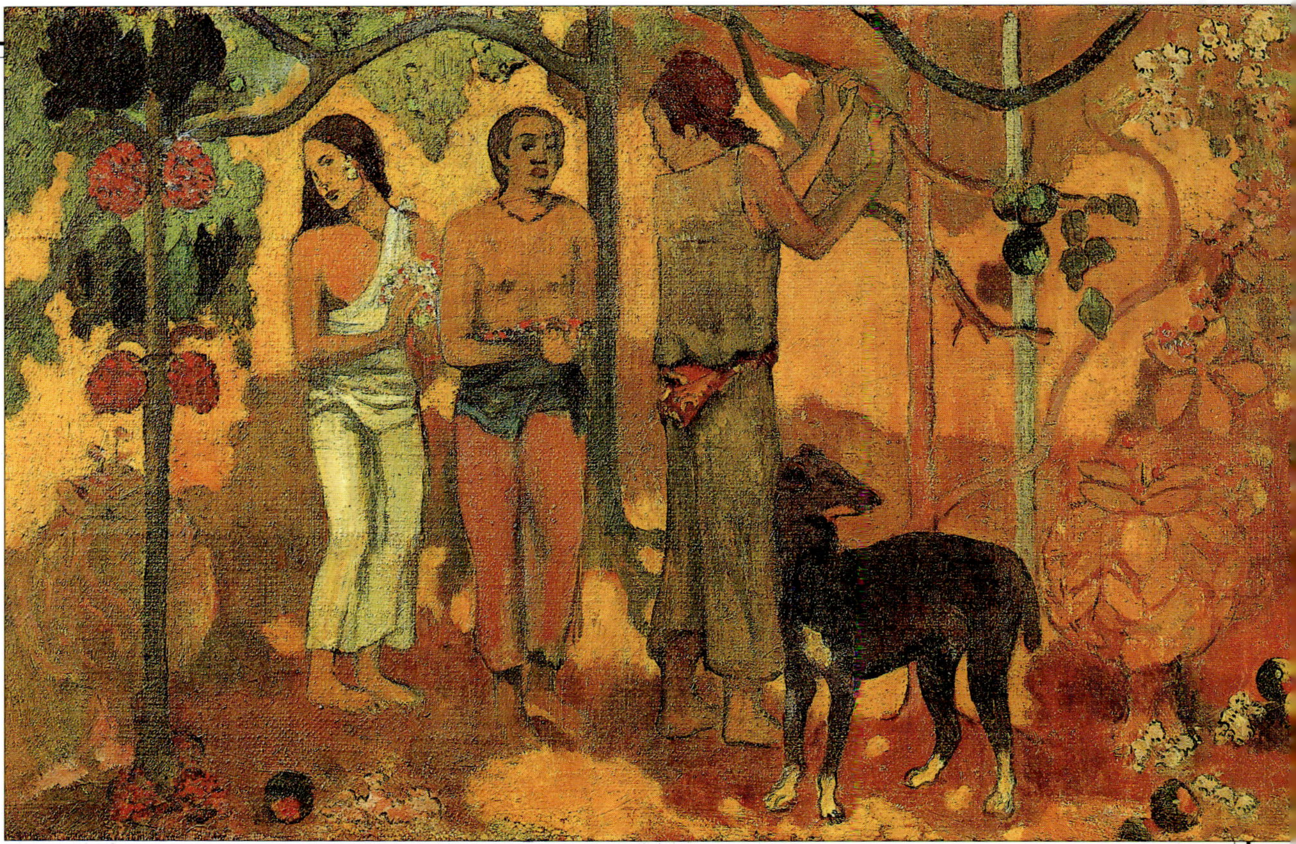

sympathetic qualities and your talent. You will remember that I never said anything about your talent until I really *felt* it; this was not malevolence on my part, but simple honesty, and I'm sure that you derived much more pleasure from an honest tribute *at the right moment* than from the sort of compliment that people make to everybody and anybody.

As an artist and in his behaviour, Degas is a rare example of what an artist should be, he who counts amongst his colleagues and admirers all those who wield power—Bonnat, Puvis, Antonin Proust—and yet who has *never* wished to receive *anything*. *From him* one has *never heard* an evil word, or anything indelicate, or anything at all unpleasant. Art combined with dignity . . .

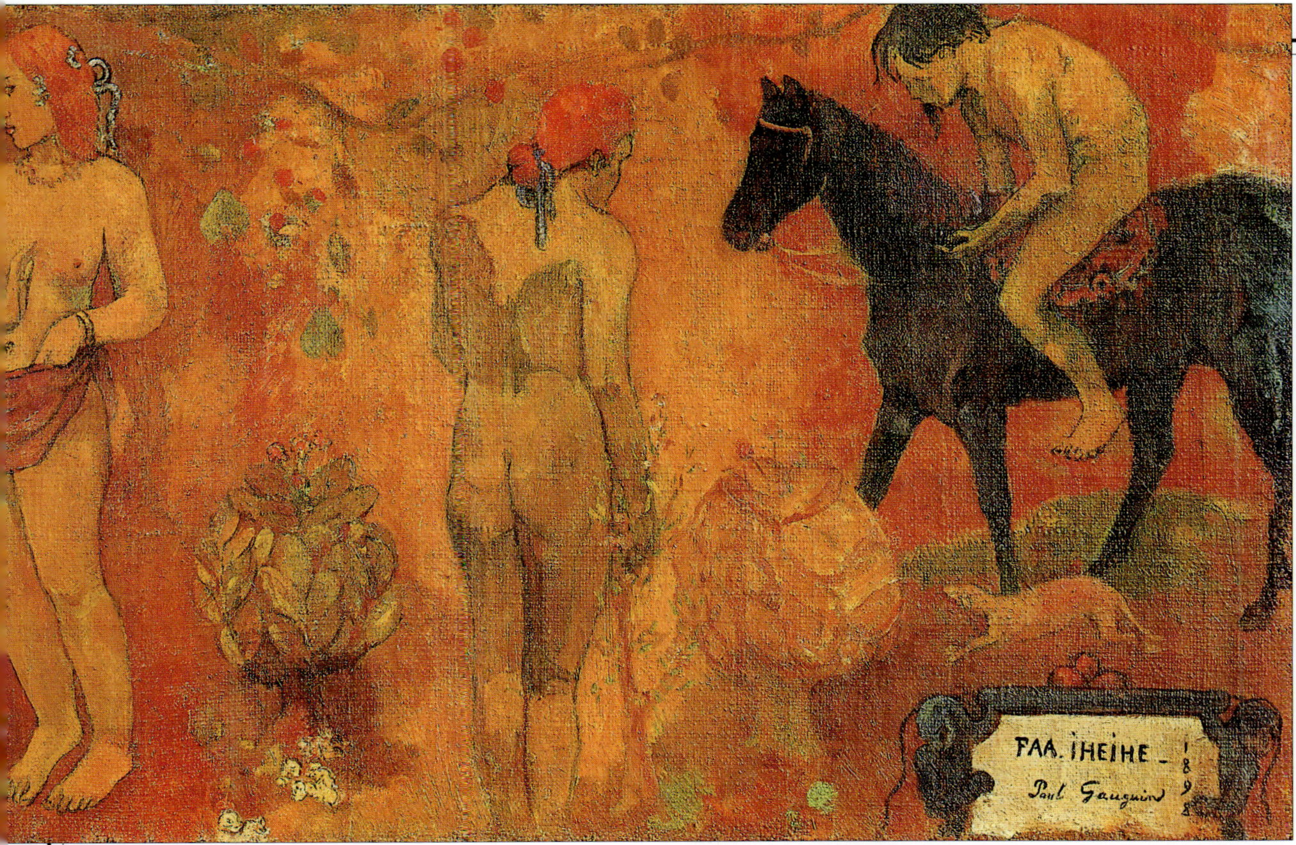

LEFT: TAHITIAN PASTORAL (FAA IHEIHE), 1898 *The title is more literally translated as 'Preparations for a Festival'. This second fresco-style canvas exchanges the dark hues of despair in 'Where have we come from?' for the warm and luminous in a celebration of life. Significantly, he writes at this time to De Monfreid asking for 'seeds and shoots' for his garden.*

DEGAS

Who knows Degas? To say nobody would be an exaggeration, but there are only a very few. I would like to say that I know him well. Even by name he is unknown to the millions of readers of the daily papers. Only painters, many out of fear, the rest out of respect, admire Degas. But do they really understand him?

Degas was born I don't know when, but he has been old for so long that he must be as old as Methuselah. I say Methuselah because I suppose that when Methuselah was a hundred, he must have been like a man of thirty in our time. Degas is in fact always young and full of energy.

He respects Ingres, which means that he respects himself. To see him with his silk top hat on his head, his blue spectacles over his eyes, and of course his umbrella, he has the air of a complete notary, of a bourgeois during the reign of Louis-Philippe.

If there is anybody less concerned about looking like an artist, it is certainly he; and yet he is so much really one. But he distrusts all liveries, even that one. He is a good man, and a witty one, but he passes for being malicious. A young critic, who has a mania for pontificating about things like the augurers used to, once said, 'Degas is a boor, a benevolent boor.' Degas a boor! He who carries himself in the street like an ambassador at court. Benevolent—that's trivial; he is something more than that . . .

Avant et Après

Tahiti To André Fontainas *March 1899*

. . . Here, near my house, in complete silence, I dream of violent harmonies in the fragrances of nature which intoxicate me.

A delight from I know not what mystic terror that I divine, going back to time immemorial; at other times, the odour of joy, which I find in the present; animal figures of statuesque rigidity, some indefinable antiquity, some august quality, some religious feeling in their rare immobility. In dreaming eyes there is the troubled surface of an insoluble enigma.

And, behold, the night comes; everything is in repose. My eyes close to see without understanding the dream in infinite space which flees before me, and I sense the mournful tread of my hopes . . .

Going back to my large painting, the idol is there not as a literary gloss, but as a statue, perhaps less of a statue than the figures of animals, less animal too, taking the shape of a body in my dream, there in front of my hut, dominating the primitive in our soul, an imaginary consolation for our sufferings in that it represents the undefined and the incomprehensible face to face with the mystery of our origins and of our future.

RIGHT: THE RAPE OF EUROPA, 1898–9
In this woodcut Gauguin's Western sources lie not in Christian but in pagan classical mythology. Illustrating the sexually charged story of the rape of Europa by Zeus in the form of a bull, Gauguin gently 'domesticates' the bull, and includes a peacock, symbol of renewal; the destructive and creative aspects of sexuality are inseparable.

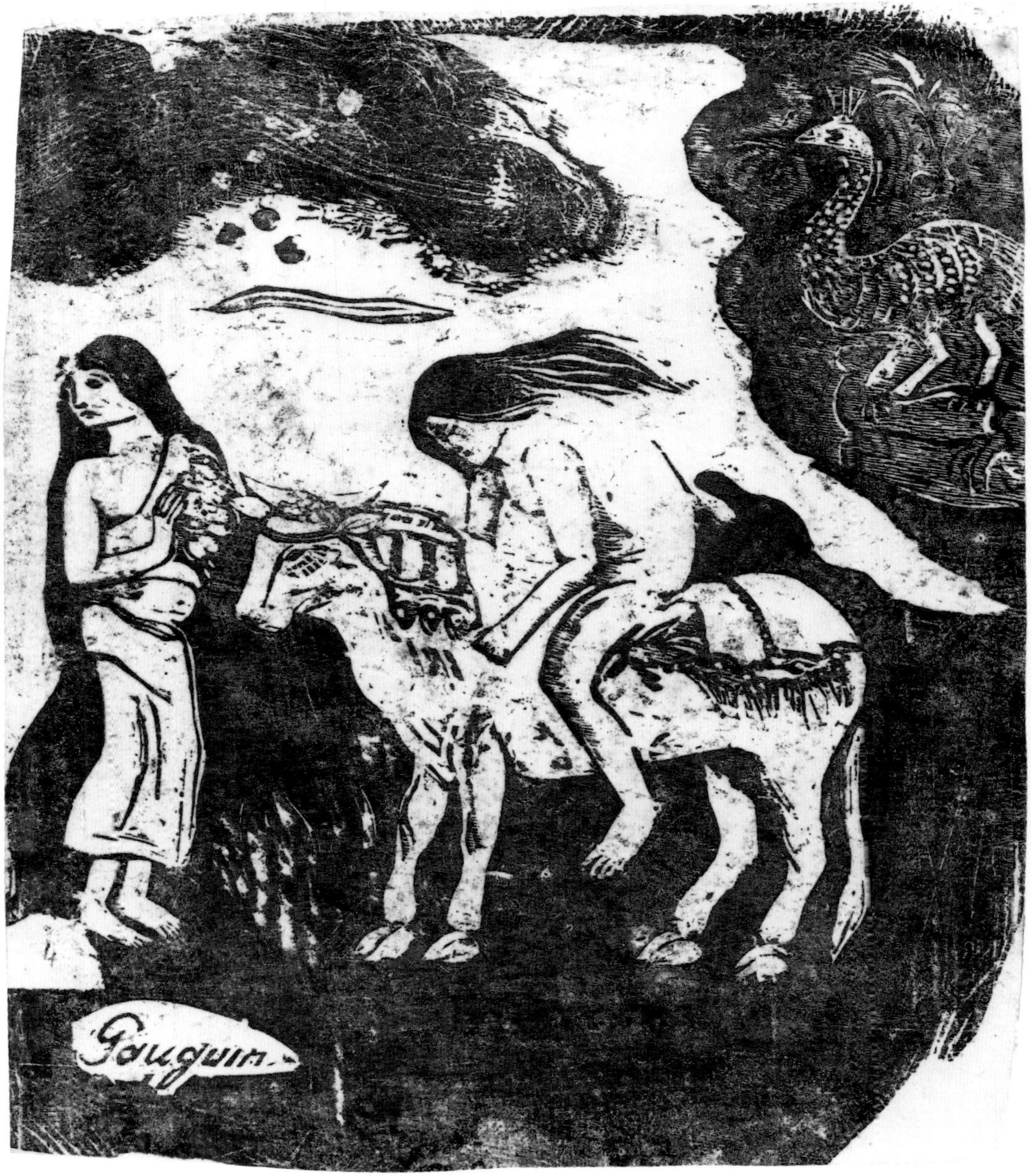
Gauguin

And all this sings sadly in my soul and in my surroundings. I am painting and dreaming at the same time, without any allegory that I can get hold of—perhaps a sign of a lack of literary education.

On awakening, I said to myself: Where do we come from? What are we? Where are we going?—a reflection which is not part of the painting, and expressed in a language quite distinct from the mural; which frames it not as a title, but as a signature.

You must understand that I have failed to comprehend the value of words—abstract or concrete—in the dictionary, and I cannot understand them any more in painting. I have tried, within a symbolic background, to translate my dream without any recourse to literary means, but with all the simplicity compatible with the demands of a craft, a difficult task. Accuse me of failing in this, but not of not having tried. Advise me to change my goal for other accepted, and indeed sanctified, goals . . .

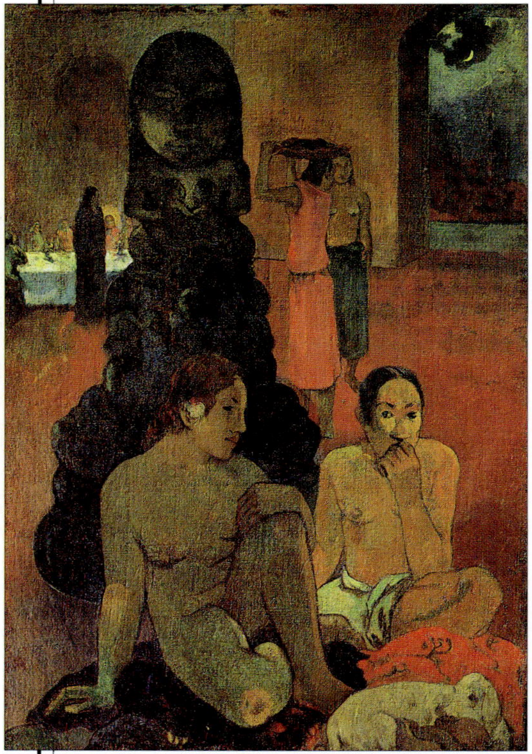

ABOVE: THE GREAT BUDDHA, 1899
'The idol is there not as a literary gloss, but as a statue,' wrote Gauguin, enigmatically, of the statue in 'Where have we come from?' (see letter to André Fontainas, page 132–4).

Tahiti To Daniel de Monfreid *May 1899*

. . . You ask me why don't I paint more *lusciously* so as to create a surface and a content which are richer?

I do not say no, and sometimes I would like to do so; but this is becoming more and more impossible for me in view of the expense of colours. Despite the economies I make, I hardly have any more, and I cannot ask you for fresh supplies until I know when my material existence will be assured. If you can find somebody who will guarantee me an income of 2,400 francs a year for five years, plus an abundant stock of colours, I would do all that was wished; I would paint with a heavy impasto, which would take me three times as long . . .

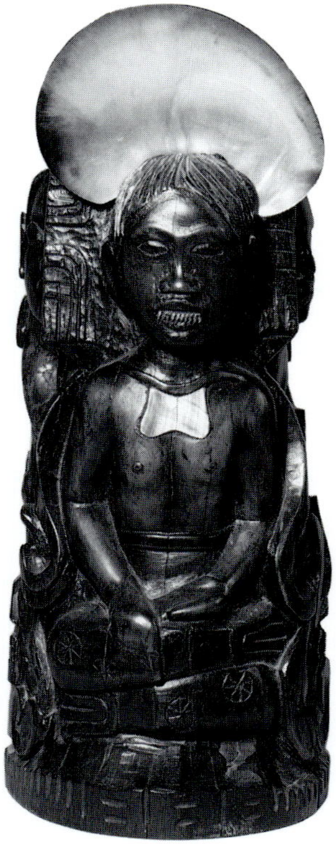

ABOVE: *Described as 'a kind of savage bibelot', this statuette is of Taaroa, creator of the 'great and sacred universe which is only the shell of Taaroa'. A mother-of-pearl halo portrays this literally.*

Tahiti To Maurice Denis *June 1899*

In response to your letter, I regret not being able to say yes. It would certainly be interesting to see the artists who formed a group at the Café Volpini reunited at ten yearly intervals,* and with them the young painters whom I admire; but my interest of ten years ago has gone today. At that time, I wished to hazard everything to *liberate* in some way the new generation, and then work to acquire a little talent. The first part of my programme has borne its fruits; today you can dare to do what you like, and, what's more, nobody will be astonished.

The second part of my programme, alas, has been less happy. Since then, I have become an old fogey, the pupil of many in your exhibition; *in my absence* that will become all too evident. Much has been written on this subject, and everybody knows that in reality I have robbed my master Émile Bernard of painting and sculpture so that he has none left. Don't believe for a moment that the thirty or so paintings that I gave him, and which he sold to Vollard, are mine; they are dreadful forgeries of Bernard.

But there is another reason, and this is absolutely true.

My work is over. My friend Daniel, to extricate me a little from my misery, has exhibited the few efforts that I have been able to make during the past three years, but without any financial success.

Ill, and obliged to undertake work of a very unintellectual kind to earn my bread, I no longer paint except on Sundays and feast days. I am not therefore able even to offer you any new delights, which in any case could not be properly framed, or be in the style of the movement. My Papuan paintings have no justification for being hung alongside the Symbolists and the Idealists. But I am sure that your exhibition will be a great success. Practically all of you have fortunes, numerous patrons and powerful friends, so it would be surprising if each of you did not reap the legitimate fruits of his talents and discoveries . . .

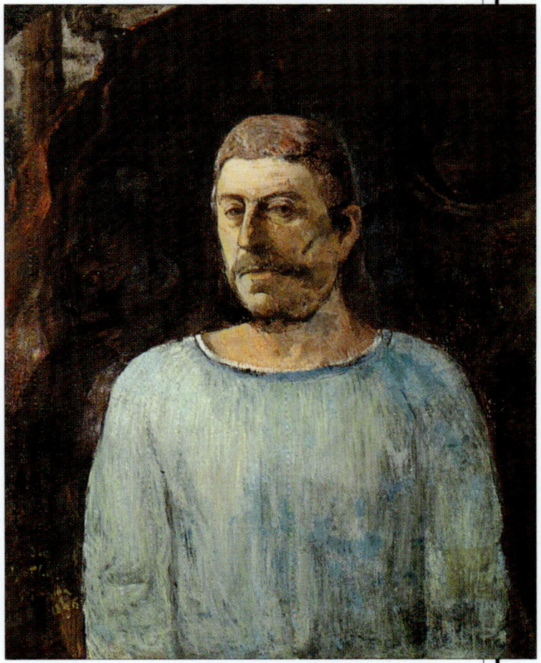

ABOVE: SELF-PORTRAIT NEAR GOLGOTHA, 1896 *This melancholy yet defiant self-image reverberates with intimations of death; in constant pain from his ulcerated leg and other ailments, Gauguin shows himself in his hospital smock, which resembles a shroud or the shift of a condemned man.*

* Denis had written to Gauguin suggesting a revival of the Café Volpini exhibition of 1889 at which Gauguin had played an important

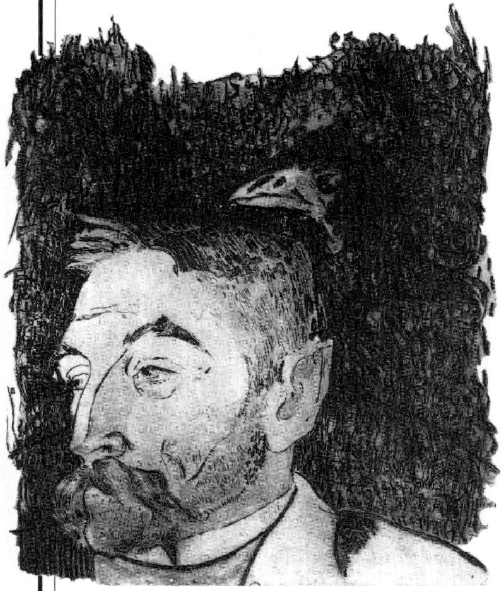

ABOVE: *This portrait of the poet Stéphane Mallarmé, a leading light of the Symbolist movement, was the only etching ever made by Gauguin. The raven, symbol of death, refers to Mallarmé's translation of Poe's poem for which Manet had made a famous series of etchings.*

RIGHT: *Puvis de Chavannes, the foremost decorative painter in the Paris of the 1880s, in his studio. He was a strong influence on the Symbolist group and his huge mural in the classical and medieval traditions is clearly echoed in many of Gauguin's great allegorical works.*

role. The sarcastic references to Bernard stem from the fact that the *Mercure de France* of June 1895 published an article in which Émile Bernard accused Gauguin of having plagiarized his works.

Tahiti — To Charles Morice — **July 1901**

. . . Today I am on my knees, overcome with misery, and especially by the disease of premature old age. Shall I have a respite to finish my work? I daren't hope for it, but I shall make a last effort by going to Fatu-iva in the Marquesan Islands, which is virtually in the Stone Age. I believe that there this altogether savage element and this absolute solitude will give me, before I die, a last blaze of enthusiasm, which will revive my imagination and bring my talent to its final consummation.

This great picture of mine is very imperfect in terms of execution; it was finished in a month without any preparation or preliminary sketches. I wanted to die and in that state of despair I painted it with a single spurt of energy. I hastened to sign it, and then took a formidable dose of arsenic. Probably it was too much; I endured terrible agony, but not death. My shattered frame, which had to cope with the shock, has been making me suffer.

Perhaps in this painting what is lacking in moderation is made up for by something inexplicable to anyone who has not suffered to the bitter end, and who does not know the soul of the painter.

Fontainas, who has always been well-disposed to me, has reproached me because he is unable to make my idea comprehensible, the abstract title not revealing itself anywhere on the canvas in concrete forms etc., and he cites as an example Puvis de Chavannes, always understandable, always knowing how to express an idea.

Puvis explains his ideas, that is very true, but he does not paint them. He is a Greek, whereas I am a savage, a wolf without a collar in the forest.* Puvis will entitle a work 'Purity', and to explain it will paint a young virgin with a lyre in her hand, a well-known symbol, which everybody can understand. Gauguin, faced with the

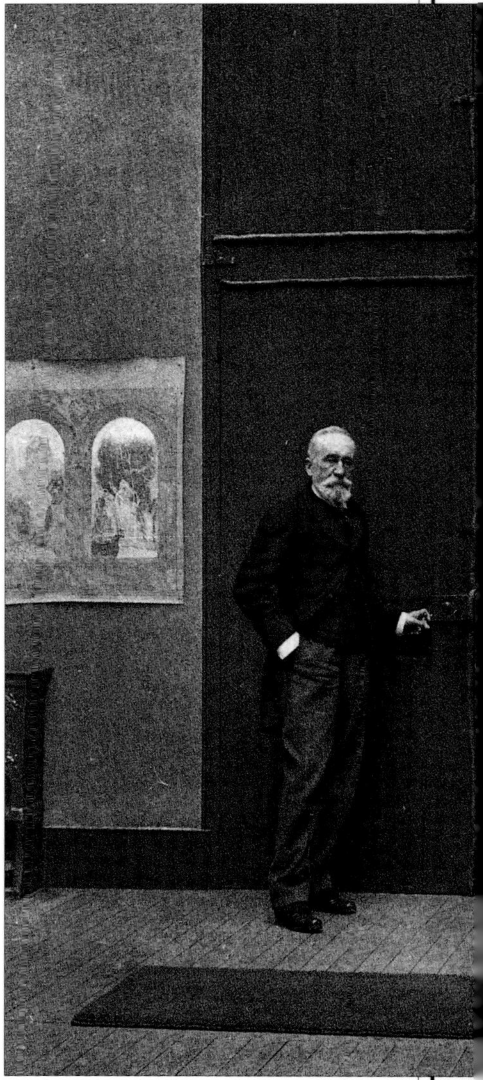

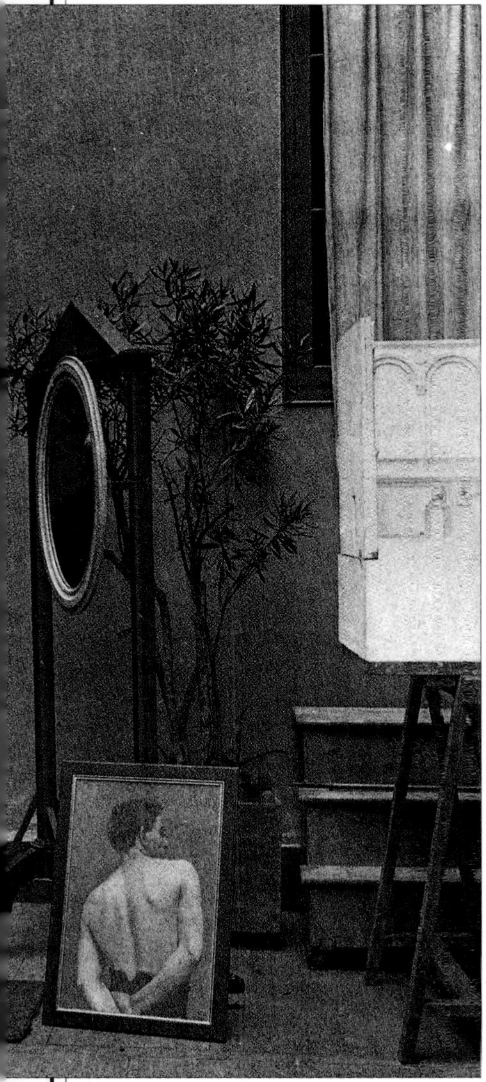

same title of 'Purity', will paint a landscape with limpid streams, no sign of pollution by man, perhaps one human being.

Without going into details, Puvis and I are divided by a whole world. Puvis, as a painter, is a wordsmith, not a man of letters, whilst I am not a wordsmith, but perhaps a man of letters.

Why is it, when faced with a painting, the critic looks for points of comparison with historical ideas and with other painters? Not finding what he thinks ought to be there, he doesn't understand anything else and is not moved. Feeling first of all, and comprehension follows.

Where are we going?

Close to the death of an old woman, a strange and stupid bird brings everything to an end.

What are we?

Daily life. The man of instinct asks himself what all that means.

Where do we come from?

The source. The child. Communal life.

The bird concludes the poem by comparing the inferior being to the intelligent one in the grand order of things propounded in the title. Behind a tree, two sinister figures dressed in robes of a melancholy hue introduce, close to the tree of science, their note of sorrow, caused by science itself, in contrast with the simple human beings in uncontaminated nature, which could be a paradise of human conception leading on to the happiness of living.

Other explanatory attributes—familiar symbols—would endow the canvas with a melancholic realism, and the problems propounded could no longer be a poem.

In these few words I explain the picture. With your intelligence you need only a few. But as for the general public, why should my brush, freed from all restraint, be obliged to open everybody's eyes? . . .

* A phrase applied to Gauguin by Degas, and one of which he was inordinately proud.

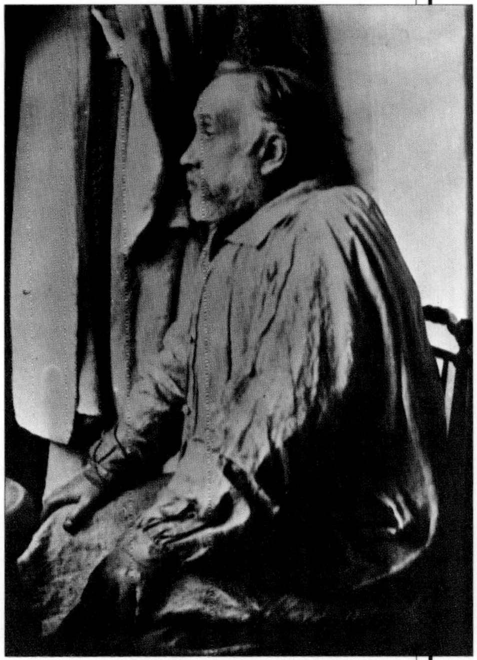

ABOVE: *A photograph of Degas in his studio, possibly taken by himself. Gauguin held him in great esteem and put great store by his criticisms and advice.*

CHAPTER 6

The Last Chance

1901–1903

IN SEPTEMBER, GAUGUIN LEFT TAHITI on the steamer *Croix du Sud*, bound for the Marquesan island of Hiva-Oa—described by Herman Melville in *Typee* as a latter-day paradise, and yet further removed from civilization, Gauguin hoped. He arrived at his chosen settlement of Atuona six days later. It was to be his final home, and in many ways the most pleasant. He acquired two plots of land from the Catholic bishop, Joseph Martin, with whom his relations were singularly unfriendly, and, with the help of local labour, built what he called his 'House of Pleasure', which had the advantage of being on the opposite side of the street to a well-stocked store run by an American, Ben Varney. A two-storey structure, its upper storey rested on a pair of wooden buildings, one a kitchen, the other a wood-carving studio, and was reached by an outside staircase. There was a small anteroom and a studio containing all his treasures, including a harmonium, a violin, his usual reproductions of works of art, forty-five pornographic photographs, and a carved bed. The entrance to the studio was through an elaborately carved doorway. The lower panels on either side of the framework had this inscription carved on them: 'Soyez amoureuses et vous serez heureuses' (Be amorous and you will be happy), surrounded by heads and figures derived from paintings he had executed in 1901 and other images. The panels on either side featured two nudes. On the lintel was inscribed 'Maison de Joie', with heads and other semi-natural decorations carved in bas-relief.

In addition to himself there were a cook, two other servants, his dog, Pegau, and a cat. Later, they were joined for a while by fourteen year old Vaeo Marie, who had been taken away from the local convent school by her father, a Marquesan chief, to become the painter's *vahine*. In August of the following year she became

RIGHT: NEAR THE HUTS, 1901
The freshness of this painting suggests Gauguin's delight in the peace and tranquillity of a new start on the Marquesas Islands.

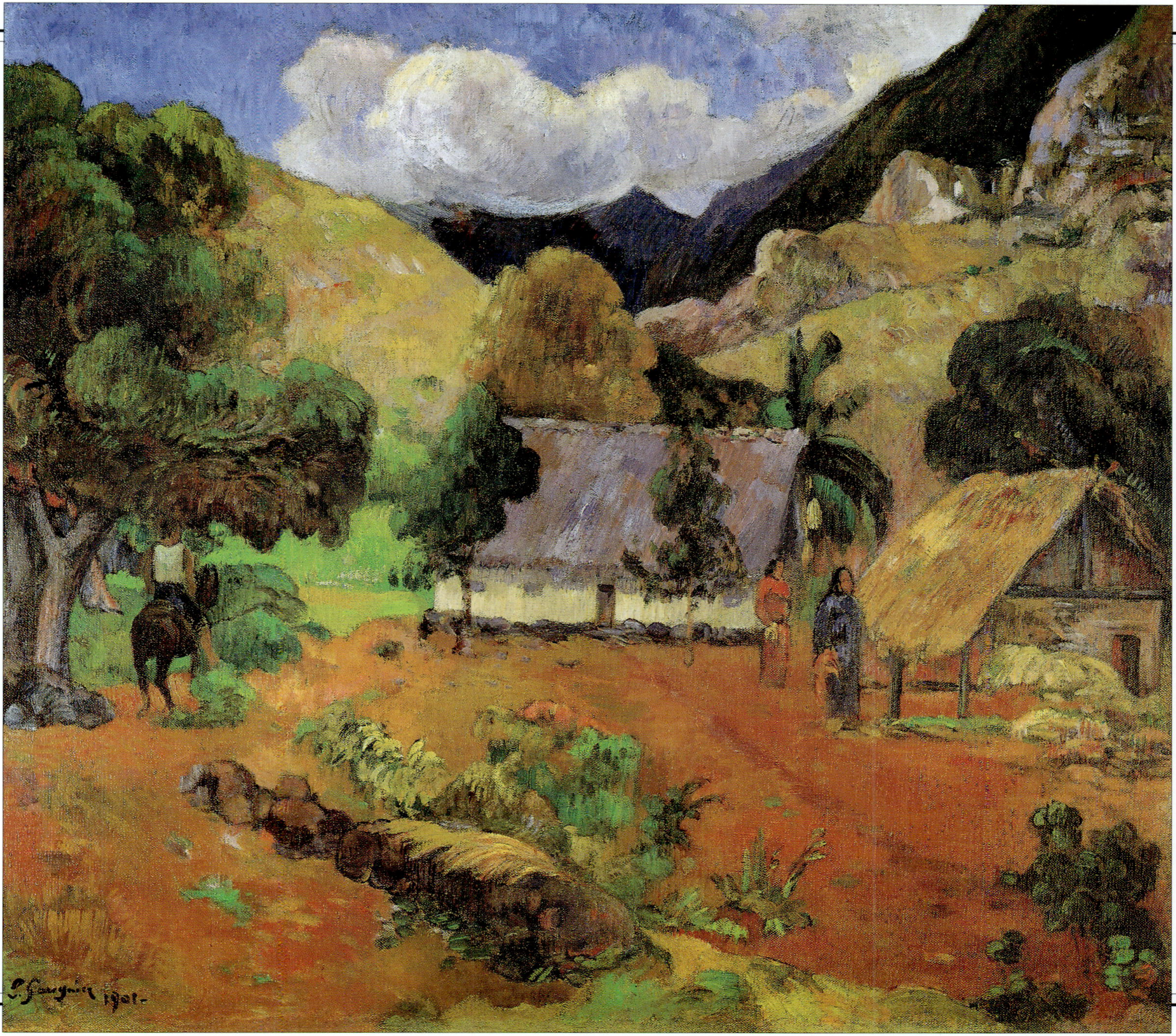
P. Gauguin 1901

pregnant and went back to her home, never to return to the House of Pleasure. Gauguin's life-style became more comfortable than it had been in Tahiti, largely because Vollard sent him a regular remittance. An idea of the very European food that he consumed can be derived from some of the items on the accounts he had with Ben Varney and the German trading company at nearby Tahuata. In the month of December 1901, for instance, he bought 98 litres of Bordeaux, 30 kilos of potatoes, 15 kilos of onions, 6 tins of tripe, 8 tins of preserved butter, 2 sacks of rice, 13 tins of asparagus, 2 tins of beans, 1 bag of salt, 1 bottle of tomato sauce, 2 packets of tea, 2 tins of anchovies, 16 litres of rum, 12 kilos of sugar, 2 kilos of garlic and 1 litre of olive oil.

He worked vigorously and rapidly, under the impetus of the allowance of 300 francs a month that Vollard had agreed to pay him, sending back to Paris as many as twenty paintings, as well as prints and engravings, in a single consignment. He also actively continued to undermine local government, taking on the Marquesan political authorities, the bishop and the police, and championing the natives. But his chronic health problems, a weak heart and ulcerous legs, sapped his energy and nagged away at his morale. At one point, it even crossed his mind to leave his South Sea paradise to seek expert medical treatment back in France and maybe fresh artistic inspiration in Spain. De Monfreid advised against this (Gauguin would probably not have survived the journey), but the incident suggests that Gauguin might have considered his search for paradise was nearly over.

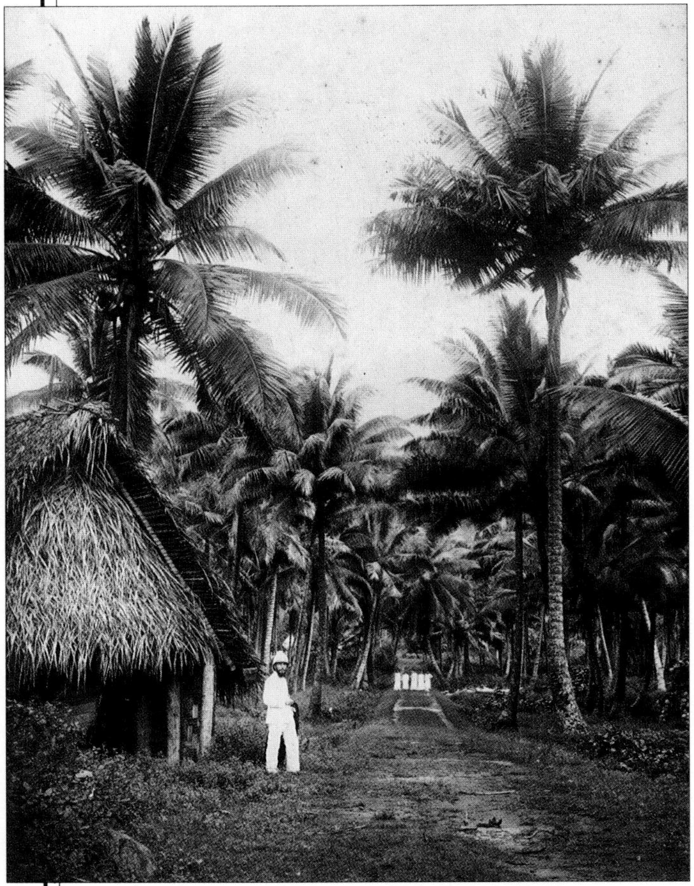

LEFT: *The road to Gauguin's new home in Atuona, as it looked in 1898. Gauguin bought a horse – they were more common here than in Tahiti – and a trap in which to get around the island.*

Hiva-Oa — To Daniel de Monfreid — **November 1901**

. . . I have everything that a modest artist could dream of: a huge studio with a small corner for sleeping in, everything to hand, arranged on shelves, the whole raised two metres high; the place

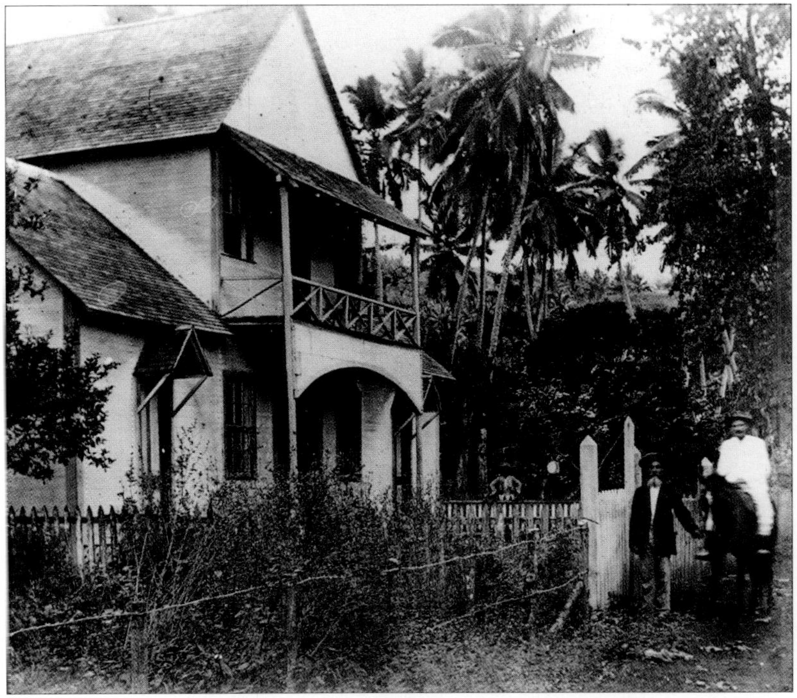

RIGHT: *Gauguin's new friend, the American storekeeper Ben Varney, stands outside his shop with the bearded Tioka, to whom Gauguin gave some land when the old man's house was destroyed in the cyclone of 1903.*

where one eats and the kitchen built by a carpenter; a hammock in which to have one's siesta shaded from the rays of the sun and freshened by the sea-breezes, which come from 300 metres away and are filtered through the coconut trees.

With some difficulty I obtained from the Mission half a hectare at the cost of 700 francs. It's expensive, but that's all there was and here the Mission *owns everything*.

Leaving on one side the drawback of the priests, I am situated in the centre of the village, but my house is so amply surrounded by trees that nobody could tell that it's there. Don't be alarmed about my provisions; my neighbour is an American, a charming fellow, who has a well-stocked *shop*, so I can get all that I need. I am more and more delighted with my determination, and I assure you that, from the point of view of painting, it is *Admirable*. The models!! They're marvellous, and I have already started to work, but I have no more canvas and I await with impatience the materials Vollard has promised me *for more than a year . . .*

In my solitude here, I have what is needed to recharge my forces. Here, poetry exudes from everywhere, and when one is painting one has only to drift away into a dream to find inspiration. All I need to achieve full maturity in my art is two years of good health and not

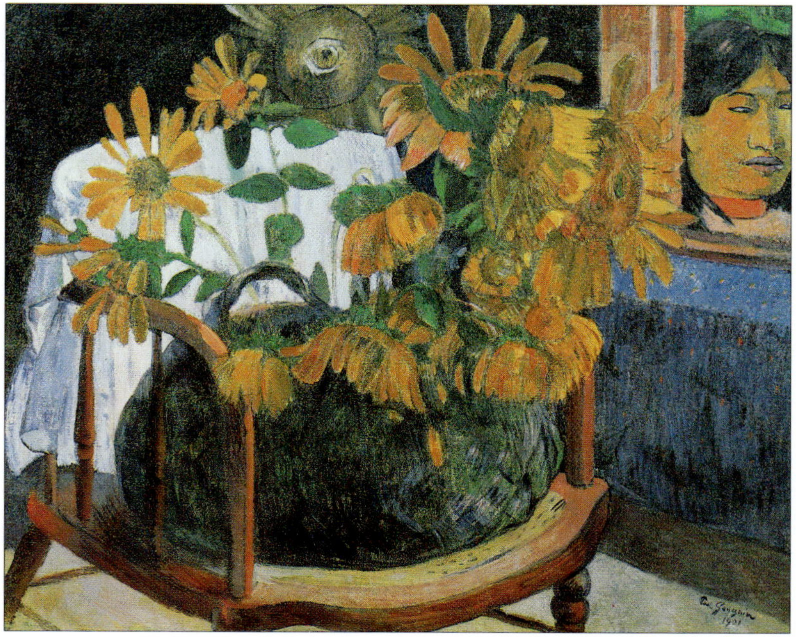

LEFT: SUNFLOWERS ON A CHAIR, 1901 *Painted just before he left Tahiti, based on the sunflowers grown from the seeds sent by De Monfreid, this still-life must surely recall Van Gogh. The all-seeing eye (staring out from the dark, and in the centre of one of the sunflowers) is a device borrowed from his friend and fellow-artist Odilon Redon.*

RIGHT: CROUCHING BATHER, *c.*1902
The technical brilliance of this work, a gouache and monotype with chalk on tan paper, underlies the brilliant simplicity of the image.

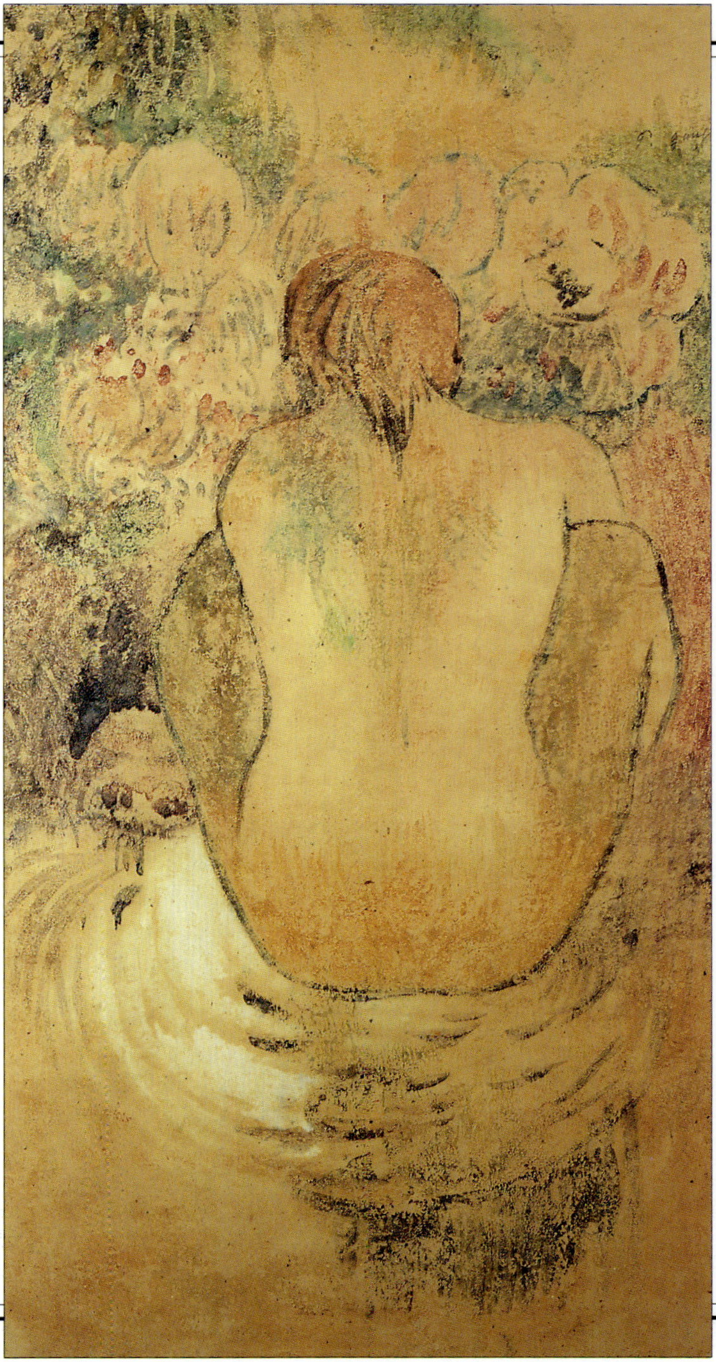

too much financial hassle, which holds a disproportionate sway over my temperament. I feel that in art *I have right on my side*, but shall I have the strength to express it forcibly in a positive way? In any case, I shall do my duty, and if my works do not last, there will always remain the memory of an artist who liberated painting from many of its old-fashioned academic faults as well as from the faults of Symbolism—another form of sentimentality . . .

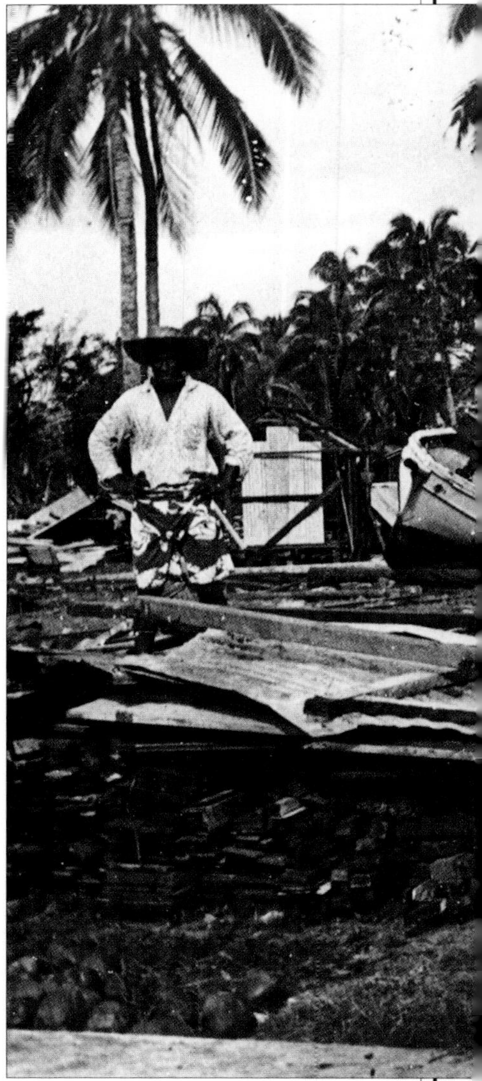

Hiva-Oa To Daniel de Monfreid *May 1902*

. . . For my part, during the past two months I have been living with a sense of deadly unease; it is because I am not the Gauguin that I was. These last terrible years and my health, *which is being very slow to improve*, have made me extremely susceptible; in this condition I lack all energy and there is nobody to comfort and console me. But things are going well for you, Annette and the child, and you have many good years of life ahead of you to paint some solid and conscientious little works. Having seen the immense steps forward you took during my first stay in Tahiti, I cannot believe that you haven't made progress since then . . .

What you have said about the collaboration with Morice in *Noa Noa** has not displeased me at all.

From my point of view, this collaboration had *two goals*. It is not like other collaborations, where two authors work in conjunction. I had the idea, talking of uncivilized people, to bring out their character side by side with our own, and I found enough new things to say about this (I myself being quite simply the savage) to contrast with the *style* of a civilized person (in this case Morice). It was in this way, therefore, that I *conceived and directed* this collaboration. Not being a professional, I would rather like to know *which of us two* was the more worthwhile, the naive and brutal savage, or the corrupted civilized man.

All the same, Morice wished the book to appear at the wrong time; and that, after all, does no harm to my reputation . . .

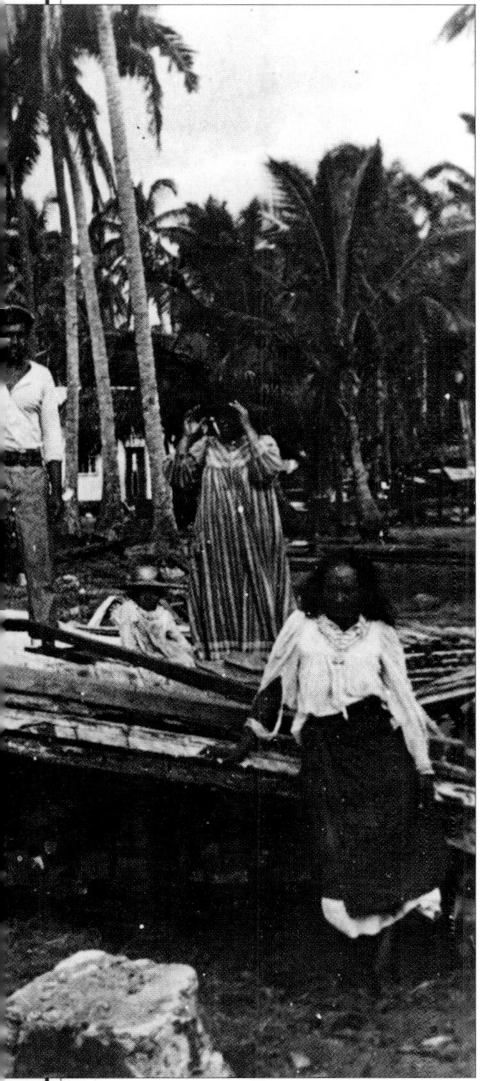

* In a letter written on 10 April 1902 De Monfreid had said, 'Everybody says your book has been absolutely ruined by the collaboration of Charles Morice, whose poems are absolutely irrelevant.'

LEFT: *A photograph of the cyclone damage in Tahiti in February 1906 shows the devastating power of tropical storms. The one which hit Hiva-Oa in January 1903 spared Gauguin's house but damaged or destroyed many of his neighbours'. The photograph shows the cutter (a small patrol boat) of the colonial administration blown 500 metres into Papeete.*

Hiva-Oa To Daniel de Monfreid *25 August 1902*

. . . You know the public, it will say: What a pity he didn't stay with his Breton style. And suppose I hadn't been there at the time to paint them? If it is fated that the chronic eczema in both my feet, which gives me such pain, is to stay incurable, it would be far better for me to come home for a change of air. I could then come and live in Provence near you, and then go on to Spain to seek some new themes. The bulls, the Spanish women, with their hair shining with grease, that has been done, overdone; still it is droll that I see them differently . . .

Hiva-Oa To Daniel de Monfreid *February 1903*

I received your two letters very late as a consequence of a cyclone here of a kind nobody had seen before, in view of the fact that it came from the north. It was, we think, caused by an earthquake on the bed of the ocean.

All the low-lying islands were overwhelmed by a frightening tidal wave, and practically the entire population has perished. We, for our part, have not been so hard hit. For forty-eight hours the rain and thunder deafened us, and one night the cyclone became terrible. Despite the fact that I am well sheltered by trees, I expected every moment that my hut would be either blown away or demolished by the wind. At ten o'clock, I heard a dull, persistent noise of a very unusual kind; it was the river, which had swept everything away in its attempt to find fresh outlets. I came out of my room to see what was happening, and to my great astonishment found myself chest-high in water. It was impossible to see anything at all; impossible to think, even for a moment, of running away. I went back into my

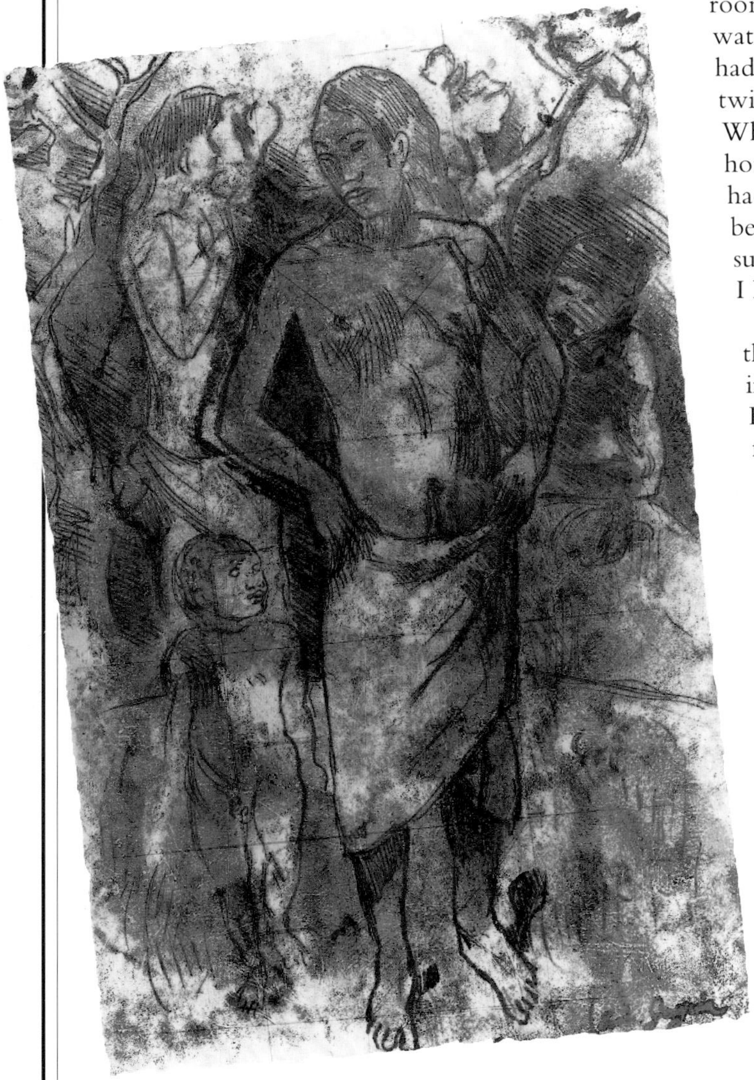

room, and so passed the night fearful that the waters would destroy my poor hut. Happily, I had built it two metres above the ground with twice as many reinforced piles as were necessary. When morning came, I was able to see the horrible condition of Atuona: bridges and roads had disappeared; everywhere huge trees had been toppled—those tropical trees which have such shallow roots—houses demolished, etc . . . I have already spent 100 francs on repairs.

I am not altogether of your opinion about the importance of my coming back to France, in the sense that I would only pass through Paris, and then go on to Spain to work there for several years. Apart from my friends, I would be entirely out of touch.

No, it is not the drawbacks of this place, but the painful condition of my eczema that inhibits me from working healthily. For nearly three months I haven't touched a brush. Besides, my future looks unsettled, and I say to myself: What would happen to me if Vollard were to renege on me? A man such as myself, always battling, even without wanting to do so, with nothing but his art, and surrounded by people who would be glad to trample on him from a great height, could hide his misery in France, but would also be pitied. To avoid all that, I must always have in front of me 4 or 5,000 francs which would allow me, were an accident to occur, to come home. Otherwise, I am well enough here in my solitude.

LEFT: *In 1902 Gauguin made a number of studies of ambiguous sexuality; this androgynous male hides his body yet the child beside him, still in his innocence, can be open and free.*

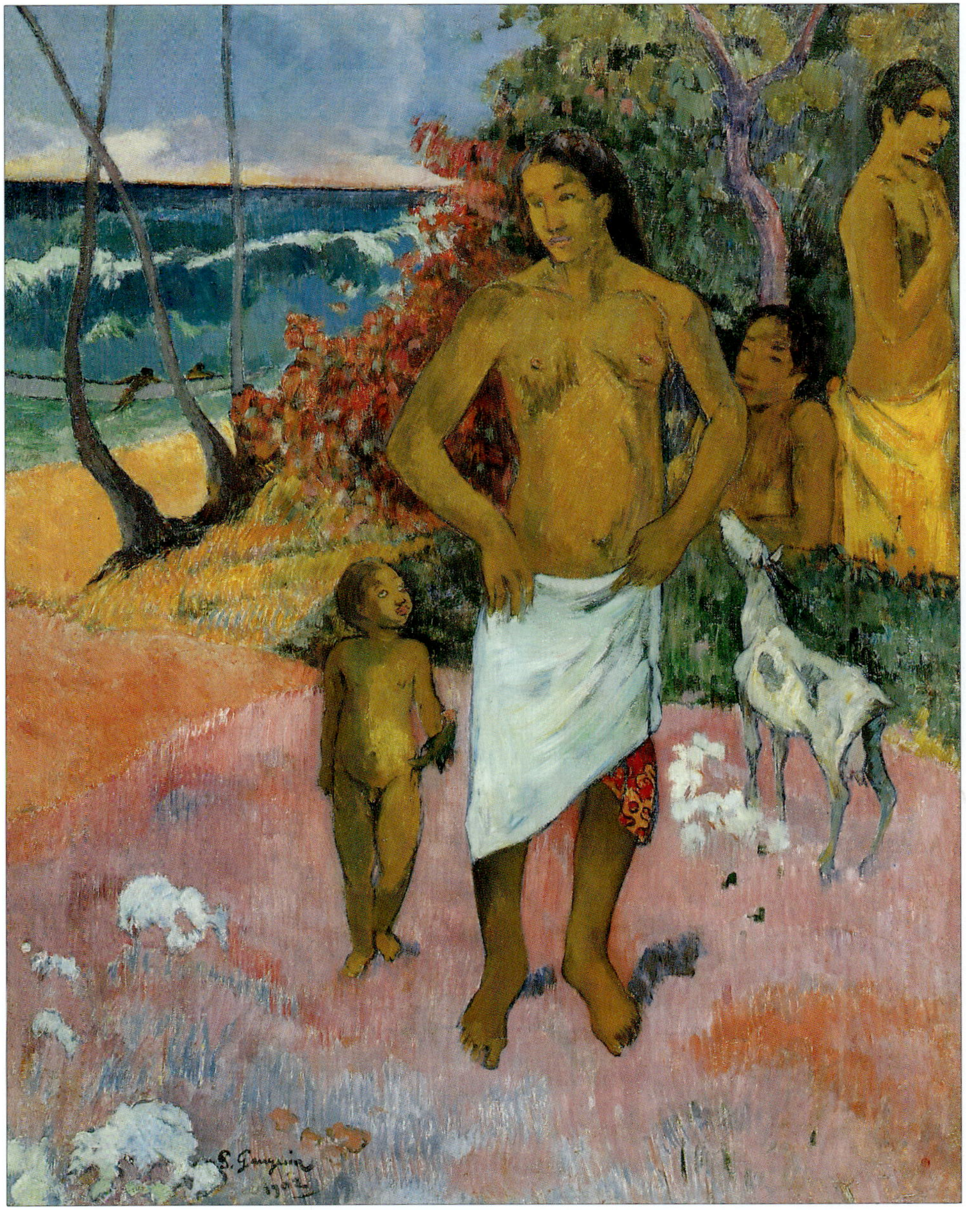

RIGHT: TAHITIAN FAMILY, *c.*1902 *An emotional charge is given to the painting by the luminescent colours of the landscape which is not present in the drawing.*

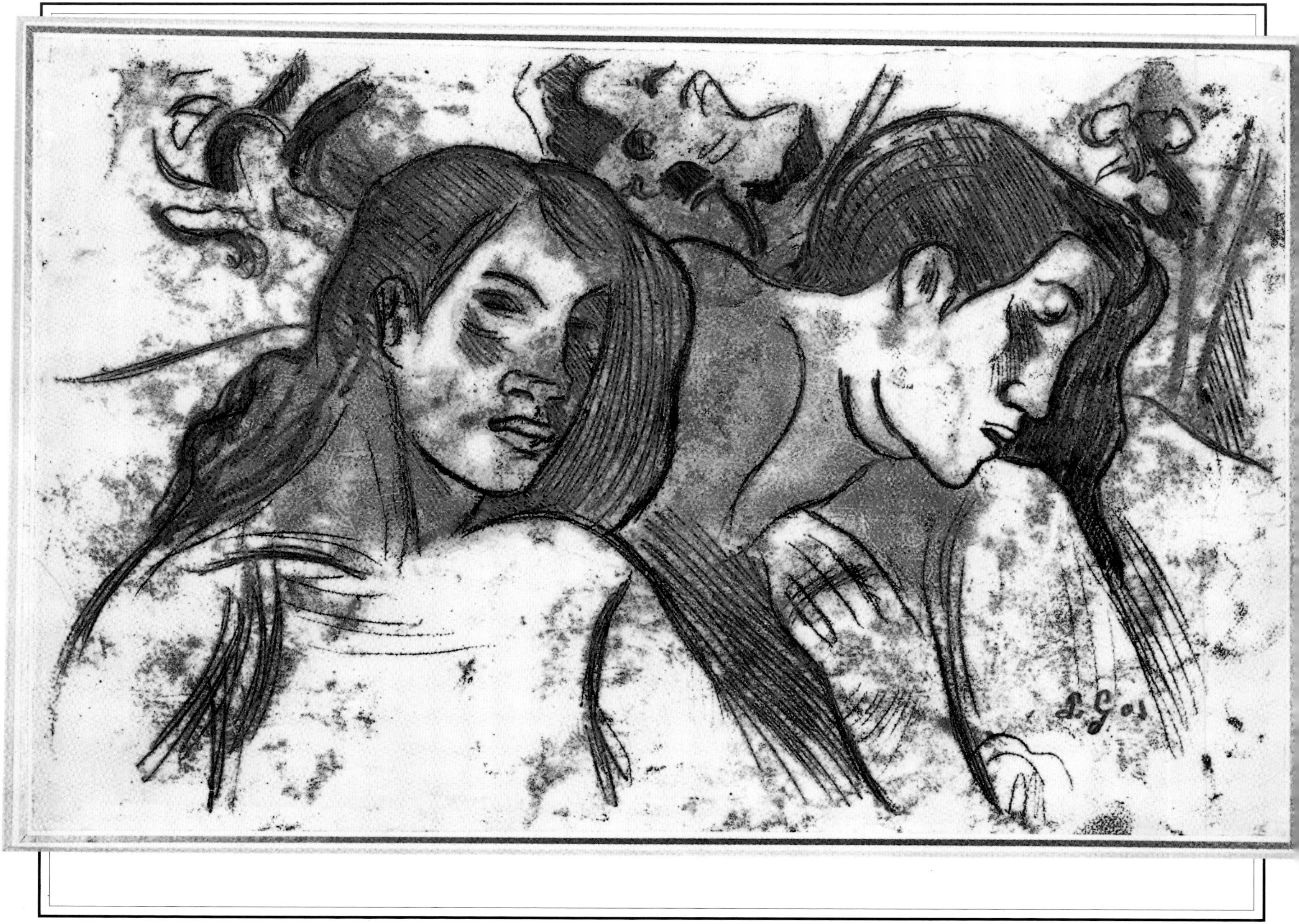

LEFT: TWO MARQUESANS, 1902 *This powerful drawing of two women is almost Expressionist in its use of line. 'Are the forms rudimentary? Yes, they have to be. Is the execution oversimplified? Yes, it is necessarily so . . . Drawing and colour must harmonize with the poem.'*

BELOW: BE IN LOVE AND YOU WILL BE HAPPY, 1898–9 *Gauguin reworked images on this theme, in a variety of media, over a period of many years. No doubt the troubled history of his own personal life was a rich source for the ironic title.*

Hiva-Oa — To Charles Morice — **April 1903**

As a result of my actions against the gendarmerie of the Marquesas that I sent you news of, I have walked into a trap set by them, and have been convicted, *despite everything*.* It spells ruin for me, and perhaps will continue to do so even if I appeal. It is essential, however, to anticipate everything and take suitable precautions. If I lose on appeal, I shall take the case to the Paris Appeal Court. I believe that Delzant, the lawyer, is somebody in those circles, and it is essential that you must straightaway find out who is the best defence lawyer in the Appeal Court if I have to take my case there.

You can see how right I was in my last letter to you to say: Act quickly and energetically. If we win, the fight will have been a good one, and I shall have achieved something for the Marquesas Islands. A lot of injustices will be abolished, and it will have been worthwhile to suffer for that.

I am down but not beaten, like the Indian who smiles whilst he is being tortured. Decidedly the savage is better than us. You were

BELOW: WOMEN, FLOWERS, AND FOLIAGE, 1899 *Woodcut in black ink on Japan paper, reworking a number of Gauguin's favourite themes.*

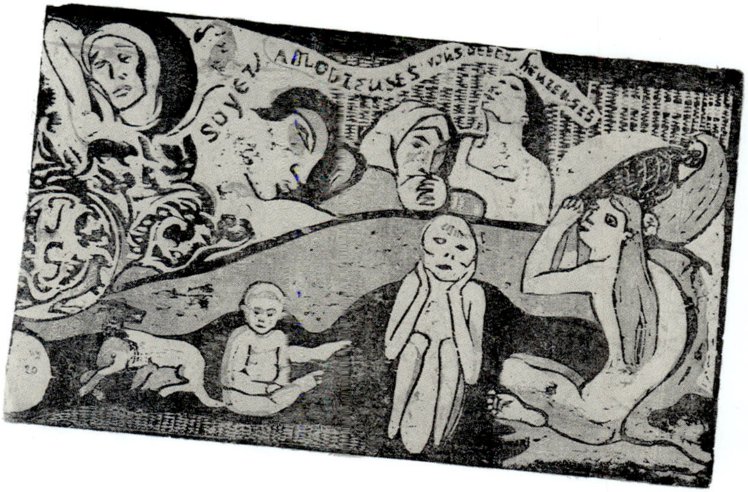

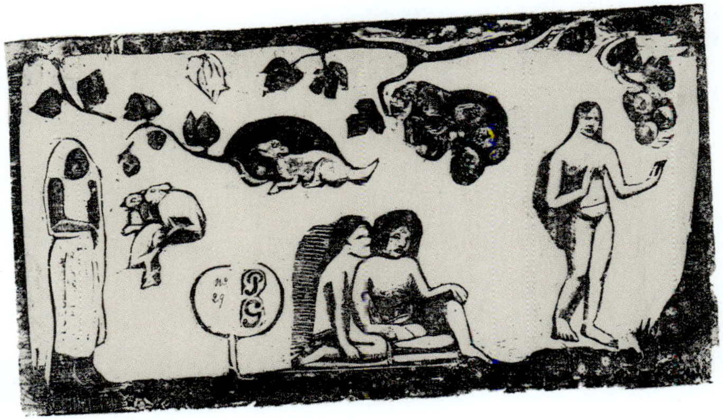

wrong when once you said that I am not a savage. I am indeed a savage. And civilized people are aware of the fact, for in my works there is nothing that surprises or shocks apart from my being 'a savage despite myself'. That is why it is inimitable. A man's work is an explanation of himself. And in this there are two kinds of beauty: that which comes from instinct, and that which comes from study. Certainly, a combination of the two, with the modifications that would entail, could give a great and complex richness which the art critic should apply himself to discovering. Today you are an art critic; let me not direct but advise you to read carefully what I am rather enigmatically going to tell you in a few lines. The great scientific skill of Raphael does not deter me, nor prevent me, from feeling and indeed understanding his primordial gift, which is an instinct for beauty. Raphael was born with beauty. All the rest with him is only a modification of this. We have just been going through a lengthy period of alienation in art caused by physics, chemistry and the study of nature. Artists, having lost all their savagery and having no more feeling for the instinctual, or, one might say, for imagination, have gone wandering off along all sorts of byways to find those productive powers which they do not have the power to create; as a result, they behave like a disordered rabble, feeling frightened and lost when they are on their own. That is why one should not force solitude on everybody, because one must be strong to act on one's own. Everything I have learnt about others has upset me. I can therefore say: Nobody has taught me anything. And it is indeed true that I know very little! But I prefer that which comes from myself; and who knows if that small amount, exploited by others, may not become a great thing? How many centuries are necessary to create an *appearance* of movement?

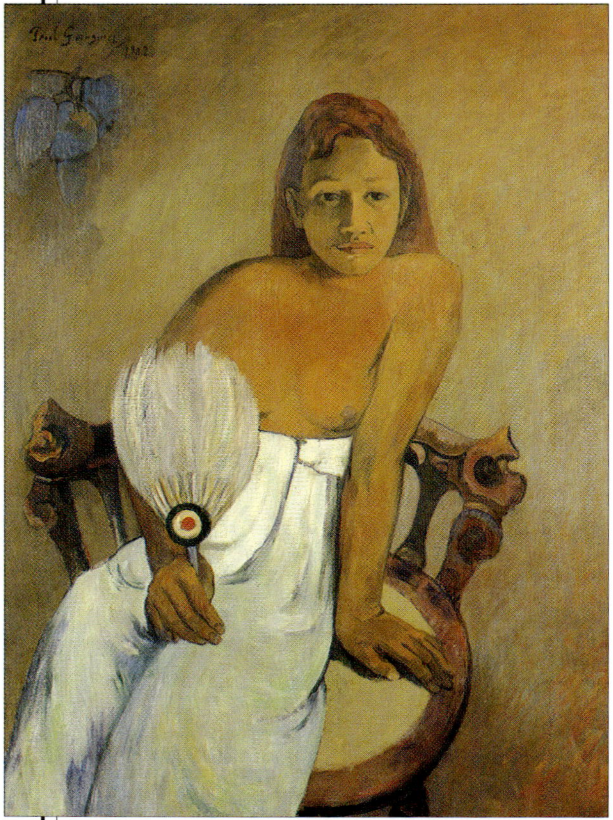

LEFT: WOMAN WITH A FAN, 1902
Using an existing photograph made in the studio of the House of Pleasure, Gauguin has changed the frontal gaze to a mysterious averted expression which distances the woman from the onlooker. The woman's fan is a symbol of aristocracy.

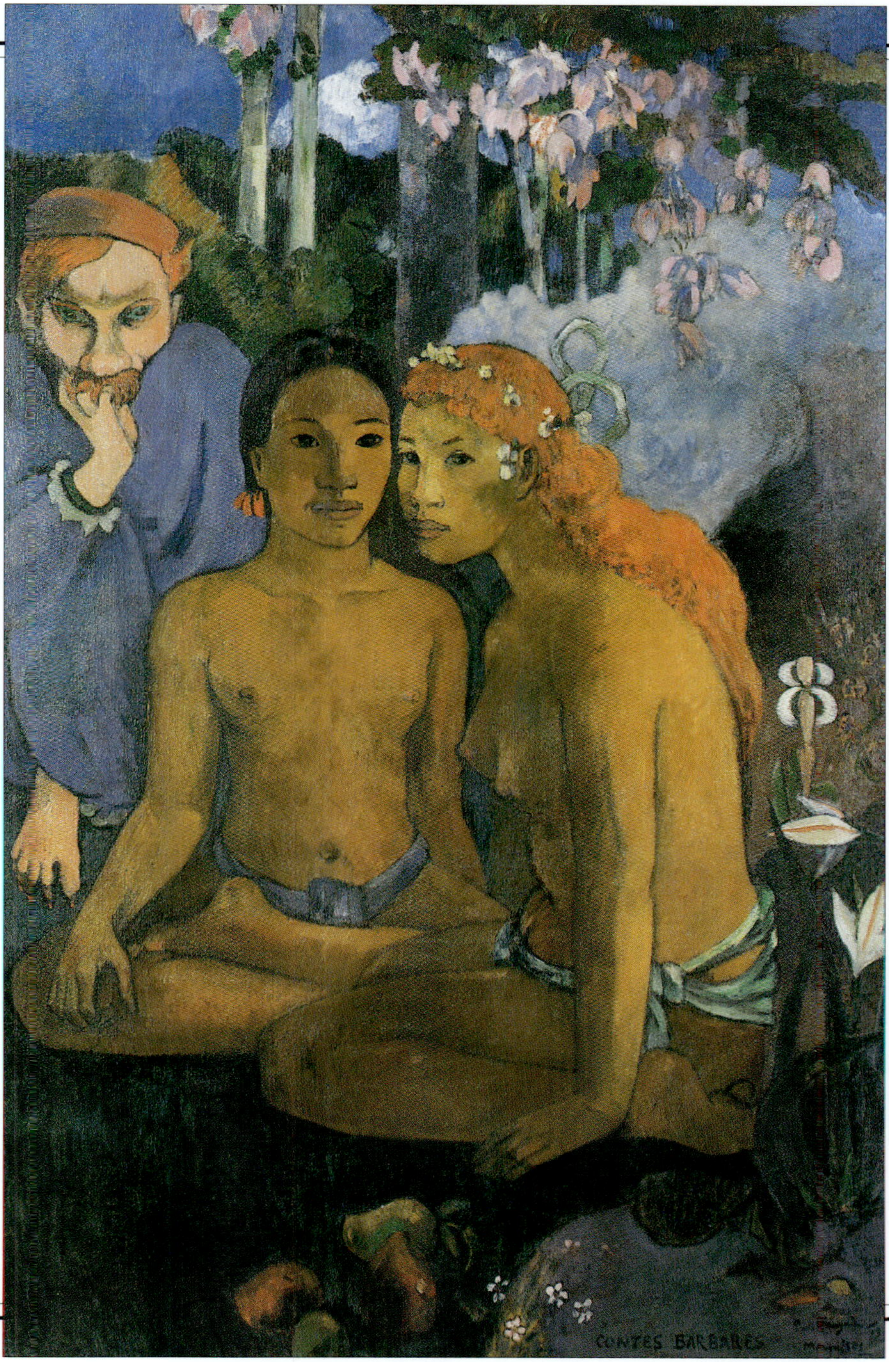

RIGHT: BARBARIC TALES, 1902
Memories of civilization continued to haunt Gauguin; the homunculus figure of the eavesdropping Meyer de Haan intrudes like the serpent in the Garden of Eden. The dwarf painter, an associate of Gauguin back in the Brittany days, had been steeped in arcane and occult knowledge, the very obverse of the serene wisdom of the Oceanic peoples.

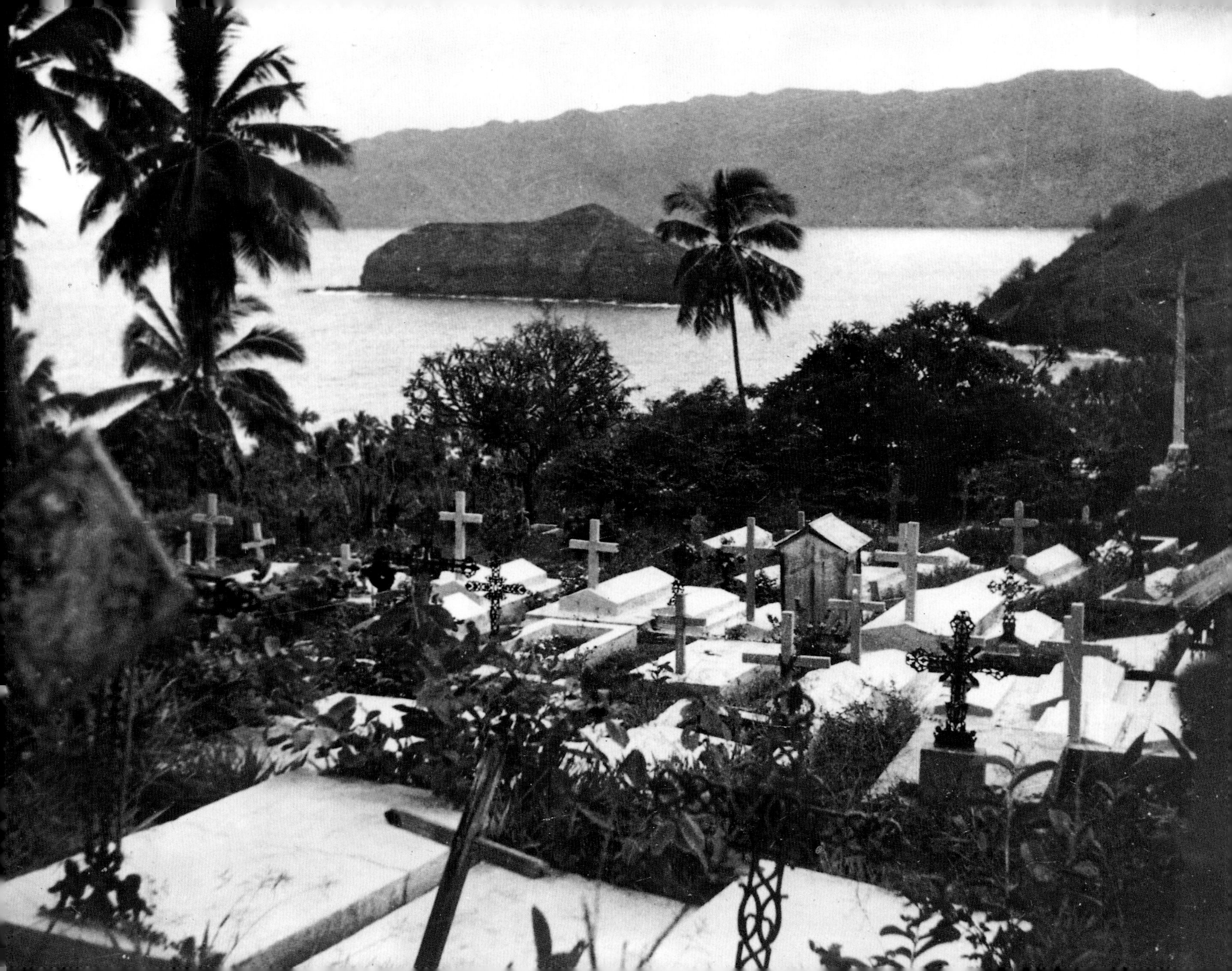

THE LAST CHANCE

LEFT: *Gauguin was buried in the graveyard at Atuona in 1903. The authorities placed a regulation white cross on his grave; his friends later had this removed and replaced it with one of his sculptures, 'Oviri', as he had wished.*

* On 31 March 1903 Gauguin was sentenced to three months' imprisonment and a fine of 1,000 francs for having 'slandered' a gendarme named Étienne Guichenay, who worked on the neighbouring island of Tahuata, by claiming that he had accepted bribes and had been guilty of smuggling during a recent visit of American whalers. He decided to apply for a new trial, at the same time claiming, with some justification, that 'The natives are lucky to have me as their protector, for, so far, the settlers, who are all poor, have always been afraid to antagonize the gendarmes, and so have kept silent. Therefore, the gendarmes, being free from control, are absolute masters . . . I am being condemned merely for defending these poor, defenceless people.'

GAUGUIN'S LAST LETTER WAS TO DE MONFREID, dated April 1903. In it he repeated the story of the sentence imposed on him, complained that Vollard hadn't sent him any money, and recorded that he owed the bank 1,400 francs. On 8 May he sent for the Protestant pastor Paul Vernier, with whom he had struck up an unexpected friendship, complaining of 'pains all over', and added that he had had two fainting fits. He then went on to talk about Flaubert's *Salammbô*. Two hours later, his servant arrived to find him dead with an empty laudanum bottle on the table beside him. It is not known whether he had consumed it or not; for years he had been heavily dependent on morphine and laudanum to soothe the pain in his leg. The cause of death seems to have been a heart attack. He was buried the next day at the Catholic cemetery just outside Atuona. The local government official reported to his superiors in Papeete:

> 'I have requested all creditors of the deceased to submit duplicate statements of their accounts, but am already convinced that the liabilities will considerably exceed the assets, as the few pictures left by the late painter, who belonged to the decadent school, have little prospect of finding purchasers.'

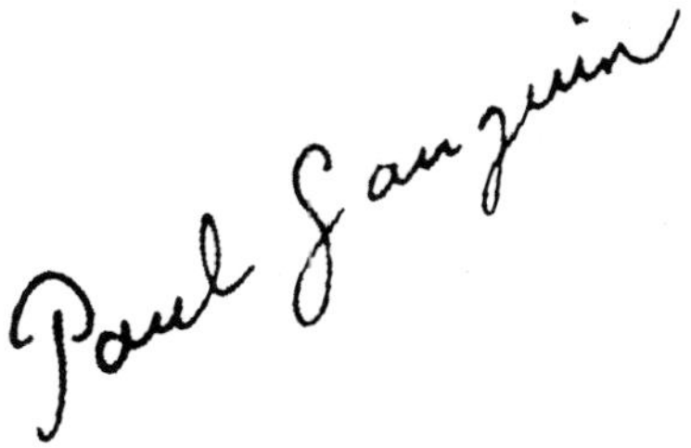

Gauguin: A Biographical Chronology

1848 7 June: born in Paris. Father, Clovis, is a journalist on the republican newspaper *Le National*. Mother, Aline, is the daughter of the socialist and feminist militant Flora Tristan (1803–1844), who was of Peruvian ancestry.

1849 August: family sails for Peru. Father suffers a ruptured artery and dies. Mother and sister Marie (born 1847) reach Lima, where live with maternal great-uncle.

1854–55 Family returns to France, moving to Orléans, where paternal grandfather and great-uncle live.

1859 Boarder at Jesuit seminary in Orléans.

1861 Mother moves to Paris as seamstress.

1862 Rejoins mother in Paris. Prepares for entrance examination to Naval Academy.

1865 Mother appoints family friend Gustave Arosa as legal guardian of children. Joins merchant marine because too old for Naval Academy; sails for Rio de Janeiro.

1866 Second voyage to Rio. October: starts 13-month voyage round the world as 2nd lieutenant on *Le Chili*.

1867 Mother dies. December: returns to France.

1868–69 Transfers to French navy; sails around Mediterranean and Black Sea on *Jérôme-Napoléon*. Inherits money and property in Orléans from mother and paternal grandfather once comes of age.

1870 Serves in North Sea during Franco–Prussian War.

1871 Gives up sea-faring; settles in Paris.

1872 Through contacts of former guardian, Gustave Arosa, enters stockbroking office of Paul Bertin; meets Émile Schuffenecker, an amateur painter. Autumn: meets Mette Sophie Gad (born 1850).

1873 22 November: marries Mette.

1874 31 August: son Émile born. Starts painting as amateur and building up collection of works by Impressionist painters.

1876 His landscape 'Sous-bois à Viroflay (Seine-et-Oise)' accepted by Salon. Winter: gives up stockbroking job. First meeting with Pissarro.

1877 Moves house; new landlord, Bouillot, introduces him to sculpture. 25 December: daughter Aline born.

1879 Employed by banker André Bourdon. Invited to take part in fourth Impressionist exhibition; he lends three Pissarros. 10 May: son Clovis born.

1880 Shows eight paintings and two sculptures at fifth Impressionist exhibition (J. K. Huysmans describes landscapes as 'watered down Pissarro' but praises nude study, 'Suzanne Sewing'). Impressionists' dealer, Paul Durand-Ruel, buys three of his canvases.

1882 Shows eleven paintings, one pastel and one sculpture at seventh Impressionist exhibition. Stockmarket crash and financial crisis in Paris; his own finances precarious. Visits Pissarro at Pontoise and Osny.

1883 Seeks employment with art dealer Georges Petit. 6 December: son Pola born.

1884 Moves family to Rouen for eight months; trip to southern France. Desperate for money, takes job with Roubaix tarpaulin factory as Danish rep. November: joins family, with his art collection (which remains in Denmark). Mette teaches French to support family.

1885 Exhibits at Copenhagen Society of the Friends of Art. Leaves Mette in Denmark and returns to Paris with son

Clovis. Short of money; works as bill-sticker, then as administrative secretary for French railway.

1886 Exhibits nineteen paintings and one wood relief at eighth and last Impressionist exhibition. June: moves to Brittany, staying at Gloanec Inn at Pont-Aven; meets Émile Bernard and Charles Laval. November: returns to Paris; meets Vincent van Gogh.

1887 Early April: Mette pays visit. 10 April: leaves for Martinique, via Panama, with Charles Laval; paints several landscapes. November: returns to Paris with fever and dysentery; stays with Schuffenecker.

1888 February–October: at Pont-Aven in Brittany with Meyer de Haan, Charles Laval and Émile Bernard; work and discussions together give rise to 'Synthetism' and 'Cloisonnism'. Théodore van Gogh organizes first one-man show in Paris. 21 October: leaves Pont-Aven for Arles. Joins Vincent van Gogh; live together for two months. 24 December: quarrels with Van Gogh; Van Gogh cuts off part of his own ear. Gauguin returns to Paris; stays with Schuffenecker.

1889 Visits Universal Exhibition in Paris. Organizes exhibition of 'Impressionist and Synthetist Group' with Schuffenecker; young Nabis, Sérusier, Maurice Denis and Bonnard, much impressed. Third, longest and most decisive stay in Brittany. Summer: at Gloanec Inn in Pont-Aven. October: moves to Le Pouldu; joined by Séguin, Filiger and Meyer de Haan.

1890 November: returns to Paris; stays with Schuffenecker. 29 July: Vincent van Gogh commits suicide.

1891 Associates with Symbolist writers at Café Voltaire. Copies Manet's 'Olympia'. Decides to go to Tahiti. 23 February: first sale, of thirty pictures, to raise money for voyage. 23 March: farewell banquet at Café Voltaire. 4 April: sails for Tahiti. 8 June: lands at Papeete. (June 1891–July 1893: first stay in Tahiti). Disgusted by European colony at capital; acquires native hut 25 miles south, in Mataiea district.

1892 Produces lots of work despite ill-health.

1893 Ill-health forces return to Europe. Goes to Orléans to collect inheritance left by uncle. Rents studio in Paris; lives with his mistress, Annah the Javanese, and her monkey. November: exhibits at Durand-Ruel's; no financial success, but Nabis impressed.

1894 January: goes to Copenhagen; last meeting with Mette. April–December: at Pont-Aven and Le Pouldu with Annah; breaks leg in fight with sailors. December: returns to Paris; Annah loots studio and disappears.

1895 Decides to return to Tahiti. 18 February: second auction-sale; a failure. July 1895–September 1901: second stay in Tahiti; settles in Punaauia district on west coast.

1896 Severe ill-health; feelings of being alone and an outcast.

1897 Daughter Aline dies in Copenhagen; stops writing to wife. Short stay in hospital. Paints 'Where have we come from, What are we? Where are we going?'. *La Revue Blanche* publishes manuscript of *Noa Noa*.

1898 Attempts suicide. Takes clerk's job in Office of Public Works at Papeete.

1899 Continually in trouble with local authorities; publishes satirical broadsheet, *Le Sourire*.

1901 August: moves to Marquesas Islands; settles on Hiva-Oa and builds 'House of Pleasure'.

1902 August: suffering heart trouble; legs covered in ulcers. Thinks of returning to France for treatment; De Monfried advises against it.

1903 March: champions natives; argues with local government, bishop and police. 31 March: sentenced to 3 months' imprisonment and fined 1,000 francs; too poor to go to Tahiti to appeal. 8 May: dies.

Friends and Acquaintances: A Biographical Index

AURIER, Georges Albert *(1865–92)* One of the founders of the *Mercure de France*, the leading French literary journal, he was an impassioned defender of Symbolist painting, and in 1891 published a laudatory article about Gauguin in the magazine.

BERNARD, Émile *(1868–1942)* A pupil of Cormon, the teacher of Toulouse-Lautrec, he became a close friend of Gauguin during the Pont-Aven period, and evolved a style which he called Pictorial Symbolism. A prolific writer, he later attacked Gauguin as a plagiarist, and devoted a great deal of his subsequent writing to denying that Gauguin had any influence on him.

BONNAT, Léon *(1833–1922)* A successful academic painter who became Director of the École des Beaux-Arts.

BRACQUEMOND, Félix *(1833–1914)* A painter and engraver, he was prominent in Impressionist circles, and gave Gauguin considerable help as a ceramicist.

CARRIÈRE, Eugène *(1849–1906)* A painter and lithographer who had a remarkable command of the effects of light and shade and was greatly admired by the post-Impressionist generation.

CHAUDET, Georges-Alfred *(died 1899)* A landscape artist turned picture dealer who exhibited and sold Gauguin's works.

DENIS, Maurice *(1870–1943)* A founder of the Nabis and an artist versatile in many media. An inveterate theoretician, he wrote extensively about art and religion.

DOLENT, Jean *(1835–1909)* A writer and art critic who was one of Gauguin's supporters and a contributor to the *Mercure de France*.

DURAND-RUEL, Paul *(1831–1922)* The main dealer of the Impressionists, he was constantly on the look-out for new talent and new schools of painting, and showed considerable courage in giving Gauguin a one-man exhibition in 1893.

FILIGER, Charles *(1863–1928)* Of Swiss parentage, after studying art in Paris, he went to Le Pouldu, where he was deeply influenced by Gauguin and Sérusier. Preoccupied with religious themes, he spent the rest of his life in Brittany.

FONTAINAS, André *(1855–1948)* One of the leading figures in the Symbolist movement, he became editor of its main literary outlet, the *Mercure de France*, which had been founded in 1889 by Alfred Vallette.

GALLET, Gustave Governor of the French possessions in the South Seas, 1895–1901.

GOGH, Théodore van *(1857–91)* Vincent's younger brother, as an art dealer, was especially helpful to Gauguin. In 1888 he organized an exhibition of his Breton paintings, and helped him in many other ways. Even Gauguin had to admit, 'When Théo van Gogh went mad, I knew I was done for. Only he knew how to sell and create a clientele.'

GOGH, Vincent van *(1853–1900)* Almost subservient to Gauguin, he spent two difficult months with him in Arles in 1888.

GOUPIL, Auguste *(1847–1921)* A rich businessman and lawyer in Tahiti, who gave Gauguin a job as a caretaker, commissioned a portrait of his daughter from him, and entrusted him for a while with the job of being drawing master to his family. They quarrelled, however, and in the satirical journal he started producing in 1899, *Le Sourire*, Gauguin wrote a bitter attack on him.

GOURMONT, Rémy de *(1858–1915)* A writer of richly textured prose, he was one of the leading figures in the Symbolist movement.

LACASCADE, Etienne Originally a doctor, then a bank manager and a member of the National Assembly, he became governor of the French colonies in the South Seas from 1886 until 1893.

LAVAL, Charles *(1862–94)* An ardent disciple of Gauguin, whose paintings his own resembled in a superficial way, he worked with him in Pont-Aven, and accompanied him on the trip to Panama and Martinique.

LECLERQ, Julien A journalist and art critic, who wrote a laudatory article about Gauguin's prints in the *Mercure de France* in 1894.

LOTI, Pierre, the pen-name of Julien Viau, *(1850–1923)* A naval officer who achieved great success as the writer of novels about exotic and unfamiliar places such as Tahiti, Japan etc. His works did much to promote interest in the non-European world.

MALLARMÉ, Stéphane *(1842–98)* The leading modern French poet of his time, and an important figure in the cultural world, he was a firm supporter of Gauguin and presided at his farewell banquet in 1891.

MAUCLAIR, Camille *(1872–1945)* A poet, novelist, critic and historian, he was a particular target for Gauguin's ire on account of his art criticism in the *Mercure de France*, which never had a good word to say for him.

MAUFRA, Maxime *(1861–1918)* A Breton by birth, he became a businessman, but, on meeting Gauguin at Pont-Aven in 1890, decided to become a painter. Taken up by Durand-Ruel, he was especially admired for his prints.

MEYER DE HAAN, Jacob *(1852–95)* From a rich Amsterdam family of merchants, he decided to become a painter, and fell under the influence of Pissarro. At first he adopted an Impressionist style, but in 1889 he met Gauguin, following him to Pont-Aven and Le Pouldu and working with him on the decoration of Marie Henry's inn there. He was of considerable financial assistance to Gauguin, who tried to persuade him to accompany him to Tahiti.

MOLARD, William *(1862–1936)* A musician and composer who was a neighbour of Gauguin at 6 rue Vercingétorix in 1894–95, and helped him extend his social contacts. Gauguin frequently made use of his services after he had returned to Tahiti to carry out commissions for him in Paris.

MONFREID, Georges Daniel de *(1856–1929)* A rich, yacht-owning painter who became Gauguin's most loyal and devoted friend, he had been one of the exhibitors at the Café Volpini. When Gauguin made his contract with Vollard in 1893 he nominated De Monfreid as his representative.

MORICE, Charles *(1861–1919)* A poet, journalist and critic, who saw in supporting Gauguin an outlet for his own talents as a publicist. He wrote the introduction to the catalogue of Gauguin's exhibition of 1893, and collaborated with him, in a manner which has for long been a subject of controversy, in the production of *Noa Noa*. This was first published in part in *La Revue Blanche*, in October and November 1897, and then in book form in 1901 at Morice's expense, both versions bearing the names of both authors.

MUCHA, Alphonse *(1860–1939)* Born in Moravia, he worked in Paris from 1888 to 1904, where his posters had a considerable influence, and promoted the acceptance and success of *art nouveau*. He was a friend of Gauguin and lent him his studio when he returned from Tahiti in 1893.

O'CONOR, Roderic *(1860–1940)* An affluent Irish painter and print-maker who met Gauguin at the Pension Gloanec in 1892 and became very friendly with him. At one point he lent Gauguin his Paris studio, and Gauguin gave him one of his prints with the inscription, 'To my friend O Conor [sic], one man of Samoa, P. Gauguin, 1894'. Presumably on the assumption that he would be financially helpful, he invited O'Conor to join him in going to Tahiti, an offer judiciously not accepted.

PAPINAUD, Pierre-Louis-Clovis *(1846–1912)* Governor of the French colonies in the South Seas from 1894 to 1895, he was responsible for an unsuccessful attempt to put down the rising on the Windward Islands in 1895.

PÉLADAN, Joseph-Aimé *(1858–1928)* Founder of the Rose & Croix movement, and author of a salacious six-volume novel.

PETIT, Edouard *(1860–1930)* Appointed governor of the French colonies in the South Seas in February 1901. A mild-mannered and generally benevolent man, who took a kindly attitude to the native population, he still managed to arouse Gauguin's hostility.

POMARÉ, V *(1839–91)* The last king of Tahiti who ruled the island under French 'patronage'. His mother, whom he had succeeded in 1870, had ruled for fifty years. Gauguin attended his funeral shortly after his arrival in Tahiti.

PROUST, Antonin *(1832–1905)* A close friend of Manet (for whom he secured the Legion of Honour), he was Minister of Fine Arts from 1881 to 1882, and Commissioner for the Universal Exhibition of 1889.

PUVIS DE CHAVANNES, Pierre *(1824–98)* Deeply influenced by early Italian paintings and predisposed to mural and decorative works with strong symbolic connotations, he was a 'father figure' to many of the Symbolists. Gauguin's reactions to him were ambiguous, part respectful, part condescending.

REDON, Odilon *(1840–1916)* A trained architect and painter, he studied under the engraver and etcher Rodolphe Bresdin, devoting himself almost exclusively to charcoal drawings, and developing a fine series of lithographs. His later explosive use of colour won him the respect of many avant-garde artists. He had a considerable influence on Gauguin, and later on the Surrealists.

SCHUFFENECKER, Émile *(1851–1934)* One of Gauguin's most devoted associates who painted pictures in a variety of styles and collected the works of others with the support of a small investment income. Heavily involved in the creation of the Volpini exhibition of 1889, he helped Gauguin a great deal but was rewarded with very little thanks.

SÉRUSIER, Paul *(1863–1927)* Meeting Gauguin at Pont-Aven, he received painting lessons from him. In 1888 he painted 'The Talisman', which created a sensation with its unrepresentational use of colour (derived largely from Gauguin), and which came to be thought of as the first Nabi work. He later became absorbed in religious art.

STRINDBERG, Johan August *(1849–1912)* One of the most distinguished and prolific of Scandinavian writers, he produced novels, plays and critical essays. (His complete works fill fifty-five volumes.) He spent a lot of time in Paris, where many of his plays were produced, and, through his friendship with Munch and other Scandinavian artists living there, became familiar with the French art scene. He himself was a gifted, though intermittent painter.

VALLETTE, Alfred *(1858–1935)* Editor of the *Mercure de France* since its foundation in 1889, he was very tolerant of Gauguin, despite the imprecations the painter rained down on the head of his art critic, Camille Mauclair.

VIÉLÉ-GRIFFIN, Francis *(1864–1937)* A symbolist poet and critic.

VOLLARD, Ambroise *(1868–1939)* One of the great dealers in the history of modern art, he was involved in selling and promoting the works of every new movement in painting. He bought his first Gauguin painting at the Durand-Ruel exhibition of 1893. Despite the fact that Gauguin was often vituperous about him, he offered to become his dealer after the death of Chaudet, and in March 1900 he agreed to pay him a monthly allowance of 300 francs in return for twenty-four paintings a year at 200–250 francs.

Acknowledgements

Letters still in copyright are reproduced by kind permission of the following:

Correspondance de Paul Gauguin edited by Victor Merlhés, © Fondation Singer-Polignac (1984): *Mette Gauguin: c.*25 July 1886; end July 1886; mid-September 1886; 20 June 1887; *c.*25 August 1887; *c.*22 January 1888. *Théodore van Gogh:* 15–18 June 1888; *c.*7 July 1888. *Vincent van Gogh:* 29 February 1888; *c.*15 March 1888; *c.*24 July 1888; *c.*27 September 1888. *Émile Schuffenecker:* 14 January 1885; early July 1887; end February 1888; 8 October 1888; 16 October 1888.
Lettres de Gauguin à Daniel de Monfreid edited by Mme Joly-Segalen, © Georges Fall, Éditions Georges Falaize (1950): 12 September 1893; November 1895; August 1896; November 1896; 14 February 1897; February 1898; 15 May 1898; 15 August 1898; May 1899; November 1901; May 1902; 25 August 1902; February 1903.
Lettres de Gauguin à sa femme et à ses amis edited by Maurice Malingue, © Éditions Bernard Grasset (1946): *Maurice Denis:* June 1899. *André Fontainas:* March 1899. *Aline Gauguin:* end December 1893. *Mette Gauguin:* 4 May 1891; 29 June 1891; March 1892; 5 November 1892; 8 December 1892; August 1897. *Dr Gouzer:* 15 March 1898. *William Molard:* May 1894; September 1894; July 1895; August 1897. *Charles Morice:* May 1896; July 1901; April 1903. *August Strindberg:* 5 February 1895.
Oviri—Écrits d'un sauvage edited by Daniel Guérin, © Éditions Gallimard (1974): *Charles Morice:* mid-January 1897. *Alfred Vallette:* July 1896. *Noa-Noa*: Marriage; The Picture I Want to Paint.

All translations are by the author.

The illustrations are reproduced by kind permission of the following:

Albright-Knox Art Gallery, Buffalo, NY: 52 left (General Purchase Funds, 1946); 83 (A. Conger Goodyear Coll., 1965). Courtesy of Alex, Reid, and Lefevre Fine Art Ltd, London: 147. Mr and Mrs Walter Annenberg Collection: 64 (Courtesy of the Philadelphia Museum of Art). Australian News and Information Bureau: 60 (Courtesy of the New South Wales Government Printer). Barnaby's Picture Library, London: 53. Musées Royaux des Beaux-Arts de Belgique, Brussels: 43 left, 53. Boston Museum of Fine Arts: 124/5 (Tompkins Collection). Bridgeman Art Library, London: 37, 87 (Private Coll., USA); 48 (Museum of Fine Art, Prague); 97 (Private Coll., Switzerland); 100 (Hermitage Museum, St Petersburg); 101 (Musée des Beaux-Arts, Lyon); 109 & front cover (Pushkin Museum, Moscow). British Museum (Dept. of Prints and Drawings), London: 148. Foundation E. G. Bührle Collection, Zurich: 18. Calmann and King Archives: 12, 32, 43 right, 46, 50, 72 left, 73, 84 centre, 103, 112. Carnegie Museum of Art, Pittsburgh: 139 (Acquired through the generosity of Mrs Alan Scaife). Art Institute of Chicago: half-title page (Albert H. Wolf Memorial Coll.); 40 (Prints and Drawings Dept. Funds); 42 (William McCallin McKee Memorial Coll.); 104 left, 105 (Clarence Buckingham Coll.); 133, 149 right (Gift of the Prints and Drawings Club); 149 left (Joseph Brooks Fair Coll.). Chrysler Museum, Norfolk, Va: 40. The Courtauld Institute, London: 120, 121. Fondation Doucet, Paris: 93 left. The Folkwang Museum, Essen: 150, 151. Photo Giraudon, Paris: 117 (Hermitage Museum, St Petersburg); 122 left (Louvre CDL); 135 (Museo de São Paulo). Larousse/Giraudon: 94. Collection Christian Gleizal: 61, 68, 72 right, 84 left, 102, 102/3, 110, 111, 114, 126, 140, 141, 144/5, 153. Gleizal/Archives d'Outre-Mer, Aix-en-Provence: 106 left, 126/7.

ACKNOWLEDGEMENTS

Josefowitz Collection: 36. Kunstindustriet Museet, Copenhagen: 47. Mansell Collection, London: 59. Metropolitan Museum, New York: 67. Museum of Modern Art, New York: 128 (Lillie P. Bliss Collection). National Gallery of Scotland, Edinburgh: 30, 41. National Gallery of Art, Washington: 23 (Coll. of Mr and Mrs Paul Mellon). Neue Pinakothek, Munich: 113 (Photo J. Blauel: Artothek). The Newark Museum, New York: 21 (Gift of Mrs L. B. Wescott, 1960). Ny Carlsberg Glyptotek, Copenhagen: 19, 74. Art Gallery of Ontario, Toronto: 75 left (The Volunteer Committee Fund, 1980). Madame Felix Pissarro: 20. Musée de Pont-Aven: 27, 38, 44, 54. Musée du Prieuré, St Germain-en-Laye: 10, 13, 14, 16 left, 16 right, 17, 25. Private Collections: 51, 65 centre, 78 right, 96. Private Collection, Switzerland: 79. Réunion des Musées Nationaux, Paris: 22, 39 centre, 63 left, 63 right, 75 right, 82 & back cover, 86 centre, 86 right, 112 (Louvre, Dept. des Arts Graphiques); 28, 45, 56, 57, 134 right (Musée d'Orsay); 119, 146 (Musée des Arts Africains et Océaniens). Photoarchive Roger-Viollet, Paris: 11, 29, 31, 35, 58/9, 65 right, 69, 76/7, 80, 85, 93 right, 107, 108 left, 118, 136, 136/7, 152. Royal Academy of Arts, London/Private Collection: 91. Scala, Florence: frontispiece, 134 left (Pushkin Museum, Moscow); 71, 142 (Hermitage Museum, St Petersburg). Collection Sirot-Angel, Paris: 25, 34, 62, 78 left, 88, 98, 106/7, 128 right. The Tate Gallery, London: 130/1. Collection of Mr and Mrs Eugene Thaw: 143. Victoria and Albert Museum (National Art Library), London: 70. Vincent van Gogh Foundation/Vincent van Gogh Museum, Amsterdam: 33, 39 left, 49, 55. The Witt Library of the Courtauld Institute, London: 66, 104 right, 108 centre, 123. The Worcester Art Museum, Worcester, Mass.: 95.